Corporate Responsibility and Human Rights

Corporate Responsibility and Human Rights

Global Trends and Issues Concerning Indigenous Peoples

Jide James-Eluyode

LEXINGTON BOOKS

Lanham • Boulder • New York • London

Published by Lexington Books
An imprint of The Rowman & Littlefield Publishing Group, Inc.
4501 Forbes Boulevard, Suite 200, Lanham, Maryland 20706
www.rowman.com

6 Tinworth Street, London SE11 5AL, United Kingdom

Some aspects of Chapters 5, 6 and 7 from Jide, James-Eluyode. "The Blurred Lines: Analysing the Dynamics of States' Duty and Corporate Responsibility to Consult in Developing Countries." *African Journal of International and Comparative Law* 23, no. 3 (October 2015): 405–434. https://doi.org/10.3366/ajicl.2015.0129. Reproduced with permission of The Licensor through PLSclear.

British Library Cataloguing in Publication Information Available

Library of Congress Control Number: 2019950449
ISBN 978-1-4985-6664-3 (cloth)
ISBN 978-1-4985-6665-0 (electronic)

To God Almighty for His countless blessings and wisdom.

In honor of the struggles of all indigenous peoples and minorities all over the globe, and to the memory of Grandpa—*a gentle and kind soul*

Contents

Acknowledgments

I am grateful to God for sustaining me throughout the challenging period of researching and writing this book.

I am also gratefully indebted to all my colleagues, friends, and professional contacts at the UIC John Marshall Law School Chicago, University of Arizona, Arizona State University, and beyond, who supported in many different ways in the making of this book. To Professors Karen Cross, Paul Lewis, Melissa Tatum, Robert Williams Jr., Leslye Obiora, James Hopkins, Rebecca Tsosie, Sergio Puig, Julie Murphy Erfani, Scott Barclay, and Natsu Taylor Saito, many thanks for their kind support. Many thanks and appreciation also go to the Maya people of southern Belize for the enduring friendship and the opportunity to work and learn within their communities.

I am especially grateful to Professors Imran Smith of SOAS University of London, for the invaluable support and critical comments about trends in the areas of law and development in Africa and international environmental law, and James Anaya, the former UN Special Rapporteur on the Rights of Indigenous Peoples, for the first-hand learning experience about critical human rights issues concerning indigenous peoples.

I express my profound thanks to Moira Gracey for reading drafts of the manuscript and for providing excellent comments and suggestions. Her insightful critique and vital suggested edits significantly strengthened this book. I am also grateful to Alysha Green, Lauren Hernandez, and Yodennis Rodriguez for assisting with editorial work in preparing the manuscript for publication.

Finally, I would like to thank and appreciate all members of my family for their loving support and encouragement. To *Grandma* and my siblings, your support and fervent prayers never went unnoticed. Most of all, my profound gratitude to my angels, Maguette and Zara, it is you who fueled this project and make it all worthwhile.

I retain the full responsibility for any errors or shortcomings in this book.

Preface

During my more than a decade of research and professional work on issues concerning international economic development and human rights, I had the privilege of interacting with many corporate personnel whose companies add great value to our society by creating beneficial goods and services, but grapple with the challenges of compliant operational conduct and corporate profit-making, especially in a changing global environment. I was also fortunate to meet and interact with several indigenous communities from different parts of the world. I learned a great deal from the experiences of these indigenous communities in rising above the legacy of historical oppressive practices that beset them and their determination to ensure that corporate projects or government initiatives occurring within their territories respect their rights and protect their interests. This book benefits immensely from these remarkable encounters, and the invaluable insights derived from them. This book has also grown out my doctoral dissertation work undertaken at the University of Arizona.

My principal goals in researching and writing this book were to facilitate the understanding of key emerging issues and trends in the areas of international human rights law and economic development policies, and issues concerning contemporary socio-cultural growths, and to advance understanding about these issues within the context of indigenous peoples' rights normative framework and the compliance responsibilities of corporations. In addition to providing much analysis and insight about critical human rights and corporate social responsibility issues and developments, I also intend to offer practical suggestions on how best corporations can address these issues in their day-to-day operations. This book is an important contribution towards the advancement of understanding about the interaction between emerging corporate social responsibility practices and the norms concerning human rights of indigenous peoples.

I have thoroughly enjoyed writing this book, and my hope is that you enjoy reading it as well. Although, I have researched and worked on many of the subjects and issues discussed in this book for many years, writing it has been as much of an educational experience for me as I hope it will be for those who read it.

Jide James-Eluyode
October 2019

Introduction

Issues concerning corporate social responsibility (CSR) and human rights of indigenous peoples have continued to generate intense debates within national and international forums. The reason, to a large extent, is the increasing role of corporations in modern society, and the impact of their operational activities. In addition, the concept of *indigenous rights*, a set of collectively enjoyed human rights meant to protect the rights of indigenous peoples as a unit, also emerged in the international arena, and created significant effects on existing socioeconomic and legal frameworks at the national and international levels. These developments have prompted debates; in some cases contentious, about what should be the proper measure of corporate responsibility, especially with respect to the human rights of communities who host corporate projects.

Traditionally, States owe the primary duty for ensuring the well-being of their populations and maintaining the effective governance of their geographical boundaries, including the regulation of corporate actors. However, in today's modern society, corporate activities and projects have had significant impact on communities in the same manner as governmental actions. Moreover, corporate entities, under the umbrella of social responsibility (corporate philanthropy) have, apparently, stepped into the role of performing some functions traditionally discharged by political governments, such as the provision of social amenities and educational infrastructures for local populations.

The reality within many national jurisdictions, especially in developing parts of the world, is that big corporations have become powerful enough to influence political and social events in those jurisdictions where they operate, in such a way that impedes a States' ability to regulate their conduct. Thus, it is imperative that these intricate cross-connections between State and corporate actions be subjected to greater scrutiny, especially in relation to the duty owed by corporate actors to society.

Since the focus of human rights has shifted from an individual-based set of rights to incorporate collective-based human rights meant to protect indigenous groups, so must shift the basis for evaluating corporate conduct. Hence the need for a text that provides illuminating perspectives on this emerging area of human rights and corporate practices. This book uses diverse case studies and illustrations to advance understanding about the various issues and trends concerning CSR and the implication of indigenous rights' normative framework. In addition, the reader is provided with informative discussion about wide-ranging human rights situations pertaining to indigenous peoples around the world, with particular emphasis on indigenous communities located in developing parts of the world.

Indeed, a basic theme explored throughout this book is the probing of the character of social responsibility practices by corporations, especially how they fulfill the responsibility to respect human rights in general, and indigenous rights in particular. This book offers new perspectives on the question of whether or not the application of the concept of CSR is adequate as the sole focal point for evaluating corporate conduct in relation to human rights of indigenous peoples. This book also considers the different propositions calling for concrete corporate human rights obligation and evaluates the various global attempts to heighten the responsibility of corporate entities to respect human rights from a mere moral platitude to a substantive legal obligation.

This book comprises of eight chapters. Chapter 1 sets the stage by previewing, in a concise manner, the many intricate issues and major conceptual challenges that are discussed in greater detail throughout subsequent chapters of the book. This chapter evaluates the nature of human rights of indigenous peoples and its evolution under the international systems, and appraises the scope of the impact of corporate operational activities on indigenous communities. This chapter also offers introductory definitions and explanations of relevant subjects and concepts underlying the thesis explored in this book.

Chapter 2 examines, in greater detail, the term *indigenous peoples* and its ramifications under international law, especially in the context of how the term is perceived and applied in different regions of the world. This chapter equally analyzes the notion of factors-based approach to defining the term *indigenous peoples*, and how such an approach affords indigenous peoples more opportunity to vindicate their claims.

Chapter 3 scrutinizes the concept of CSR, its essential elements as currently understood and practiced, its application and effectiveness in dealing with issues relating to human rights of indigenous peoples, as well as the implication of the concept's misperception and practices in different parts of the world. In order to provide a proper context for measuring corporate responsibility for human rights of indigenous peoples, chapter 3 evaluates the scope of corporate *due diligence duty* for human rights of indigenous peoples, and looks at emerging corporate approaches to ensuring compliance with international human rights standards.

Chapter 4 examines the challenge posed by the lack of desire and practical capacity by States, especially on the part of governments in developing countries, to impose strict regulatory limitations on corporate entities. In addition, this chapter examines various global efforts to redefine corporate responsibility through the establishment of a universal binding code of conduct to regulate multinational corporations.

Chapter 5 discusses one of the most common problems facing indigenous groups throughout the world; lack of implementation of a good faith consultation process before governmental authorities make decisions about measures or permit corporate projects that may affect indigenous communities. This chapter also examines the current international normative standards on the right of indigenous peoples to consultation, as well as the various *soft* regulatory frameworks concerning corporate responsibility to consult.

Chapter 6 focuses on the challenge associated with the operationalization of indigenous peoples' right to consultation in developing, and to a reasonable extent, developed countries. In this regard, chapter 6 evaluates the strengths, or weakness thereof, of several legislative and constitutional provisions, and other regulatory frameworks, existing in different jurisdictions across the world.

Chapter 7 evaluates issues concerning corporate approaches in terms of ensuring that their operational activities fully respect the consultation right of indigenous peoples, along with the various compliance challenges associated with a corporation's fulfillment of its due diligence duty to consult. This evaluation was done within the context of the current framework which maintains a distinction between State's duty to consult (obligatory) and a corporation's due diligence duty to conduct consultation (non-obligatory). In this regard, chapter 7 considers situations where the business interests of corporations and those of States are intertwined or contractually merged under a single corporate structure. Furthermore, chapter 7 examines whether the rationale for maintaining the distinction between the substantive legal duty of States and non-binding corporate due diligence duty to consult presents a great challenge in terms of the effectiveness of the consultation right as a valuable safeguard that indigenous communities can depend on.

Lastly, chapter 8 analyzes the evolving patterns in project development and implementation, such as the proactive participation of indigenous peoples in natural resource project development and the idea of independent third-party monitoring of corporate projects (as a safeguard for securing the rights of indigenous communities). An examination of these emerging patterns is particularly essential, considering that the preexisting model for project implementation within indigenous peoples' territories is one that oftentimes excludes the affected communities from the decision-making process concerning development and implementation of such projects. This final chapter offers closing remarks and suggestions on how best corporations can incorporate indigenous peoples' compliance protocol as part of their day-to-day operations.

The author notes that some aspects of chapters 5, 6, and 7 of this book were part of the author's earlier published journal article with the Edinburgh University's *African Journal of International & Comparative Law*.[1] However, the issues as discussed throughout this portion of the book were expanded and updated with new research materials and insights.

NOTE

1. *See* Jide James-Eluyode, The Blurred Lines: Analyzing the Dynamics of States' Duty and Corporate Responsibility to Consult in Developing Countries, *AJICL*, Vol. 23, No. 3 (2015), 405–434.

Chapter 1

Overview of Challenges and Conceptual Notes

THE BACKDROP

Indigenous peoples often live in the most biodiverse regions on earth, and many indigenous communities occupy areas of the world with an abundance of natural resources. These indigenous communities, who frequently experience marginalization and discrimination, are uniquely impacted by the intense bio-prospecting and resource extraction activities of both private corporations and governmental authorities conducted within or near their territories. In many cases, this difficult state of affairs brings about strife, especially considering that extractive projects are oftentimes associated with environmental pollution, land dispossession, and human rights infractions.[1] The predicament faced by the indigenous Shuar village in Ecuador typifies the kind of situation in question here.

Military drones and police helicopters circle above the Shuar indigenous village of *El Tink*, an Amazonian community in Ecuador where a high-profile dispute against a Chinese copper mine has become a standoff and a siege. Some wear masks to hide their faces. Others appear so casual they could be out for an afternoon stroll. But together, they take it in shifts to guard the crossing 24 hours a day. Friendly vehicles are allowed through. Government forces are turned back, but the siege is exacting a humanitarian toll on the villagers. Aerial surveillance is the only way the authorities can monitor this cloud forest enclave because residents have blocked the sole entrance to their home: a bouncing plank-and-cable bridge suspended 15 meters above the brown torrents of the Zamora river. The river protects us. The military can't cross the bridge because we guard it day and night. If they come, we'll set fire to it . . . . But we feel like we are captives.

1

We can't leave this place because we fear we will be arrested. That means we can't work so we have to forage deep into the forest for food. Some days our children go to sleep without eating a single meal.[2]

With increasing frequency, there have been disputes between indigenous communities and governmental authorities around the world. These disputes are usually over lands and natural resources found within those communities: Who owns these lands and resources, who can exercise control over them, and who has the power to allow corporate entities to extract and commercialize those resources? The global community saw this type of contention play out for many years in the Marlin mine case in Guatemala.[3] In that case, the Maya indigenous people within the San Marcos area of northwestern Guatemala persistently protested GoldCorp Incorporation's operation of the Marlin gold and silver mine within their territory. They alleged, among other things, that GoldCorp's operations at the mine, including its use of cyanide and possible release of metals into the water system, posed severe environmental risks to the communities, and that the operation would cause a disruption to local agricultural activities. The Guatemalan government permitted GoldCorp's mining operation in that area.[4]

Similarly, in Nigeria, the Ogoni people, who live within the Niger Delta region of that country, were, for decades, embroiled in a struggle with the government of Nigeria, the Shell Petroleum Development Company of Nigeria, Royal Dutch Shell, and other oil and gas companies, over the community's unrelenting protests against the environmental degradation and human rights violations arising from the Nigerian government-sanctioned exploitation of the natural resources located within Ogoniland.[5] Like the Marlin mine case in Guatemala, the Ogoni peoples' struggle with governmental authority and oil companies in Nigeria turned violent on some occasions, resulting in death and injury to several people, including key community leaders.[6]

A rather captivating illustration of this type of conflict was recently displayed in the Dakota Access pipeline case in the United States.[7] The Standing Rock Sioux Native American Tribe led one of the biggest congregations of indigenous groups in recent American history to protest a U.S. Army Corps of Engineers–approved pipeline construction project. The pipeline built by Energy Transfer Partners L.P., run within close proximity to the Standing Rock Sioux reservation. The pipeline was designed to pass underneath the Mississippi and Missouri rivers, and Lake *Oahe* near the Tribe's reservation. According to the Tribe, the construction of the pipeline poses a risk to the community in terms of possible significant disturbance and destruction of sacred tribal sites and cultural heritages along its path.[8]

Oftentimes, the types of situations highlighted above are played out in long-running and bitter litigation, in the media, at community centers, and on city streets. In the majority of these cases, there is a common theme: it is no longer a bilateral struggle between the communities and governmental authorities, but rather, a trilateral one—involving the communities, government, and corporations. What role do corporations play? Do they owe any duties to their host communities under international and national human rights law, and if so, what? What is the nature of CSR implicated thereby and how does it fit in the overall scheme of indigenous peoples' rights? This book explores those questions, from a pragmatic perspective.

MAJOR CHALLENGES

A number of practical and conceptual challenges impede efforts to advance and protect the human rights of indigenous peoples. Chapter 1 previews some of these challenges; they will, however, be discussed in greater detail in subsequent chapters throughout this book. Discussions in this chapter also lay the foundation for substantive issues that will be addressed in subsequent chapters and offer introductory definitions and explanations of relevant subjects and concepts.

With the advent of globalization and rapid technological advancements, there has been a remarkable expansion of corporate ventures into and within several regions of the world. These developments have significantly widened the exposure of both State and non-state actors, such as corporations, to sets of diverse stakeholders, and thereby increasing the likelihood of human rights violations occurring. Additionally, the notion of collective human rights and its application to situations of indigenous peoples, which received recognition under international law, have generated significant compliance complexities for corporations. Thus, it is imperative for corporations to re-evaluate their operational activities and to appraise the nature of the responsibility they owe to indigenous peoples and their communities. It is apparent now more than ever, that the pursuit of profit and respect for human rights are not mutually opposing objectives: rather, they are intricately connected.[9]

In the past, corporate entities have strived to meet their human rights compliance burden by developing formal corporate policies that reflect the corporations' commitment to respect general human rights standards, including indigenous peoples' rights. Oftentimes these types of corporate policies are formulated by relying on the traditional individual-based human rights framework. However, a corporation may fail to fully discharge its human rights compliance burden by simply responding to the compliance challenges associated with human rights of indigenous peoples using the same corporate policy measures meant for traditional individual-based human rights. While indigenous peoples' rights may fittingly be deemed conceptually analogous to traditional individual-based human rights, the nature of the constituent rights that indigenous peoples' rights embody is characteristically unique.[10]

Developing countries,[11] especially, struggle to embrace the notion of indigenous people's rights. As a result, they have lagged behind in ensuring effective promotion and protection of the human rights of their indigenous populations. In addition, the intense desire by corporate entities to exploit and commercialize the diverse natural resources found within the territories of many indigenous communities has led to the destruction of, and interference with, the socio-cultural and economic way of life of those communities. For instance, the nearly forty-two million indigenous people spread across Latin America continue to experience a widening development chasm between their communities and those of the dominant societies in which they live.[12] While there has been progress in some Latin American countries to develop legislations and policies for protecting rights of their indigenous populations, the fact that a notable disconnect still exists between these legislations and policies, and their implementation, has been fatal to much of the progress made thus far.[13] James Anaya, the former United Nations (UN) Special Rapporteur on the rights of indigenous peoples, placed this challenging situation in proper context when he stated that

> in many cases in which extractive companies have been identified as responsible for, or at least associated with, violations of the rights of indigenous peoples, those violations occur in countries with weak regulatory regimes, and the responsible companies are domiciled in other, typically much more developed, countries.[14]

It is apparent that the practical and conceptual challenges that impede the advancement of indigenous peoples' human rights are more prevalent in developing parts of the world. By way of example, in Africa, efforts aimed at protecting the human rights of indigenous peoples and ensuring corporate accountability for violations of such rights at the same time have been particularly constricted by two broad factors. One is the general misperception about the concept of *indigenous peoples* or *indigenous rights*, which created a perplexing conundrum within the African continent, as to whether the concept of indigenous rights even applies to their populations.[15] This dilemma was equally echoed by the African Commission's Working Group of Expert on Indigenous Populations/Communities, when the body described the situation as follows:

The Resolution on the Rights of Indigenous Populations/Communities in Africa reflects the ambiguity felt within the African Commission about this initiative. It also reflects a divergence of conceptual thought between French and English-speaking members. The expression "indigenous" had long been problematic within the African Commission and the report attempts to deal with the matter.[16]

Another factor is differences in how the concept of CSR is generally perceived or practiced in developing countries, in contrast to how it is understood in developed countries around the world. While discretionary philanthropic acts seem to be the major component of CSR in many developing countries, strict legal compliance, superior ethical practice, and adequate public health and environmental safeguards have been the prime requisites of CSR in developed countries.[17] The effect of these conceptual differences is significant because it has, for a long time, formed the basis for corporate attitude in developing countries, and has influenced how well corporations react to the legal and moral demands of communities in those countries. An appreciation of this factor is particularly important for any evaluation of corporate operational activities within, or near, territories of indigenous communities in developing countries, where domestic regulatory frameworks and safeguards for corporate conduct are weak, inadequate, or lacking. To the extent that corporations in these places tend to implement double standards in their operational codes of conduct—one, which treats the human rights of host communities in developing countries without due regard—and another, incorporating sufficient human rights safeguards and ethical standards as it pertains to their activities in developed countries.[18]

This plight was compounded by the fact that currently, under international law, a binding and direct legal duty to uphold human rights standards has been attributed only to States.[19] Corporations are, therefore, not subject to direct binding legal obligations to uphold human rights standards, except to the extent of regulations imposed upon them through States' domestic laws, whether or not such domestic laws incorporate important and adequate international human rights standards and environmental safeguards. As a result, corporations have been, for the most part, guided by an array of non-binding voluntary codes or self-regulation, a situation that has encouraged offhand attitudes towards the human rights safeguards necessary to protect the communities who host corporate projects. Some have suggested that when dialogue involves the determination of what corporations' legal responsibility for human rights ought to be, they should be subject to the scrutiny of a substantive set of laws with respect to, at minimum, core issues such as environmental degradation, human rights abuse, and corruption.[20]

NATURE AND DEVELOPMENT OF HUMAN RIGHTS OF INDIGENOUS PEOPLES

From Individual Human Rights to Collective Human Rights

Human rights relate to the essential rights and protections enjoyed by all humans. The assurance of these rights is of vital importance to the establishment of fair, just, and civilized societies.

> Human rights are rights inherent to all human beings, whatever our nationality, place of residence, sex, national or ethnic origin, color, religion, language, or any other status. We are all equally entitled to our human rights without discrimination. These rights are all interrelated, interdependent and indivisible.[21]

Traditionally, the focal point of human rights has been the freedoms and protections due to individual members within the society. In contrast, the cornerstone of human rights as a fundamental framework for indigenous peoples' rights is the *communal* rights possessed by groups, jointly.[22]

The concept of human rights has generally referred to possession of innate privileges that a person is entitled to enjoy simply because of his/her humanity.[23] Human rights are composed of those basic standards of human existence, the absence of which restrain the capacity of every person to live in dignity and undermines their self-worth.[24] These rights are based on the principle that every person, irrespective of who or where he or she is, is the subject of rights and is entitled to all civil, political, economic, social, and cultural rights.[25] The idea of human rights has been recognized globally as the fundamental requirement for upholding human dignity, freedom, peace, and justice in all societies.[26] It is now a common understanding at the international, regional, and domestic levels that the concept of human rights encompasses a certain sum of values necessary to preserve the worth of people everywhere—irrespective of national boundaries and cultural affiliations.[27]

The modern conception of internationally affirmed human rights arose in the twentieth century.[28] This era, marked by brutish wars and unimaginable atrocities, especially among the most developed countries, saw countries around the world come together and collectively resolve to tackle increasing infractions on the liberty, freedom, dignity, and worth of a person.[29] This common global understanding resulted in the establishment of the UN in 1945 and later, the adoption of the Universal Declaration of Human Rights (UDHR) by the UN General Assembly in December of 1948.[30] Undoubtedly, the adoption of the UDHR constitutes a turning point in the development of human rights as a cardinal concept. The UDHR memorializes the firm collective commitment of governments all over the world, to ensure the promotion and realization of universal respect for and observance of human rights and fundamental freedoms.[31]

However, historical accounts have suggested that the evolution of human rights can be traced as far back as medieval times.[32] During this period, the theory of natural law and natural rights began its rapid expansion as the bedrock of human rights as we now know it today. To this extent, the natural rights theory provided secure grounding for contemporary international human rights standards.[33] Natural rights proponents have argued that the existence of certain fundamental inalienable human rights such as the right to life, liberty, and property are traceable to natural law.[34] They contend that such rights exist as a result of a higher law rather than man-made law, and that such a higher law constitutes a universal and absolute set of principles, which governs all human beings.[35]

An oft-recited historical account about the evolution of contemporary human rights standards is that they were conceived as rights enjoyed by individuals only. Under the natural rights theory, it is presumed that an individual (*not groups or collectives*) enters into the community of other human beings, with some basic rights of which no authority or government can deprive the person. As Thomas Aquinas puts it, natural law, which he asserted as being the foundational basis for the evolution of human rights, confers certain immutable rights upon *individuals*.[36] Some have justified their characterization of human rights standards as inhering only in individuals by arguing that the contours of human rights of peoples, as a social construct, is repugnant to the notion of human rights of a person, and constitute a snag to its advancement.[37] They add that the abstract concept of collective human rights, often, presents significant obstruction, which stultifies the enjoyment by individuals of their human rights.[38] To bolster these kinds of assertions, critics of collective human rights tend to claim that, because most traditional human rights instruments only admit individuals as the principal beneficiaries of rights proclaimed by such instruments, this reality undermines the value of the notion of collective human rights.[39] They argue that this type of *lacuna* impugns the utility of such a conceptual framework.[40]

Clearly, such assertions by critics of collective human rights are incongruous with the prevailing international consensus on this issue. Such claims are incompatible in tone with the position of the UN, as reflected in the UN Declaration on the Rights of Indigenous Peoples.[41] In contrast, other scholars have argued that an insistence that human rights can only be held as individual rights will be, for all practical purposes, at variance with the social realities of human situations.[42] They contend that conjoined rights, such as the rights of people or the rights of cultural minorities, are valid constituents of human rights.[43]

Moreover, the claim that the objectives of collective human rights are unattainable because most primary human rights instruments only admit individual beneficiaries is not merely misleading, but erroneous. This is so because the UN Charter of 1945, International Convention on the Elimination of All Forms of Racial Discrimination (ICERD) of 1965, International Covenant on Civil and Political Rights (ICCPR) of 1966, and the International Covenant on Economic, Social, and Cultural Rights (ICESCR) of 1966 contain provisions that protect and respect collective rights. Article 1(2) of the UN Charter states that one of the important purposes and principles of the UN is developing friendly relations *among nations* based on respect for the principle of equal rights and self-determination of peoples.[44] In addition, Article 1, common to both ICCPR and ICESCR, also clearly provides as follows:

(1) All peoples have the right of self-determination. By virtue of that right they freely determine their political status and freely pursue their economic, social and cultural development.
(2) All peoples may, for their own ends, freely dispose of their natural wealth and resources without prejudice to any obligations arising out of international economic co-operation, based upon the principle of mutual benefit, and international law. In no case, may a people be deprived of its own means of subsistence.
(3) The States Parties to the present Covenant, including those having responsibility for the administration of Non-Self-Governing and Trust Territories, shall promote the realization of the right of self-determination, and shall respect that right, in conformity with the provisions of the Charter of the UN.[45]

Developments within the area of international human rights in the past three decades also reinforce the triumph of the notions that human rights of peoples are compatible with the tenets of traditional human rights.[46] For instance, to underscore the relevance of the primary international human rights instruments for the promotion and protection of both human rights of persons, and peoples, the Committee on the Elimination of Racial Discrimination (CERD), a UN treaty monitoring body, has on some occasion declared that securing the protection of the right of indigenous peoples, as collective units, to be free from discrimination falls within the scope of the International Convention on the Elimination of all forms of Racial Discrimination of 1965.[47] The CERD concluded that the Convention on the Elimination of all forms of Racial Discrimination will apply to any form of discriminatory acts perpetrated against peoples.[48]

Certainly, the endorsement of the concept of human rights of peoples, through its wide international support, has removed any skepticism as to the applicability of primary international human rights instruments to the situation of indigenous peoples. Nowhere is this endorsement more distinctly encapsulated than in the pronouncements of several UN institutions, including the Secretariat of the UN Permanent Forum on Indigenous Issues. Due to the peculiar circumstances of indigenous groups within society, the disproportionate discrimination they have suffered, and in line with the fundamental human rights principles of universality, equality, and non-discrimination, the UN Permanent Forum on Indigenous Issues concluded the following:

> Indigenous peoples are entitled to the full range of rights established under international law. However, indigenous peoples have distinct and unique cultures and world views that are part of their collective rights, and their needs, aspirations and development strategies for the future may differ from those of the mainstream population. Their equal worth and dignity can only be assured through the recognition and protection not only of their individual rights, but also of their collective rights as distinct peoples. It is when these rights are asserted collectively that they can be realized in a meaningful way.[49]

The Fundamentals of Indigenous Peoples' Rights

In recent times, many indigenous groups have adopted the platform provided by international law as their preferred functional tool for asserting their collective rights and ensuring their cultural survival, within their various national boundaries. The ILO Convention (No. 169) concerning Indigenous and Tribal Peoples in Independent Countries (1989)[50] and the UN Declaration on the Rights of Indigenous Peoples (UNDRIP) 2007[51] are the two preeminent international instruments that recognize indigenous peoples as an important subject of human rights concerns, and provide the footing for the concept of indigenous rights to thrive. These two instruments established the broad normative framework for the promotion and protection of human rights of peoples. As earlier noted in this chapter, other international human rights instruments, such as the ICESCR,[52] ICCPR,[53] and ICERD,[54] have also been applied to deal with indigenous rights issues.[55]

Both the UNDRIP and ILO Convention (No. 169) have been lauded for establishing a cognizable scheme for the recognition and protection of indigenous peoples' collective rights. It is, however, worth pointing out here that there some who hold critical views about UNDRIP, alleging, for example, that the document is inherently flawed, and, therefore, cannot effectively serve as a fundamental framework for protecting the rights of indigenous peoples.[56] Those who find fault with UNDRIP argued that the document is significantly weakened because it fails to address the issue of domination and indigenous peoples, and that its Article 4 and Article 46 constitute an encumbrance for limiting the ability of indigenous peoples to fully enjoy their right to self-determination.[57]

Nevertheless, UNDRIP represents the sheer determination of indigenous peoples to ensure the protection of their rights by the international community. This collective aspiration, overwhelmingly adopted by the global society, was evidently echoed in the first article of UNDRIP, which affirms that indigenous peoples have the full enjoyment, as a collective or as individuals, of all human rights and fundamental freedoms as recognized in the Charter of the UN, the UDHR, and international human rights law.[58]

Admittedly, the breadth and limits of indigenous rights are still evolving, but the questions as to the nature of those rights are largely settled. More to the point, indigenous rights are mainly a collection of distinctive normative prescriptions codified for the purpose of protecting and promoting the human rights of indigenous peoples or groups, which they enjoyed in community. Indigenous-specific rights evolved as a result of the conscious attempt by the international community to apply certain aspects of general human rights standards in dealing with a peculiar form of violations and marginalization in society.[59] This array of rights was meant to afford indigenous groups an opportunity to enjoy human rights as a societal unit. The scope and variety of collective human rights covered by the UNDRIP and ILO Convention (No. 169) include the following:

- right to collective survival;[60]
- right to life and security;[61]
- right to self-determination/self-government;[62]
- rights to participation and prior consultations;[63]
- rights to land, territories and natural resources;[64]
- right to health;[65]
- right to religion;[66]
- right to education;[67]
- right to environmental conservation and protection;[68]
- right to live in freedom;[69] and
- rights to language, cultural identity, and intellectual property.[70]

Indigenous Peoples: Connotation and Denotation

There is no universally applicable definition of the term *indigenous peoples*. A majority within the international arena is of the view that a formal universal definition is inessential.[71] Interestingly, both the UNDRIP and

ILO Convention (No. 169), the two foremost international instruments on indigenous rights, do not offer any formal definition of the term *indigenous peoples*, but rather validate the rights of indigenous groups to determine their own identity in accordance with their customs and traditions, to show their distinct cultural features and a collective attachment to the territory where they are located.[72]

Nonetheless, in a general sense, the term *indigenous peoples* refers to members of a distinct cultural group having customary, economic, social, or political ways of life that may be different from those of the dominant society, and who possess special traditional attachment to the lands or territories they occupy.[73] The most widely cited description of the term *indigenous peoples* was that proposed by José R. Martínez Cobo, the former UN Special Rapporteur of the Sub-Commission on Prevention of Discrimination and Protection of Minorities, in his report titled "the Study on the Problem of Discrimination against Indigenous Populations."[74] Cobo defines indigenous peoples as "those which, having a historical continuity with pre-invasion and pre-colonial societies that developed on their territories, consider themselves distinct from other sectors of the societies now prevailing in those territories, or parts of them."[75]

Cobo's definition and other related conceptual challenges highlighted in this chapter will be discussed in greater detail in chapter 2 of this book.

Indigenous peoples constitute a significant and important part of the global society, occupying about 20 percent of the world's land surface.[76] The combined population of indigenous peoples around the world is about four hundred million people, spread across numerous territories and over more than ninety countries in all continents.[77] Even in the Arctic regions, there are several indigenous groups who have developed unique ways, and livelihood strategies, to adapt to the harsh climatic conditions of the region.[78] Examples of indigenous groups include the First Nations in Canada, Aboriginal and Torres Strait Islander people in Australia, Maori people in New Zealand, Guaraní Indians in Brazil, the Maya people in Central America, the Sami ethnic group in Norway, the Hill tribes in Thailand, the Adivasi people in India, the San tribe in South Africa, the Ogoni people in Nigeria, the Maasai people in Kenya, and of course, Native Americans in the United States. One common defining feature of indigenous peoples is that they have close relationships with, and are inextricably connected to, the lands they traditionally occupy and the attached natural resources on which they rely.

A discussion of indigenous peoples' rights is more pertinent to the overall landscape of our global economy and social makeups than many people recognize. Even though the total population of indigenous groups throughout the world is less than half a billion, the majority of the world's remaining natural resources lie within territories of indigenous peoples.[79] For instance, in the

United States, over 50 percent of the country's uranium deposits, and one-third of its low-sulfur coal reserves are located within territories of Native American tribes.[80] Also, in India, more than 70 percent of the country's bauxite deposits spread across South Odisha and Andhra Pradesh are found on lands and forests occupied and used by the Adivasis and other indigenous peoples.[81] Similarly, a 2014 report examining energy development on Native American lands found that the energy resources beneath those lands contain about 30 percent of the United States' coal reserves, more than 50 percent of potential uranium reserves, and over 20 percent of the country's known oil and gas reserves, worth nearly US$1.5 trillion.[82]

Indigenous territories in Latin American countries have also served as a vital source for the global supply of solid minerals, including nickel, gold, and silver. Brazil is the source of over 90 percent of the world's niobium reserves; Chile and Argentina provide about 65 percent of the world's lithium reserves; about half of the world's known economically recoverable silver deposits are located in Peru, Chile, Mexico, and Bolivia combined; and over 40 percent of the global copper reserves are found in Peru, Chile, and Mexico.[83] Similarly, in Nigeria, over 70 percent of the country's total oil and gas production output, which equates to about 75 percent of the national government's annual revenue, is derived from the indigenous territories within the Niger Delta region of the country.[84]

Evolution of Indigenous Peoples' Rights under the International Systems

Indigenous peoples are very diverse, in terms of their cultural and linguistic attributes, as well as their defining way of life. Nonetheless, one commonality is that indigenous communities across the world share a history of marginalization, discrimination, and injustice.[85] These critical experiences of indigenous peoples are traceable to long-standing patterns of oppression and subjugation associated with the period of conquest and the colonization of territories occupied by indigenous peoples around the world.[86] The *doctrine of discovery*, widely used by the colonists as the basis for a unilateral takeover of indigenous people's lands and resources, embody the patterns of oppression and subjugation prevalent during that era.[87] The 1494 *Treaty of Tordesillas*, by which Portugal and Spain divided up the Americas between themselves, while ignoring the indigenous communities already occupying the area,[88] and the 1885 *General Act of the Berlin Conference*, used by the colonial powers of Europe to partition and expropriate lands belonging to indigenous communities in Africa, without their consent, are both legacies of colonialism, and serve as a pointer to the continuing reality faced by these indigenous communities today.[89]

Struggle by indigenous peoples to make their voices heard and ensure protection for their collective rights has been going on within many national boundaries for more than a century. As an example, the 1763 Royal Proclamation[90] fueled the movement by Canada's First Nations to secure legal basis for their aboriginal rights during that period,[91] and the 1832 landmark case of *Worcester v. Georgia*,[92] in which the U. S. Supreme Court recognized Native American tribes as sovereign and self-governing entities, resulted from the unrelenting advocacy effort of the Cherokee Nation.[93]

Despite the immense challenges, indigenous rights advocates around the world made a concerted effort, especially, in the past three decades to keep indigenous peoples' issues at the center stage within the international discourse, notably since the establishment of the UN Working Group on Indigenous Populations (WGIP) in 1982.[94] The adoption of UNDRIP in 2007 resulted from that effort, and is now widely acknowledged as the greatest singular accomplishment in the area of indigenous peoples' human rights to date.

However, organized efforts to protect the rights of indigenous peoples, at the international level, really began in the early twentieth century. Historical accounts suggest that, as far back as the 1920s, indigenous leaders such as T.W. Ratana, a Maori religious leader in New Zealand, and Chief Deskaheh of the Six Nations, a confederation of Native American Indian tribes, organized a visit to the defunct League of Nations in Geneva on an advocacy mission to seek protection for the rights of their peoples.[95] But, the international institutional system only began to give meaningful attention to issues concerning indigenous peoples from the 1980s onward,[96] and in particular the turning point in 1982 with the establishment of the WGIP.[97] The Working Group provided the first and, at the time, the only consequential platform within the UN systems for dealing with issues relating to the indigenous peoples' human rights.[98]

The subsequent establishment of the UN Voluntary Fund for Indigenous Populations (VFIP) in 1985 greatly assisted the work of the WGIP.[99] The VFIP constituted a pivotal development at the time and became a valuable catalyst that accelerated the promotion and protection of the human rights of indigenous populations.[100] The fund provided the much-needed financial assistance to various representatives of indigenous communities and organizations, which enabled them to attend and actively participate in the deliberations of the WGIP.[101] The activities of the WGIP eventually led to the historic adoption of the UNDRIP in 2007.[102]

Beyond the impact of the WGIP and VFIP, other factors aided the development of indigenous rights. Some of these factors include the adoption of the ILO Convention (No. 169) concerning Indigenous and Tribal Peoples in Independent Countries by the General Conference of the International

Labour Organization in June 1989,[103] the foremost international convention
that directly addresses the rights of indigenous peoples.[104] The 1992 United
Nations Conference on Environment and Development (UNCEED), otherwise referred to as the Rio Earth Summit, also played an important role in
providing global visibility for indigenous issues. The Earth Summit resulted
in the adoption of the Rio Declaration on Environment and Development,
which incorporates provisions recognizing the role of indigenous peoples
within the global environmental and developmental system. The Declaration
sets an important precedent, by stating the following in Principle 22:

> Indigenous people and their communities, and other local communities have
> a vital role in environmental management and development because of their
> knowledge and traditional practices. States should recognize and duly support
> their identity, culture and interest and enable their effective participation in the
> achievement of sustainable development.[105]

Furthermore, the 1993 United Nations World Conference on Human
Rights held in Vienna, Austria, was equally a key contributing factor in
accelerating the development of indigenous peoples' rights.[106] Given its status
as one of the largest congregations ever on the issue of human rights, it is
not surprising that the Vienna Conference, in its concluding Declaration and
Programme of Action, recommended that new steps be taken to promote and
protect the rights of indigenous peoples.[107] These new steps led to the creation
of the permanent forum for indigenous peoples' rights within the UN institutional system and its first meeting.[108] Another major outcome of the new
steps called for by the Vienna Conference was the designation, by the UN
General Assembly, of the year 1993, as the International Year of the World's
Indigenous People,[109] as well as the subsequent proclamation of 1995–2004
as the International Decade of the World's Indigenous Peoples.[110]

Indeed, indigenous peoples' rights continue to gain momentum, with
global awareness about the nature of these rights growing rapidly.[111] These
foregoing important developments in the area of indigenous peoples' rights,
and the consistent discussions about issues concerning indigenous peoples
within the international arena in the past three decades that brought them
about, have greatly influenced instrumentalization of indigenous rights
standards within domestic jurisdictions.[112] Countries around the world are
responding to the emergence of these normative rules by enacting new laws
or modifying internal policies to reflect the international standards on indigenous rights within their domestic jurisdictions.[113] Many international human
rights treaties monitoring bodies have also found ways to use preexisting
traditional international human rights instruments to promote and protect
indigenous rights as part of their implementation processes.[114]

Likewise, development of institutional codes of conduct and policy initiatives are now on the rise, as they have become necessary to directly address the issue of corporate responsibility with regard to these new human rights normative standards. As an example, in 2011, the Organization for Economic Cooperation and Development (OECD) adopted a guiding framework (OECD Guidelines for Multinational Enterprises), directed at multinational enterprises operating within OECD countries.[115] The OECD Guidelines for Multinational Enterprises require that all business enterprises respect the internationally recognized human rights of local communities affected by their activities. The Guidelines demand that such multinational enterprises make conscious efforts to engage with local communities as important stakeholders, in order to provide meaningful opportunities for their views to be taken into account in relation to planning and decision-making for any project or other activities that may significantly impact them as host communities.[116]

Similar institutional codes and policy initiatives that were subsequently developed include the World Bank Operational Policy on Indigenous People;[117] the International Financial Corporations (IFC) Performance Standard Code;[118] the World Resource Institute (WRI) Principles for Community Engagement;[119] the International Council on Mining and Metals (ICMM) Position Statement and Good Practice Guide;[120] and the *Akwé: Kon Guidelines.*[121]

CORPORATIONS AND HUMAN RIGHTS
OF INDIGENOUS PEOPLES

The importance of a vibrant commercial climate and resilient business entities to the progress and prosperity of the global economy cannot be overemphasized. In spite of this importance, the stark reality confronting our world today is that, just as corporations, through the products they create and the services they render, add great value, so also, they cause immense negative impacts on the society.[122] The contexts in which corporations operate, as well as the societal expectations regarding their role, have shifted significantly in the past few decades. To this extent, corporate entities now have to reconcile their strong attachment to the traditional objective of maximizing profits with the idea of seeking sustainable profits—that is, creating products or services in a way that is socially responsible, with production processes that are compatible with basic human rights standards.

The concept of CSR is oftentimes perceived as a necessary tool for harmonizing the widening differences between a corporation's business pursuits and societal demand for sound legal and ethical values, with the ultimate objective of encouraging socially responsible corporate behavior. However, the question of whether or not CSR, as a concept, can be an effective tool for appraising corporate conduct with respect to the human rights of indigenous peoples is debatable, and constitutes an integral part of the core issues examined throughout this book.

Across the world, the dialogue is still ongoing as to whether or not governments and corporations should share the legal and moral responsibility for the social and economic well-being of the community of people who are impacted by their activities or initiatives,[123] and if so, to what extent. Whatever the case, achieving a balanced apportionment of responsibilities in this regard is a difficult task, considering that government and corporations have traditionally been allocated separate roles and legal responsibilities within our society. The governmental structure of States, as organized political entities, customarily sets the legal rules and regulations to guide the affairs of their population, including the conduct of corporations operating within their jurisdiction. At the same time, over the years, many corporations have grown larger and more powerful than some national governments.[124] The suspicions about the rapidly increasing influence of corporations within our societal structure are rooted in the belief, shared by some, that a relatively small group of multinational corporations now wield considerable influence over the global economy.[125] They believe that this small group of multinational corporate entities, which collectively control about 60 percent of worldwide revenues, is in a vantage position to drive global events.[126] Joel Bakan, in an attempt to draw attention to what could become a difficult predicament if not addressed, also argued that corporations around the world are gradually transforming into mammoth institutions, dangerous possessors of the great power which they can now wield over people and societies.[127]

As we see today, the assessments of Bakan and others are not far off the mark. Some corporate entities have, in fact, become sizable and have amassed enough influence to impact political events and engage in some form of control over society.[128] The *Chiquita* case[129] provided a good illustration of this situation. In 2007, Chiquita Brands International Inc., one of the world's foremost produce companies, pled guilty to federal charges in the United States for knowingly providing material support to Columbia's right-wing paramilitary group, Autodefensas Unidas de Colombia (AUC), and the left-wing Revolutionary Armed Forces of Colombia (FARC). According to the allegations, Chiquita paid these groups more than US$1.7 million, between 1997 and 2004, as security payments, driven, in part, by the company's desire to influence the sociopolitical dynamics in Columbia in order to secure its continuing access to Colombia's banana growing regions. [130]

With this kind of clout, corporations have been quite successful in carrying on their commercial enterprises in some regions around the world without sufficient regulation or functional safeguards.[131] The most serious concern created by this problematic situation seems to be over corporate operational conduct in developing countries, where economic developmental expediency and national financial constraints have made it more difficult for such countries to impose adequate environmental, labor, and human rights regulatory standards against influential corporations, to the same extent as developed countries.[132] Some have therefore suggested that the governmental authorities of these developing countries are simply not in a position to stand up to the influence of the powerful corporations.[133] This is especially so because, in a bid to spur national economic development, they are compelled to put in place lax regulations or minimal statutory burdens as an incentive to attract foreign direct investments (FDIs).[134]

Corporate Extractive Activities and their Impact on Indigenous Communities

Global demand for oil and gas, solid minerals, and related commodities has continued to grow steadily.[135] As already noted, some of the largest natural resource deposits needed to sustain the ever-growing global demands are found in the territories of indigenous peoples spread across different parts of the world, including developing regions.[136] According to a report about the extractive industry, more than half of the top ten destinations for global mining investments are located in Latin America.[137] Another report of the Inter-American Development Bank, which examined natural resource extraction in Latin America and the Caribbean, concluded that, in the past decades alone, the average FDI in mineral extraction projects poured into Latin American and Caribbean countries reached up to US$800 billion, and is projected to increase to a record high by the year 2020.[138]

A parallel situation subsists with respect to the African continent, which has always been a hotbed for land and natural resource grabs.[139] According to reports, Africa contributed one in every four barrels of new petroleum discovered outside of North America.[140] As early as 2001, seven billion of the total eight billion barrels of new oil reserves worldwide were discovered on the African continent.[141] By the late 2000s, the total FDI streaming into African countries reached an all-time high of US$72 billion, with the majority share of these investments going into the extractive industries such as mining, and oil and gas exploration.[142] In addition, in the decade of the 2000s, an estimated US$1 trillion worth of minerals, metals, and oil had already been extracted from the continent.[143] Interestingly, despite the recent global depreciation in commodity prices, and a depressed economic environment, by 2015, many African countries with substantial natural resource deposits still managed to attract significant foreign investment for the development of their natural resource assets.[144]

By all accounts, patterns of disproportionate impact created by extractive projects on indigenous communities who live within, or are in close proximity to, the area where these projects are located, are quite common.[145] As Naomi Kipuri,[146] a renowned Maasai and anthropologist, pointed out:

> The discovery of oil and precious stones almost always involves violation of the rights of indigenous peoples in order to benefit from the resource areas. The case of the *Ogoni* of Nigeria is a familiar one. Similarly, where tanzanite has been mined in Tanzania, the *Maasai* have been pushed away.[147]

The condition of the indigenous communities who host extractive projects is particularly acute. In the majority of cases, host communities are overburdened by the harsh impact of such projects on their territory, cultural values, way of life, and environmental assets, all of which are essential to their survival. These host communities have demanded respect of their human rights for decades and have been continuously ignored by corporate entities. To make the situation worse, the socio-cultural and economic growth of these indigenous communities is often significantly disrupted, and their way of life as a people undermined, by unmindful corporate extractive activities. The essence of the dire predicament commonly confronted by indigenous communities as a result of extractive activities was appositely captured in the following words:

> Evidence shows that indigenous peoples bear the costs of resource-intensive projects disproportionately, and the human rights effects include loss of traditional territories and land, eviction, migration and eventual resettlement, depletion of resources necessary for physical and cultural survival, destruction and pollution of the traditional environment, social and community disorganization, long-term negative health and nutritional impacts as well as, in some cases, harassment and violence.[148]

Beyond question, indigenous communities have suffered numerous cases of human rights violations, loss of traditional land and resources, environmental pollutions, and long-term adverse health impacts as a result of extractive projects within or around their territories. The Marlin mine and its impact on the indigenous peoples settled within the municipalities of San Miguel Ixtahuacán and Sipacapa in the San Marcos department of northwestern Guatemala is illustrative.[149] As stated above, for many years the communities protested the operation of the Marlin gold and silver mine by GoldCorp Inc. within their territory. They alleged, among other things, that GoldCorp's activities at the mine, particularly its use of cyanide and potential release of metals into the water system, posed severe environmental risks to the communities.[150] A Tufts University report that examined, among other things, the environmental risks of the Marlin mine similarly found that local communities, on the other hand, bear 100 percent of environmental risk. Environmental risk at Marlin is exceptionally high and likely to increase over the remaining life of the mine and into the post-closure phase. Gold mining poses generic hazards related to cyanide and heavy metals contamination of water from acid mine drainage (AMD).[151]

In June of 2010, James Anaya, the then UN Special Rapporteur on the situation of human rights and fundamental freedoms of indigenous people, visited Guatemala to access the situation of the indigenous communities impacted by the Marlin mine. Anaya, in his assessment report, concluded that

> the existence of legitimate demands on the part of the indigenous peoples is undeniable. These demands are founded not only on Guatemala's international human rights obligations but also on elementary considerations of humanity, given the impact of the projects on their ancestral lands. There is obviously a considerable degree of opposition among the indigenous peoples to mining and other extractive industry projects. Their opposition is understandable in the light of the repeatedly reiterated perception that such projects invariably have a negative impact, damaging the land on which the affected communities have always lived and fueling conflict between communities.[152]

The story is no different for indigenous communities who host extractive and other resource-intensive projects in Africa.[153] The African Working Group of Experts on Indigenous Populations/Communities once reported that, in the Great Lakes Region of Africa, activities of corporations executing mining, logging, plantations, and oil exploration concessions continued to have severe consequences for the region and posed a significant threat to the lives and survival of many of the indigenous communities throughout the area.[154] The Republic of Angola, a south-central African country, is another case in point. In Angola, Chevron's oil and gas operation caused massive damage to the environment and livelihood of the indigenous fishing communities in the Cabinda Province of the country.[155] Fishing, which embodies the cultural identity within the community and serves as one of the main source of their sustenance, is now almost impossible due to constant oil spills and leakages.[156] On a number of occasions, Chevron has been admonished by many local and international watchdogs for its disastrous oil spills in Angola and elsewhere, and even penalized for some of its environmental damages caused to communities in that country.[157]

Only few communities have witnessed the extent of monumental environmental disasters and human right violations as the indigenous communities across the Niger Delta region of Nigeria. The Niger Delta region extends over more than 70,000 km square of south-eastern Nigeria and makes up about 7.5 percent of the country's total land mass.[158] The region is reputed to be one of the world's largest deltas, and Africa's most extensive mangrove/swamp forests, comparable to the Mekong, the Amazon, and the Ganges.[159] The Niger Delta has a combined population of about forty million people, including several indigenous ethnic groups, such as the Efik, Ibibio, Ogba, Itsekiri, Urhobo, Isoko, Anang, Ijaw, and the Ogoni people, who spread across nine of the thirty-six constituent states of Nigeria.[160] The Niger Delta states produce over 70 percent of Nigeria's total oil and gas production output, and at times provided more than 70 percent of the national government's annual revenue.[161] However, the intense level of oil and gas exploration activities by multinational corporations, including Shell, Chevron, Texaco, Agip, Exxon-Mobil, Elf, Pan Ocean, and Phillips Oil, has exposed the communities within the Niger Delta region to one of the most grievous human rights violations and environmental degradations ever recorded against a corporation.[162] To cite one example, an environmental impact assessment of Ogoniland in Niger Delta, conducted by United Nations Environment Programme (UNEP), concluded that pollution of soil by petroleum hydrocarbons in Ogoniland was quite extensive inland areas, sediments, and swampland.[163] The UNEP's assessment found that groundwater contamination was prevalent within the communities, with about 8 cm thick layer of refined oil observed floating over the community's wells, contaminating that drinking water with benzene, a known carcinogen, at levels over 900 times above the World Health Organization (WHO) guideline.[164]

Other observers of the situation in the Niger Delta have also pointed out that more than one-half million metric tons of oil, equivalent to fifty times the pollution of Exxon Valdez tanker spill event of March 24, 1989, in Alaska, USA, has been dumped into the Niger Delta area over the course of fifty years.[165] The parlous predicament that became the norm across the Niger Delta region was described as follows:

> What the Niger Delta people used to call upon for their livelihood and well-being has been wrecked for eternity by the coming of oil and its exploration . . . they cannot fish because marine life has been flushed out, they cannot hunt because the game fled a long time ago, thanks to the oil hunters, and their land no longer yields good harvest. The destruction of flora and fauna has been compounded by endemic poverty, the absence of basic social amenities, and at best primitive health and educational facilities.[166]

This account of the extraordinary adverse impact created by extractive projects on indigenous communities is not a categorical conclusion that corporations, and in particular, extractive companies, offer no positive contributions within our societal structure. Nor is it true that there are no instances of successful, productive, and mutually respectful, partnerships between extractive companies and indigenous communities.[167] However, it is important first to highlight ongoing distressing experiences of indigenous communities all over the world, and the disproportionate adverse impact that corporate activities continue to have on their neighborhoods and existence. Second, to invite rigorous dialogue around the question of whether the international community should once again, without delay, take on the challenge of articulating, via international legal instruments, a direct and binding legal duty on corporations with regard to human rights safeguards.

The remainder of this book will examine the conceptual challenges and the implications of the divergent CSR practices, as well as all the other barriers previewed here.

NOTES

1. See, for example, David A. Lertzman and Harrie Vredenburg, Indigenous Peoples, Resource Extraction and Sustainable Development: An Ethical Approach, *Journal of Business Ethics*, Vol. 56, No. 3 (Feb., 2005), pp. 239–254; and, Ruslan Garipov, Resource Extraction from Territories of Indigenous Minority Peoples in the Russian North: International Legal and Domestic Regulation, *Arctic Review on Law and Politics*, Vol. 4, No. 1 (2013), pp. 4–20, at p. 7.

2. See Jonathan Watts, Amazon Land Battle Pits Indigenous Villagers against Might of Ecuador State, *The Guardian* (March 19, 2017), available at https://ww w.theguardian.com/world/2017/mar/19/ecuador-indigenous-shuar-el-tink-mining -land-dispute (last accessed March 18, 2019).

3. See Lyuba Zarsky and Leonardo Stanley, *Searching for Gold in the Highlands of Guatemala: Economic Benefits and Environmental Risks of the Marlin Mine* (GDAE/Tuft Univ., September 2011). See also, Shin Imai, Ladan Mehranvar, and Jennifer Sander, Breaching Indigenous Law: Canadian Mining in Guatemala, *Indigenous Law Journal*, Vol. 6, No. 1 (2007): 101–139, at 108.

4. *Id.*, Zarsky and Stanley, *Searching for Gold in the Highlands of Guatemala*, pp. 10–13, 30–33; *Id.*, Imai, Mehranvar, and Sander, Breaching Indigenous Law, p. 108.

5. See, for example, *Social and Economic Rights Action Centre (SERAC) & Another v. Nigeria* (2001) AHRLR 60 (ACHPR 2001). Communication 155/96, Decided at the 30th ordinary session, October 2001.

6. See, for example, *Id. SERAC & Another v. Nigeria* (2001); Bronwen Manby, *Shell in Nigeria: Corporate Social Responsibility and the Ogoni Crisis* (SAGE Knowledge. Cases/SAGE, 2016); and, Ogoni: Timeline of the Ogoni Struggle, March 30, 2018. Available at https://unpo.org/article/20716 (last accessed February 29, 2019).

7. See, for example, Stephen Young, The Sioux's Suits: Global Law and the Dakota Access Pipeline, *American Indian Law Journal*, Vol. 6, No. 1, Article 4 (2017); Kate Harris and Michael Gonchar, Battle Over an Oil Pipeline: Teaching About the Standing Rock Sioux Protests, *New York Times*, November 30, 2016;

and Steven Mufson, A Dakota Pipeline's Last Stand, *The Washington Post*, November 25, 2016.

8. *Id.*, Young, The Sioux's Suits; *Id.*, Harris and Gonchar, Battle Over an Oil Pipeline; and *Id.*, Mufson, A Dakota Pipeline's Last Stand.

9. It has been argued that "improvements in human rights are good for business. So, when you advocate more respect for human rights, you're really directly promoting better business conditions." See John Kamm, Business and Human Rights Do Mix, *State Bar of California International Law Section Newsletter* (September 2014). See also generally, Bryan Horrigan, Fault Lines in the Intersection Between Corporate Governance and Social Responsibility, *UNSW Law Journal*, Vol. 25, No. 2 (2002), pp. 515–553; and, Jide James-Eluyode, The Notion of Collective Human Rights and Corporate Social Responsibility: Issues and Trends in International Law, *International Company and Commercial Law Review*, No. 5 (2013), p. 209, at 211.

10. See Report of the Special Rapporteur on the Rights of Indigenous Peoples, *James Anaya*, A/66/288, August 10, 2011, at para 92.

11. The author recognized that there are mushrooming of classifications and categorizations of countries within the international arena, particularly in relation to the constructs of *developed* and *developing*. However, the historical and theoretical basis for such classifications and categorizations is not within the scope of this book. The classification of *developing* (and *developed*) *countries* used throughout this book was simply for the purpose of helping to understand and unravel the various challenges discussed in the book.

12. See, for example, *Indigenous Latin America in the Twenty-First Century: The First Decade* (International Bank for Reconstruction and Development/The World Bank, 2015), pp. 10, 18.

13. See, for example, Rainer Grote, The Status and Rights of Indigenous Peoples in Latin America, *Heidelberg Journal of International Law.*, Vol. 59 (1999), p. 497 at 526–527.

14. See Report of the Special Rapporteur on the rights of indigenous peoples, James Anaya, Extractive Industries and Indigenous Peoples, A/HRC/24/41, July 1, 2013, para 47.

15. See, for example, Naomi Kipuri, The UN Declaration on the Rights of Indigenous Peoples in the African Context, in Claire Charters and Rodolfo Stavenhagen (eds.), *Making the Declaration Work: The United Nations Declaration on The Rights of Indigenous Peoples* (IWGIA, 2009), pp. 252, 255, and 256.

16. See Report of the African Commission's Working Group of Expert on Indigenous Population/Communities, Adopted by the African Commission on Human and Peoples' Rights at its 28th ordinary session, 2005, p. 11.

17. See generally, Jedrzej George Frynas, *Beyond Corporate Responsibility: Oil Multinationals and Social Challenges* (Cambridge, 2009).

18. See, for example, Jedrzej George Frynas, The False Developmental Promise of Corporate Social Responsibility: Evidence from Multinational oil Companies, *International Affairs*, Vol. 81, No. 3 (2005), pp. 581–598, at p. 584. See further, *Id.*, Frynas, *Beyond Corporate Responsibility*.

19. See generally, Emeka Duruigbo, Corporate Accountability and Liability for International Human Rights Abuses: Recent Changes and Recurring Challenges, *Northwestern University Journal of International Human Rights*, Vol. 6 (2008), p. 222.

20. See Bede Nwete, Corporate Social Responsibility and Transparency in the Development of Energy and Mining Projects in Emerging Markets: Is Soft Law the Answer? *German Law Journal*, Vol. 8, No. 4 (2007), p. 312 at 339.

21. See *What Are Human Rights?* The Office of the UN High Commissioner for Human Rights (OHCHR), available at http://www.ohchr.org/EN/Issues/Pages/WhatareHumanRights.aspx (last accessed March 30, 2019).

22. See generally, Will Kymlicka, *Multicultural Citizenship: A Liberal Theory of Minority Rights* (Oxford University Press, 1996); and, Human Rights and Rights of Peoples, in Fons Coomans, Cees Flinterman, Fred Grunfeld, Ingrid Westendorp and Ian Willems (eds.), *Human Rights from Exclusion to Inclusion: Principles and Practice* (Kluwer Law, 2000), p. 277.

23. See Preamble to the UN Universal Declaration of Human Rights (UDHR) of 1948. Human rights include several universally recognized protections like right to life, liberty and security; freedom from discrimination, slavery, torture, cruel, inhuman or degrading treatment or punishment; privacy; and freedom of movement. See further UDHR 1948, articles 1–30.

24. See *Id.*, UDHR 1948, preamble and articles 1–30.

25. See In Order that People be Given their Due, in Fons Coomans, Cees Flinterman, Fred Grunfeld, Ingrid Westendorp and Ian Willems (eds.), *Human Rights from Exclusion to Inclusion: Principles and Practice* (Kluwer Law, 2000), pp. 17–18.

26. See Malcolm Shaw, *International Law*, 5th ed (Cambridge University Press, 2003), p. 247.

27. See Richard Lillich, Hurst Hannum, James Anaya, and Dinah Shelton, *International Human Rights Problems of Law, Policy, and Practice*, 4th Ed. (Aspen 2006), p. 2.

28. See Jan Herman Burgers, The Road to San Francisco: The Revival of the Human Rights Idea in the Twentieth Century Author, *Human Rights Quarterly*, Vol. 14, No. 4 (November, 1992), pp. 447–477.

29. See Johannes Morsink, *The Universal Declaration of Human Rights: Origins, Drafting, and Intent* (University of Pennsylvania Press, 1999), pp. 36–91.

30. *Id.*, Morsink, *The Universal Declaration of Human Rights*, pp. 1–35. See also *Id.* UDHR 1948, *preamble*.

31. *Id.* UDHR 1948, *preamble*.

32. See generally, Micheline Ishay, *The History of Human Rights: From Ancient Times to the Globalization Era* (University of California Press, 2004).

33. See Jack Donnelly, Human Rights as Natural Rights, *Human Rights Quarterly*, Vol. 4, No. 3, (Autumn, 1982), pp. 391–405. See also, Hugo Grotius, *De jure belli et pacis* (Book 1, 1689); John Locke, *The Second Treatise of Government* (1690; 1952 edn).

34. See St Thomas Aquinas, *Summa Theologica*, Lib. Pt. II (1475). See also Robert McCorquodale, *Human Rights* (Ashgate, 2003), p. 3.

35. See *Id.* Shaw, *International Law*, p. 248. See also John Finnis, *Natural Law and Natural Rights* (Oxford University Press, 1980). According to the Free Dictionary, natural law is seen as "the unwritten body of universal moral principles that underlie the ethical and legal norms by which human conduct is sometimes evaluated and governed." See http://legal-dictionary.thefreedictionary.com/natural+law (last accessed on February 1, 2019). According to Cicero, both justice and law evolved from what nature has given to man, from what the human mind embraces, from the function of man, and from what serves to unite humanity. Natural law obliges us to contribute to the general good of the larger society. See Marcus Tullius Cicero, *de Legibus*, Vol. 1: Libri Tres; Prolegomena Et Uerba Scriptoris Cum Scripturae Discrepantia Continens (Classic Reprint-Latin, Forgotten Books, 2016); and W. D. Pearman, *De legibus libri tres: A Revised Text with English Notes* (Cambridge, 1881). See further, Paul A. Boer Sr. and Francis Barham, *The Political Works of Cicero: Treatise on the Republic and Treatise on the Laws* (Veritatis Splendor Publications, 2014).

36. *See Id.* Aquinas, *Summa Theologica*; and *Id.* Robert McCorquodale, *Human Rights* (2003), p. 3.

37. "Ayn Rand, the developer of the philosophy of objectivism, asserted that a group, as such, has no rights. She maintained that only an individual can possess rights, and therefore the expression '*individual rights*' is a redundancy while the expression '*collective rights*' is a contradiction in terms." *See* Rakesh Chandra, Collective Rights vs. Individual Rights, *International Journal of Multidisciplinary Research and Development*, Vol. 4, No. 7 (July 2017), pp. 51–55, at p. 52.

38. See P. Sieghart, *The International Law of Human Rights* (Oxford University Press, 1983), p. 368. *See also Id.,* Chandra, Collective Rights vs. Individual Rights, p. 52.

39. See *Id. Human Rights and Rights of Peoples Rights*, ed. Fred Grunfeld et al. (Kluwer Law, 2000), p. 277 at 285.

40. See *Id., Human Rights and Rights of Peoples Rights*, p. 285. See also Miodrag Jovanovic, Recognizing Minority Identities Through Collective Rights. *Human Rights Quarterly,* Vol. 27 (2005), pp. 625–651; and, *Id.*, Chandra, Collective Rights vs. Individual Rights, pp. 51–55.

41. The UNDRIP was adopted by the General Assembly in September of 2007, with overwhelming support by majority of UN Member-States. See Resolution A/RES/61/295/ October 2, 2007, adopted by the General Assembly on September 13, 2007.

42. See, for example, Peter Jones, Human Rights, Group Rights, and Peoples' Rights, *Human Rights Quarterly*, Vol. 21, No. 1 (February 1999), pp. 80–107. See also *Id.*, Shaw, *International Law*, pp. 262 and 272; and *United Nations Training Module on Indigenous Peoples Issues* (UNPFII Publications, 2010), p. 3.

43. See generally *Id.,* Jones, Human Rights; *Id.,* Shaw, *International Law*; and *Id. United Nations Training Module on Indigenous Peoples Issues. See further* Peter Jones, Group Rights, *The Stanford Encyclopedia of Philosophy* (Summer 2016 Edition), ed. Edward N. Zalta, para 8 and 9.

44. See UN Charter 1945, article 1 (2).

45. See International Covenant on Civil and Political Rights (ICCPR), 1966, art 1; and, International Covenant on Economic, Social and Cultural Rights (ICESCR), 1966, article 1.

46. See, for example, *Indigenous Peoples' Rights in International Law: Emergence and Application*, ed. Roxanne Dunbar-Ortiz, Dalee Sambo Dorough, Gudmundur Alfredsson, Lee Swepston, and Petter Wille (Gáldu & IWGIA, 2015), at 98. See also Indigenous Peoples at the UN, https://www.un.org/development/desa/indigenouspeoples/about-us.html (last accessed January 02, 2019).

47. See CERD General Recommendation No. 23: Indigenous Peoples: 08/18/1997-Gen. Rec. No. 23 (General Comments), para 1.

48. *Id.,* CERD General Recommendation No. 23.

49. See *Id. United Nations Training Module on Indigenous Peoples Issues*, p. 3.

50. Adopted by the General Conference of the International Labour Organization in June 1989.

51. Adopted by the UN General Assembly in September 2007.

52. See ICESCR 1966.

53. See ICCPR, 1966, particularly art. 27.

54. See International Convention on the Elimination of All Forms of Racial Discrimination, 1965.

55. See, for example, CERD General Recommendation No. 23 (08/18/1997), para 1.

56. See, for example, Irene Watson, The 2007 Declaration on the Rights of Indigenous Peoples, *Griffith Law Review*, Vol. 20, No. 3 (2011), pp. 507–514; Steven T. Newcomb, The UN Declaration on the Rights of Indigenous Peoples and the Paradigm of Domination, *Griffith Law Review*, Vol. 20, No. 3 (2011), pp. 578–607; Ward Churchill, A Travesty of a Mockery of a Sham, *Griffith Law Review*, Vol. 20, No. 3 (2011), pp. 526–556; Irene Watson, Aboriginal(ising) International Law and Other Centres of Power, *Griffith Law Review*, Vol. 20, No. 3 (2011), pp. 619–640; Aileen Moreton-Robinson, Virtuous Racial States: The Possessive Logic of Patriarchal White Sovereignty and the United Nations Declaration on the Rights of Indigenous Peoples, *Griffith Law Review*, Vol. 20, No. 3 (2011), pp. 641–658; and Sharon H. Venne, The Road to the United Nations and Rights of Indigenous Peoples, *Griffith Law Review*, Vol. 20, No. 3 (2011), pp. 557–577.

57. *Id.* Watson, The 2007 Declaration on the Rights of Indigenous Peoples; *Id.* Newcomb, The UN Declaration on the Rights of Indigenous Peoples; *Id.* Churchill, A Travesty of a Mockery of a Sham; *Id.* Aileen Moreton-Robinson, Virtuous Racial States; and *Id.* Venne, The Road to the United Nations.

58. See, for example, UNDRIP, article. 1. *See also* ILO No. 169, article 3, for similar provision.

59. See *State of the World's Indigenous Peoples* (UN Publications, 2009), p. 1. See also, the preamble to UNDRIP.

60. See, for example, UNDRIP, article 1 & 8.

61. See, for example, UNDRIP articles. 7–10.

62. See, for example, UNDRIP articles 3, 4 & 33–37. *See also* ILO No. 169, articles. 3–4.

63. See, for example, UNDRIP articles. 18–24. *See also* ILO No. 169, articles. 6–7.

64. See, for example, UNDRIP articles 26, 27 & 28. *See also* ILO No. 169, articles. 13–18.

65. See, for example, UNDRIP, article 24.

66. See, for example, UNDRIP, articles 11 & 12.

67. See, for example, UNDRIP, articles. 14, 15 & 21.

68. See, for example, UNDRIP article 29.

69. See, for example, UNDRIP article 7 (2), 8, 9 &10.

70. See, for example, UNDRIP articles 11, 12, 13, 24 & 25. *See also* ILO No. 169, article. 5.

71. According to the Secretariat of the UN Permanent Forum on Indigenous Issues, historical accounts about development of International Law within the UN system have shown instances where various terms have not been formally defined. "[T]he most vivid examples being the notions of 'peoples' and of 'minorities.' Yet, the United Nations has recognized the right of peoples to self-determination and has adopted the Declaration on the Rights of Persons Belonging to National or Ethnic, Religious and Linguistic Minorities. The lack of formal definition of 'peoples' or 'minorities' has not been crucial to the Organization's successes or failures in those domains nor to the promotion, protection or monitoring of the rights recognized for these entities." See *the Concept of Indigenous Peoples,* Background paper prepared by the Secretariat of the Permanent Forum on Indigenous Issues [PFII/2004/WS.1/3], Workshop on Data Collection and Disaggregation for Indigenous Peoples (New York, January 19–21, 2004). *See also Indigenous and Tribal Peoples' Rights over their Ancestral Lands and Natural Resources: Norms and Jurisprudence of the Inter-American Human Rights System* (OAS, 2010), at p. 9.

72. See UNDRIP (2007), article 33 (1) & (2), and ILO Convention No. 169, article 1 (2).

73. See James Anaya, *International Human Rights and Indigenous Peoples* (Aspen, 2009), p. 27.

74. See José R. Martínez Cobo, *United Nations Sub-Commission on Prevention of Discrimination and Protection of Minorities, Study on the Problem of Discrimination against Indigenous Populations,* E/CN.4/Sub.2/1983/21/Add. 8, September 1983.

75. *Id.,* José R. Martínez Cobo, at Paras 379–382.

76. See *Id. State of the World's Indigenous Peoples*, p. 84.

77. *Id., State of the World's Indigenous Peoples*, pp. 1 & 84.

78. See Robert T. Watson, Marufu C. Zinyowera and Richard H. Moss, *The Regional Impacts of Climate Change: An Assessment of Vulnerability* (Cambridge, 1997), p. 89; David W. H. Walton, *Antarctica: Global Science from A Frozen Continent* (Cambridge, 2013), pp. 319–320.

79. See *Id. State of the World's Indigenous Peoples*, p. 88. *See also* Cathal Doyle, *Indigenous Peoples' Right to Free Prior & Informed Consent (FPIC) and the Extractive Sector*, the IPLP Speaker Series, University of Arizona Rogers College of Law, August 31, 2010.

80. See, for example, Mark Allen, Native American Control of Tribal Natural Resource Development in the Context of the Federal Trust and Tribal Self-Determination, *Boston College Environmental Affairs Law Revie*, Vol. 16 (1989), p. 857, at 871.

81. See Cathal Doyle, Helen Tugendhat, and Robeliza Halip, *Mining, the Aluminium Industry, and Indigenous Peoples: Enhancing Corporate Respect for Indigenous Peoples' Rights* (AIPP/FPP/IUCN, 2015), pp. 103–104.

82. See Shawn Regan, *Unlocking the Wealth of Indian Nations: Overcoming Obstacles to Tribal Energy Development*, PERC Policy Perspective-No. 1-February 2014.

83. See Martin Walter, *Extractives in Latin America and the Caribbean: The Basics* (Inter-American Development Bank, 2016), p. 5.

84. See P. O. Oviasuyi and Jim Uwadiae, The Dilemma of Niger-Delta Region as Oil Producing States of Nigeria, *Journal of Peace, Conflict and Development*, No. 16, November 2010. *See also* The Oil Industry and Human Rights in the Niger Delta: *Report of the Testimony of Nnimmo Bassey*, Executive Director of Environmental Rights Action (ERA)/Friends of the Earth Nigeria (FoEN), before the United States Senate Judiciary Sub-committee on Human Rights and the Law, September 24, 2008.

85. See *Id., State of the World's Indigenous Peoples*, p. 1. *See also* Philip Mulligan, The Marginalization of Indigenous Peoples from Tribal Lands in Southeast Madagascar, *Journal of International Development*, Vol. 11, No. 4 (special Issue), June 1999, pp. 649–659; and, Samuel Ruiz and Alina Rocha Menocal, The Politics of Marginalization: Poverty and the Rights of the Indigenous People in Mexico, *Journal of International Affairs*, Vol. 52, No. 1 (Fall 1998), pp. 85–100.

86. See, for example, Colin Samson, Carlos Gigoux, *Indigenous Peoples and Colonialism: Global Perspectives* (Polity, First edition, 2016); and, Robert A. Williams Jr., *Savage Anxieties: The Invention of Western Civilization* (St. Martin's Press, 2012).

87. See, for example, Philip P. Frickey, Marshalling Past and Present: Colonialism, Constitutionalism, and Interpretation in Federal Indian Law, *Harvard Law Review*, Vol. 107 (1993), p. 381; and, Blake A. Watson, The Impact of the American Doctrine of Discovery on Native Land Rights in Australia, Canada, and New Zealand, *Seattle University Law Review*, Vol. 34 (2011), p. 507.

88. The Treaty of Tordesillas, which was signed on June 7, 1494, between Spain and Portugal to memorialize the agreement concerning settlements of their conflicts over lands said to have been "discovered" by Christopher Columbus and other voyagers.

89. See *the General Act of the Berlin Conference on West Africa*, signed on February 26, 1885, signed by the representatives of the United Kingdom, France, Germany, Austria, Belgium, Denmark, Spain, the United States of America, Italy, the Netherlands, Portugal, Russia, Sweden-Norway, and Turkey. See further, Endalcachew Bayeh, The Legacy of Colonialism in the Contemporary Africa: A Cause for Intrastate and Interstate Conflicts, *International Journal of Innovative and Applied Research*, Vol. 3, No. 2 (2015), pp. 23–29.

90. See the Royal Proclamation of 1763, which was issued by King George III on October 7, 1763.

91. See Terry Fenge and Jim Aldridge (eds), *Keeping Promises: The Royal Proclamation of 1763, Aboriginal Rights, and Treaties in Canada* (Montreal and Kingston: McGill-Queen's University Press, 2015), p. 296.

92. See *Worcester v Georgia*, 31 U.S. (6 Pet.) 515 (1832).

93. See generally David Getches, Charles Wilkinson, Robert Williams, Matthew Fletcher, and Kristen Carpenter, *Cases and Materials on Federal Indian Law 7th ed.* American Casebook Series (West Academic, 2016).

94. See Economic and Social Council Resolution 1982/34 of May 7, 1982.

95. See *Id.* Anaya, *International Human Rights and Indigenous Peoples*, p. 3; and *Id., State of the World's Indigenous Peoples*, p. 1.

96. See *Id., State of the World's Indigenous Peoples*, p. 3.

97. The WGIP was established pursuant to Economic and Social Council Resolution E/RES/1982/34. However, the process that culminated in the creation of the WGIP actually began in 1972, with the authorization, by the UN Sub-Commission on Prevention of Discrimination and Protection of Minorities, of a Study on the problem of discrimination against indigenous populations. José R. Martínez Cobo, from Ecuador, was appointed as the Special Rapporteur for the study. The final report, which included the most widely cited definition of indigenous peoples, later became popularly known as the Martínez Cobo Study. The public and governmental interest created by the Martínez Cobo Study led to the establishment of the WGIP. See *The Rights of Indigenous Peoples*, OHCHR Fact Sheet No.9 (Rev.1), at http://www.ohch r.org/documents/publications/factsheet9rev.1en.pdf (last accessed January 20, 2019). See also *Id. State of the World's Indigenous Peoples*, p. 2.

98. The WGIP rounded up its activities in July 2007, and has since been replaced with the UN Permanent Forum on Indigenous Issues (UNPFII), which was established in July 2000. See UN Economic and Social Council Resolution E/2000/22, July 28, 2000.

99. See UN General Assembly Resolution, A/RES/40/131, December 13, 1985.

100. See Anna Meijknecht, *Towards International Personality: The Position of Minorities and Indigenous People in International Law* (Intersentia, 2001), p. 111. See also *UN Voluntary Fund for Indigenous Peoples: 30 Years of Empowering Indigenous Peoples to Claim their Rights*, available at https://www.ohchr.org/Document s/Issues/IPeoples/Fund/BookletVoluntaryFund.pdf (last accessed January 12, 2019). This document was developed by the Office of the High Commissioner for Human Rights, to provide an overview of the activities and accomplishments of the *UN Voluntary Fund for Indigenous Peoples, Id.*

101. See UNGA Resolution A/RES/40/131 (1985), para c.

102. See, for example, *Making the Declaration Work: The United Nations Declaration on the Rights of Indigenous Peoples*, ed. Claire Charters and Rodolfo Stavenhagen (IWGIA, 2009), p. 32.

103. The ILO has been engaged with indigenous rights issues long before the adoption of Convention No. 169 in 1989. As early as 1957, the ILO adopted the Convention on Indigenous and Tribal Populations (No. 107), which is the first international legal instrument concerning indigenous rights. Convention No. 107 was, however, fundamentally flawed in terms of content and character. Convention No. 107 was widely criticized for its patronizing outlook, and for encouraging the idea of

assimilation and integration in its estimation of indigenous groups. A decision was therefore made to revise Convention No. 107, and that ultimately led to the adoption of Convention (No. 169) in June of 1989. It should be noted that, even though a decision to foreclose any further ratification of Convention No. 107 was made; it remains binding upon those State parties who have already ratified it, until they take steps to ratify Convention No. 169. See *ILO Convention on Indigenous and Tribal Peoples, 1989 (No.169): A Manual* (Geneva, International Labour Office, 2003), at 3.

104. See generally, *Understanding the Indigenous and Tribal People Convention, 1989 (No. 169): Handbook for ILO Tripartite Constituents* (Geneva: ILO, 2013). *See also, ILO Convention on Indigenous and Tribal Peoples, 1989 (No.169).*

105. See the Rio Declaration on Environment and Development of 1992, principle 22.

106. See OHCHR, *World Conference on Human Rights*, June 14–25, 1993, Vienna, Austria. Available at http://www.ohchr.org/EN/AboutUs/Pages/ViennaW C.aspx (last accessed July 20, 2018).

107. See Vienna Declaration and Programme of Action (A/CONF.157/23), adopted by the World Conference on Human Rights in Vienna on June 25, 1993, para 20. See further *Id.*, A/CONF.157/23, (Part I), chap. III, sect. II.B, para. 32.

108. In summer of 2000, pursuant to the resolution of the UN Economic and Social Council, the UN Permanent Forum on Indigenous Issues (UNPFII) was established to serve as the principal body for coordinating, at the international level, issues concerning indigenous peoples around the world. See Economic and Social Council Resolution E/RES/2000/22, July 28, 2000.

109. See UN General Assembly Resolution A/RES/47/75, December 14, 1992.

110. See UN General Assembly Resolution A/RES/48/163 of December 21, 1993. A second International Decade of the World's Indigenous People which commenced on January 1, 2005 was also adopted by the General Assembly in 2004. See UN General Assembly Resolution A/RES/59/174 of December 20, 2004.

111. See generally UN Permanent Forum on Indigenous Issues (UNPFII), *State of the World's Indigenous Peoples* (UN Publications, 2nd Vol., 2015), available at: http://www.refworld.org/docid/55c89dac4.html (last accessed July 20, 2018). See also *Id. State of the World's Indigenous Peoples.*

112. See, for example, Christian Courtis, *Notes on the Implementation by Latin American Countries of the ILO Convention 169 on Indigenous Peoples, Sur. Rev. Int. direitos Human*, Vol.6, No.10 (Sao Paulo, June 2009). See also *Overview of the State of Indigenous Peoples in Asia* (AIPP, May 2014), p. 2. Available at http://www .gapeinternational.org/wp-content/uploads/2011/08/asia-ip-overview-final.pdf (last accessed February 01, 2019).

113. See, for example, Constitution of the Republic of Ecuador 2008, Chapter 4 & 5; Constitution of the Plurinational State of Bolivia 2009; Indigenous Peoples Rights Act of Philippine 1997; Constitution of the Republic of Kenya 2010; and, *Law on the Promotion and Protection of Indigenous Populations*, Act No. 5-2011 of Republic of Congo, 2011.

114. For illustrations, article 27 of ICCPR has been widely applied to indigenous issues. *See* General Comment 23, UN Human Rights Committee, U.N. Doc. CCPR/C/21/Rev.1/Add.5. Likewise, the UN Committee on the Elimination of Racial

Discrimination (CERD) has, on occasion, protected indigenous rights, using the general framework of the non-discrimination normative standards under the Convention on the Elimination of All Forms of Racial Discrimination. See *Id.,* CERD General Recommendation No. 23, U.N. Doc. A/52/18, Annex V.

115. The Organization for Economic Cooperation and Development (OECD) Guidelines form part of the OECD Declaration on International Investment and Multinational Enterprises, adopted by the 42 OECD adhering governments on May 25, 2011.

116. See OECD Guidelines for Multinational Enterprises, Part II, General Policies.

117. This policy requires that all development projects proposed for financing by the World Bank, and which impacts Indigenous Peoples, should fully respect the dignity, human rights, economies, and cultures of the peoples. See *World Bank Operational Manual on Indigenous Peoples, OP 4.10* (Indigenous Peoples, 2005).

118. The IFC Performance Standard directs both public and private companies to always observe respect for international indigenous rights standards in their operations. See IFC Policy and Performance Standards on Social and Environmental Sustainability – PS-7, April 2006.

119. See WRI Reports, *Breaking Ground: Engaging Communities in Extractive and Infrastructure Projects* (2009), p. 2.

120. See ICMM Indigenous Peoples and Mining Position Statement 2008; ICMM Good Practice Guide, 2010. The WRI Principles & Good Practice Guide prescribes compliance standards for indigenous rights, by corporations operating in the extractive industry sectors. Commitment 1 of the ICMM Guide requires that corporations aligned with the extractive industry institution, should acknowledge and respect Indigenous Peoples' rights and interests as expressed in all provincial, national and international law in the process of conducting their operations. *Id.,* para 1.4, p. 7.

121. Properly referred to as Akwé: Kon Voluntary Guidelines for the Conduct of Cultural, Environmental and Social Impact Assessment regarding Developments Proposed to Take Place on, or which are Likely to Impact on, Sacred Sites and on Lands and Waters Traditionally Occupied or Used by Indigenous and Local Communities. The Voluntary Guidelines were adopted in February 2004, published by Secretariat of the Convention on Biological Diversity. The Akwé: Kon Voluntary Guidelines require both private enterprises and governmental agencies proposing any project that may affect lands or waters of indigenous communities to acknowledge the peoples' rights, and engage in a process of notification and public consultation about the intention to carry out such project. *Id.,* part III, para 10.

122. See, for example, The Price of Oil: Corporate Responsibility and Human Rights Violations in Nigeria's Oil Producing Communities, *Human Rights Watch* (January 1999). See also, Melik Özden, *Transnational Corporations and Human Rights: What Is at Stake in The United Nations Debate Over the Norms on The Responsibilities of Transnational Corporations and Other Business Enterprises with Regard to Human Rights* (CETIM Publications, 2005).

123. See generally *Id.,* Duruigbo, Corporate Accountability and Liability for International Human Rights Abuses.

124. See, for example, M.T Kamminga, S. Zia-Zarifi, *Liability of Multinational Corporations Under International Law* (Kluwer Law, 2000), pp. 209–210.

125. See, for example, Anup Shah, Corporate Power Facts and Stats, *Global Issues*, November 12, 2011. See also Andy Coghlan and Debora MacKenzie, Revealed: the Capitalist Network That Runs the World, *New Scientist*, October 24, 2011.

126. *Id.*, Shah, Corporate Power Facts and Stats; and *Id.*, Coghlan and MacKenzie, *Revealed*.

127. See Joel Bakan, *The Corporation: The Pathological Pursuit of Profit and Power* (Free Press, 2004), p. 2.

128. See, for example, Parag Khanna, and David Francis, These 25 Companies Are More Powerful Than Many Countries: Going Stateless to Maximize Profits, Multinational Companies Are Vying with Governments for Global Power, Who Is Winning? *Foreign Policy*, (March/April 2016 Issue), available at http://foreignp olicy.com/2016/03/15/these-25-companies-are-more-powerful-than-many-countri es-multinational-corporate-wealth-power/ (last accessed January 23, 2019). See also, Google's Revenue Beats the GDP of Several Major Countries, *Investopedia*, June 11, 2015.

129. See *Doe v. Chiquita Brands International Inc.*, Case 0:08-md-01916-KAM (FLSD, 2008).

130. See Jason Ryan, Chiquita Pleads Guilty to Paying Terrorists, *ABC News*, March 19, 2007. See *further Id., Doe v. Chiquita Brands International Inc.* (FLSD, 2008); and Michael Anderson, Transnational Corporations and Environmental Damage: Is Tort Law the Answer? *Washburn Law Journal* (2001–2002), p. 399.

131. An example of this type of dilemma was aptly reflected in the advertisement placed by the government of Philippines in the Fortune Magazine in 1975, in order to attract foreign investments. The advertisement, in part, stated thus: "To attract companies like yours . . . we have felled mountains, razed jungles, filled swamps, moved rivers, relocated towns . . . all to make it easier for your business to do business here." See David C. Korten, *When Corporations Rule the World* (Kumarian/Barrett-Koehler, 1995), p. 159; *Id.*, 2nd Ed. (Kumarian/Barrett-Koehler, 2001), at p. 293.

132. See Shedrack C. Agbakwa, A Line in the Sand: International (Dis)Order and the Impunity of Non–State Corporate Actors in the Developing World, in Antony Anghie et al. eds., *Third World and International Order, Law Politics and Globalization* (Martinus Nijhoff Publishers, 2003), pp. 1–18.

133. See *Id.*, Korten, *When Corporations Rule the World* (1995, 2001); and, *Id.* Shedrack C. Agbakwa, A Line in the Sand, pp. 1–18.

134. See *Id.*, Nwete, Corporate Social Responsibility and Transparency in the Development of Energy and Mining Projects in Emerging Markets, p. 312 at 316. See also *Id.* Korten, *When Corporations Rule the World*, (2001), pp. 159, 293.

135. See, for example, *Commodity Markets Outlook*, World Bank Quarterly Report, January, 2017.

136. See, for example, *Indigenous Peoples – Lands, Territories and Natural Resources*, available at http://www.un.org/esa/socdev/unpfii/documents/6_session _factsheet1.pdf (last accessed September 17, 2018). See also *Id.* State of the World's Indigenous Peoples (2009), p. 87. See generally, *The Role of Indigenous Peoples in Biodiversity Conservation: The Natural but Often Forgotten Partners* (IBRD/World Bank, 2008).

137. See *Extractive Industries and Conflict Prevention in Latin America*, 7 (UNDP Regional Centre Panama), at http://www.undp.org/content/dam/undp/lib rary/Democratic%20Governance/OGC/Rebecca%20A%20Extractive%20Industries %20and%20Conflict%20Prevention%20in%20LAC.pdf (last accessed on February 04, 2019).

138. See Martin Walter, *Extractives in Latin America and the Caribbean: The Basics*, (Inter-American Development Bank, 2016); and Latin America Mining Summit paper, LatAMin 2013, at http://www.magenta-global.com.sg/mining-latin-amer ica-2013/index.php (last accessed February 04, 2019).

139. Historical accounts have shown that as early as 1884, a conference was convened in Berlin, Germany, by fourteen major colonial powers that prevailed across Africa then—including France, Germany, Great Britain, Portugal, and the United Sates. The Berlin conference was held without the participation of Africans. The conference ultimately recreated the geography for Africa, and laid the road map for how the natural resources, and markets of the continent would be shared among the then reigning colonial powers. See generally Alvin Josephy, *The Horizon History of Africa* (American Heritage Publications, 1971).

140. See Michael Watts, *Petro-Insurgency or Criminal Syndicate? Conflict, Violence and Political Disorder in the Niger Delta*, Working Paper No. 16 (University of California, Berkeley, 2008), p. 3.

141. See John Ghazvinian, *Untapped: The Scramble for Africa's Oil* (Harcourt Books, 2007), pp. 11–12.

142. See UNCTAD World Investment Report 2010 (Developing Countries), p. 32. It is important to note that FDI to Africa slowed in the later years due the distress in global economy, and particular national challenges. See World Investment Report 2016 (UNCTAD, 2016), p. 38, at p. 40.

143. See *Corporate Responsibility in African Development: Insights from an Emerging Dialogue*, Working Paper No. 60 of the Corporate Social Responsibility Initiative (John F. Kennedy School of Government, October 2010).

144. See *African Economic Outlook 2016: Sustainable Cities and Structural Transformation*, AfDB/OECD/UNDP (OECD Publishing, Paris, 2016), pp. 51–55, available at http://dx.doi.org/10.1787/aeo-2016-en (last accessed February 04, 2019). See also, World Investment Report 2016 (UNCTAD, 2016).

145. See, for example, United Nations Environmental Programme, Environmental Assessment of Ogoniland, (UNEP, 2011). See also *Id.,* Michael Watts, *Petro-Insurgency or Criminal Syndicate?*, p. 3. See further Stewart M. Patrick, Why Natural Resources Are a Curse on Developing Countries and How to Fix It, *The Atlantic*, April 30, 2012.

146. See Naomi Kipuri, cited *in Fossil Fuels, Oil Companies and Indigenous Peoples: Strategies of Multinational Oil Companies, States, And Ethnic Minorities Impact on Environmental, Livelihoods and Cultural Change* (Tobias Haller, Annja Blochlinger, Markus John et.al eds., LIT Verlag/Transactions Publishers, 2007).

147. *Id.*, Naomi Kipuri, in *Fossil Fuels, Oil Companies and Indigenous Peoples*, p. 19.

148. See *Id., State of the World's Indigenous Peoples*, p. 84, at 88.

149. See *Id.* Zarsky and Stanley, *Searching for Gold in the Highlands of Guatemala,* p. 9. *See also Mining in Guatemala: Rights at Risk* (Amnesty International, 2014), p. 9.

150. *Id.* Zarsky and Stanley, *Searching for Gold in the Highlands of Guatemala;* and *Id., Mining in Guatemala.* See also, Inter-American Commission on Human Rights, Precautionary Measures, in *Communities of the Maya People (Sipakepense and Mam) of the Sipacapa and San Miguel Ixtahuacán Municipalities in the Department of San Marcos, Guatemala,* (IACHR, 2010: PM 260-07), available at http://www.oas.org/en/iachr/indigenous/protection/precautionary.asp (last accessed February 06, /2019).

151. See *Id.,* Zarsky and Stanley, *Searching for Gold in the Highlands of Guatemala,* pp. 4–5. The author notes that, while a majority of studies conducted show that the Marlin Mine posed grave environmental risks to the surrounding communities. However, there are few others that found that Goldcorp was in compliance with good practice standards in all environmental areas. See, for example, Executive Summary, *Human Rights Assessment of Goldcorp's Marlin Mine* (On Common Ground Consultants Inc., May 2010).

152. See Report of the Special Rapporteur on the situation of human rights and fundamental freedoms of indigenous people, James Anaya, Preliminary note on the application of the principle of consultation with indigenous peoples in Guatemala and the case of the Marlin mine, A/HRC/15/37/Add. 8 (July 8, 2010), at para 11.

153. See for example Diana Vinding ed., *The Indigenous World* (IWGIA, 2004), p. 372; Hughes Lotte, Mining the Maasai Reserve: The Story of Magadi, *Journal of Eastern African Studies,* Vol. 2, No. 1 (2008), pp. 134–164. See also, Meitiaki Ole Soikan, *The Social, Environmental and Cultural Effects of Extractive Industries in Kajiado District, Rift Valley Province, Kenya—A Case Study of (Gypsum and Limestone) Cement Factories and Soda Ash Companies,* Mainyoito Pastoralist Integrated Development Organization (MPIDO) Kenya, *Paper Presented at the International Conference on Extractive Industries and Indigenous Peoples,* March 23–25, 2009, Manila Philippines.

154. See *Id.,* Report of the African Commission's Working Group of Expert on Indigenous Population/Communities (28th Ordinary Session, 2005), p. 26.

155. See generally Elias Mateus Isaac and Albertina Delgado, Chevron in Angola, in *The True Cost of Chevron – An Alternative Annual Report,* ed. Michelle Kinman & Antonia Juhasz (May 2011).

156. See *Id.,* Isaac and Delgado, Chevron in Angola, p. 23.

157. See, for example, Angola Fines Chevron for Pollution, *BBC News World Edition,* Monday July 1, 2002.

158. See *Id.,* UNEP Environmental Assessment of Ogoniland (2011). See also: Akachi Odoemene, Social Consequences of Environmental Change in the Niger Delta of Nigeria, *Journal of Sustainable Development,* Vol. 4, No. 2 (April 2011); *and* O.O. Emoyan, I. A. Akpoborie and E. E. Akporhonor, The Oil and Gas Industry and the Niger Delta: Implications for the Environment, *Journal of Applied Sciences and Environmental Management,* Vol. 12, No. 3 (September 2008), pp. 29–37.

159. See *Id.,* UNEP Environmental Assessment of Ogoniland, p. 20; E.A. Ajao and Sam Anurigwo, Land-Based Source of Pollution in the Niger Delta, Nigeria,

Ambio, Vol. 31, No. 5 (August, 2002), pp. 442–445; and Chinedum Ile and Chinua Akukwe, *Niger Delta, Nigeria: Issues, Challenges and Opportunities for Equitable Development*, Niger Delta Environmental Network paper, Washington, DC (2001).

160. See Odoemene, Social Consequences of Environmental Change in the Niger Delta of Nigeria, p. 124.

161. See Oviasuyi and Uwadiae, The Dilemma of Niger-Delta Region as Oil Producing States of Nigeria. See also *Id.*, Emoyan, Akpoborie and Akporhonor, The Oil and Gas Industry and the Niger Delta, pp. 29–37, at p. 29.

162. See generally, *Id.*, UNEP, Environmental Assessment of Ogoniland (2011). It should be pointed out that, Shell Petroleum Development Company of Nigeria (SPDC) was at one time charged before a District Court in the United States for grave human rights violations in the Niger Delta, including the company's complicity in the torture, killing, and other abuses of some prominent community leaders of Ogoniland; the company eventually agreed in 2009 to settle the case out of court for US$15.5 million. See Wiwa v. Royal Dutch Petroleum/Shell Transport and Trading and Wiwa v. Anderson (Otherwise known collectively as *Wiwa v. Shell*) US District Court for the Southern District of New York 96 CIV. 8386. See also 226 F 3d 88 (2d Cir. 2000). History of proceedings and other relevant documents can also be accessed at http://www.earthrights.org/legal/wiwa-v-royal-dutchshell (last accessed February 03, 2019).

163. *Id.*, UNEP Environmental Assessment of Ogoniland, p. 9.

164. *Id.*, UNEP Environmental Assessment of Ogoniland, pp. 10–11. UNEP ultimately concluded that the clean-up and restoration effort to redeem the Ogoniland could take up to thirty years to complete. *Id.*, at p. 12.

165. See: Jonathan Brown, Niger Delta Bears Brunt after 50 Years of Oil Spills, *The Independent (UK)*, Thursday October 26, 2006; and John Vidal, Nigeria's agony Dwarfs the Gulf Oil Spill—The US and Europe Ignore It, *The Observer (Guardian News UK)*, Sunday May 30, 2010. *See further:* Okonkwo et al., The Niger Delta wetland ecosystem: What Threatens it and Why Should We Protect It? *African Journal of Environmental Science and Technology*, Vol. 9, No. 5 (May 2015), pp. 451–463, at 454: *and* the Joint Report Compiled by the WWF, *The World Conservation Union, the Nigeria's Federal Government, and the Nigerian Conservation Foundation* (October 2006). *See also Id.*, Brown, Niger Delta Bears Brunt After 50 Years of Oil Spills; and *Id.*, Vidal, Nigeria's Agony Dwarfs the Gulf Oil Spill.

166. See Wale Adebanwi, Nigeria: Shell of a State, *Dollar and Sense Magazine*, July/August 2001.

167. For example, in Australia, there have been cases of fruitful partnership between resource extraction companies and Aboriginal groups settled within the area of a proposed resource development project. These types of partnerships have led to mutually beneficial agreements between the parties, setting out the terms upon which the project proceeds, and in a way, that secures the rights of the affected communities. See generally, David Triggera, Julia Keenanb, Kim de Rijkea, and Will Rifkinb, Aboriginal Engagement and Agreement-making with a Rapidly Developing Resource Industry: Coal Seam Gas Development in Australia, *The Extractive Industries & Society*, Vol. 1 (2014), pp. 176–188. Another example of successful partnership is

the collaboration between the Blood Tribe First Nation in southern Alberta, Canada, and Native American Resource Partners (NARP), a private company, to create Kainai Energy Company (KEC). The Blood Tribe subsequently entered into an investment agreement with Indigena Capital, a private investment firm focused on indigenous nations. See http://bloodtribe.org/entities; and, https://indigenacapital.com/ (last accessed March 7, 2019). See also Blood Tribe Announces Formation of New Tribal Energy Company in Partnership with Native American Resource Partners, *Marketwired News* (April 4, 2011).

Chapter 2

The Rubric of Indigenous Peoples

A REFLECTION ON THE TERM *INDIGENOUS PEOPLES* AND ITS CONCEPTUAL RAMIFICATIONS

The Definitional Conundrum

Indigenous peoples are spread across all parts of the world, from the Amazon rainforest to the Nordic region, as far as the Arctic territories, and all the way to the deserts of Africa.[1] These various indigenous communities possess unique traditional beliefs, cultural and social values, and economic livelihood characteristics that are often recognizably different from those of the dominant societies in which they live.

The concept of indigenous peoples' rights has assumed a major role in reshaping discussion at the international level and in influencing policies of many national governments. However, one question persists: who does the term *indigenous peoples* cover? Which groups are indigenous? A review of normative developments and academic literature in the area of indigenous peoples' rights in the past several years suggest that there is no broad agreement on the definition of *indigenous peoples*. The challenge associated with constructing a consensus and generally applicable definition of *indigenous peoples* was reflected in the 1996 Report of the Working Group on Indigenous Populations during its fourteenth session.[2] The Working Group was established within the UN system in the early eighties to coordinate the development of international standards to protect the rights of indigenous peoples.[3] As indicated in the 1996 Report, a glaring schism unfolded that put cross sections of participants who attended the Working Group's fourteenth session at odds with each other. For instance, on one side, many indigenous participants attending the session fervently stressed that a *scientific* definition of the term *indigenous peoples* would be problematic, as was illustrated in a joint resolution expressing their common position:

> We, the Indigenous Peoples present at the Indigenous Peoples Preparatory Meeting on Saturday, 27 July 1996, at the World Council of Churches, have reached a consensus on the issue of defining Indigenous Peoples and have unanimously endorsed Sub-Commission resolution 1995/32. We categorically reject any attempts that Governments define Indigenous Peoples.[4]

They reiterated that it was not unprecedented for a term to lack strict definition under international law and that the framework of indigenous rights could be accomplished without a universal definition. As an example, they pointed to the term *minorities*, which currently does not have a generally applicable definition under international law.[5]

On the other side, representatives (otherwise called "observers") for some UN Member States clamored for a more universal definition.[6] In particular, the representatives for Bangladesh, India, and Nigeria insisted that

> a definition of indigenous people was essential if the cause was to move forward. The observer for Bangladesh said, inter alia, that a definition was an essential step in institutionalizing guarantees for safeguarding the rights of indigenous people . . . . The observer for India expressed the view that the Working Group, by avoiding the critical issues of identifying through a definition the actual beneficiaries of the concept, would lose its focus on the human rights questions of the truly indigenous peoples. The observer for Nigeria said that a clear-cut definition was necessary to identify the essential distinction between indigenous peoples and minorities.[7]

Indeed, finding a universal definition has thus far remained a subject of vigorous debate, and scholars and advocates alike are increasingly confounded by the elusiveness of a faultless and all-embracing meaning. The paradoxical situation created by the persistent search for a pristine meaning of the term *indigenous peoples* is now more glaring than ever. This definitional predicament is two-fold. As Jeff Corntassel aptly characterized it, on one level, formulating a rigid universal definition could preclude certain indigenous groups, who ought to qualify, from securing the needed protections provided under the indigenous peoples' rights framework.[8] A point of view shared by some indigenous advocates who argue that "it would be an error, and indeed, discriminatory for one group of human beings to try to define another."[9] On another level, a lack of a generally applicable definition could throw the door wide-open to groups who are not the intended beneficiary of the indigenous rights framework to unduly obtain protection thereunder, while disadvantaging groups who are entitled to be considered indigenous.[10] The persistent call, during the first session of the Working Group on Minorities by the representatives for Nigeria, to incorporate the terms *refugees* and *indigenous peoples* under an all-embracing universal definition of "minorities" is a case in point that reflects this dilemma.[11]

Mindful of the expression of concern by indigenous groups and the protracted debate that ensued over which definition is most suitable, the predominant view shared by indigenous rights advocates is that any endeavor to carry out an exhaustive search for a universally applicable definition of *indigenous peoples* is not only unnecessary but may actually be counterproductive.[12] Because of the manifest uniqueness and diversity of indigenous groups all over the world, it is, therefore, not surprising that this point of view garnered significant traction over a short period.[13] The definitional approach now widely favored is one that encourages a focus on the identification, rather than definition, of who *indigenous peoples* are.[14] Certainly, this approach aligns well with the position broadly held by the majority of indigenous organizations who appeared before the now defunct UN Working Group on Indigenous Populations.[15]

In spite of the definitional quandary that kept indigenous scholars and advocates busy for quite some time, one definition gained widespread popularity. It was formulated by José Martínez Cobo, the former UN Special Rapporteur of the Sub-Commission on Prevention of Discrimination and Protection of Minorities, in his often-cited Study on the Problem of Discrimination against Indigenous Populations.[16] Cobo stated in his report as follows:

> Indigenous communities, peoples and nations are those which, having a historical continuity with pre-invasion and pre-colonial societies that developed on their territories, consider themselves distinct from other sectors of the societies now prevailing in those territories, or parts of them. They form at present non-dominant sectors of society and are determined to preserve, develop and transmit to future generations their ancestral territories, and their ethnic identity, as the basis of their continued existence as peoples, in accordance with their own cultural patterns, social institutions and legal systems.[17]

This widely applauded definition, which was frequently regarded as an acceptable working definition of *indigenous peoples*, is not without flaws. For instance, the nature of the historical continuity, as Cobo stated, includes occupation of part or whole of ancestral land, common ancestry with the original occupants of the lands, and the manifestation of culture.[18] Cobo's characterization of indigenous communities in this manner is somewhat narrow in outlook and preclusive in effect. This constrictive characterization could be quite challenging for some indigenous groups as they seek protection of their collective rights in accordance with the rubric of indigenous peoples within the context of an international human rights framework, especially, considering that Cobo's definition was specifically formulated for the purpose of articulating the collective global action that would impact the future existence of these groups.[19]

The Saramaka people of Suriname, for example, would not necessarily fit squarely within Cobo's suggested criteria. The Saramakas are neither settled on the lands of their original forbearers nor share common ancestry with the earliest inhabitants who may have dwelled in the area they now occupy prior to the arrival of African slaves in the northeastern Atlantic coast of South America in the seventeenth century.[20] In fact, ancestors of the Saramaka people were among groups of liberated African slaves that decided to settle in the Suriname territory in the early eighteenth century.[21] Since doing so, the Saramaka people continue to administer the affairs of their community in accordance with their own norms, customs, and traditions.[22] This historical reality about the Saramaka peoples was given prominence in *Saramaka v. Suriname*.[23] The Inter-American Commission on Human Rights submitted this case to the Inter-American Court of Human Rights in June 2006.[24] In *Saramaka v. Suriname* the State of Suriname argued that the Saramaka people did not qualify for treatment as indigenous peoples in accordance with international law, because they were not native to the territory they occupy in Suriname.[25] Notwithstanding, the court concluded that members of the Saramaka people form a distinct tribal community.[26] The court held that the State of Suriname must recognize the group's juridical capacity to fully exercise their rights in a collective manner, and guarantee them the use and enjoyment of their territory in accordance with their communal property system.[27] According to the court:

> With regard to members of indigenous peoples, the Court has stated that "it is essential for the States to grant effective protection that takes into account their specificities, their economic and social characteristics, as well as their situation of special vulnerability, their customary law, values, and customs."[28]

The court concluded further that, the State must

> grant the members of the Saramaka people legal recognition of their collective juridical capacity, pertaining to the community to which they belong, with the purpose of ensuring the full exercise and enjoyment of their right to communal property, as well as collective access to justice, in accordance with their communal system, customary laws, and traditions . . . adopt legislative, administrative and other measures necessary to recognize and ensure the right of the Saramaka people to be effectively consulted, in accordance with their traditions and customs, or when necessary, the right to give or withhold their free, informed and

prior consent, with regards to development or investment projects that may affect their territory, and to reasonably share the benefits of such projects with the members of the Saramaka people, should these be ultimately carried out.[29]

The "pre-invasion and pre-colonial" element suggested by Cobo is similarly incongruous with the situation of some indigenous groups, such as the Adivasi Janajati community, whose ancestors form part of the earliest inhabitants of present-day Nepal, a country that was never colonized.[30] Even though Nepal was neither a colony of another country nor invaded by another State,[31] the Adivasi Janajati group was recognized as indigenous peoples within the framework of international indigenous rights.[32] Similarly, the Bedouins in Palestine were recognized as indigenous peoples based on cultural distinctiveness and attachment to their lands, despite argument by some that the group cannot show that their presence within the territory they occupy preceded the arrival of a colonial power.[33]

By focusing on historical continuity with pre-invasion and pre-colonial societies, Cobo's definition emphasizes the idea of aboriginality. In doing so, Cobo seems to suggest that being the original inhabitants of a territory and physically possessing the territory before the intrusion of any foreign elements or culture is a paramount factor for identifying a group as indigenous. On this point, it could be argued that contemporary thinking regarding the meaning of *indigenous peoples* has departed from Cobo's emphasis on historical continuity with pre-invasion and pre-colonial societies as a fundamental defining parameter.[34] The modern thought is that the term *indigenous peoples* should be viewed beyond the idea of aboriginality. It should be understood as a special lexicon conceived to address serious discrimination, marginalization, and human rights violations against indigenous groups within the society.[35] Consistent with this modern notion, indigenous peoples were therefore credited with the right to determine their own identity in accordance with their customs and traditions, in order to show their distinct cultural features and a collective attachment to the territory where they are located.[36]

Plainly, the idea of aboriginality may be pertinent to the situation of indigenous groups like the Australian Aborigines, First Nations in Canada, Native American Indians in the United States of America, and the numerous tribes in Africa. Even in the context of Africa, where many countries across the continent share colonial experiences, a focus on the element of aboriginality raises some challenges.[37] As the African Commission on Human and Peoples' Rights (ACHPR) noted:

> The question of aboriginality or of "who came first" is not a significant characteristic by which to identify indigenous peoples in itself. Limiting the term "indigenous peoples" to those local peoples still subject to the political

domination of the descendants of colonial settlers makes it very difficult to meaningfully employ the concept in Africa.[38]

Indigenous Identity in the Context of Africa

Many African countries contested the meaning of the term *indigenous peoples,* and some even strove to curtail the application of indigenous peoples' rights itself within their national boundaries. Across Africa, the term *indigenous peoples* was initially perceived as a veiled descriptor for an undertaking to examine and ascertain the aboriginal connection of the various African tribes to the continent. Accordingly, the idea of indigenous peoples' rights was largely denounced as a malicious attempt by the West to relive Africa's bitter colonial experience.[39] African countries' critical reception of the rubric of indigenous peoples was fairly predictable because Africans have generally not entertained any doubts as to their native attachment to the continent. Even the ACHPR, prior to becoming a champion for indigenous rights advancement in Africa, initially spurned the idea on the basis that the term *indigenous peoples* cannot be relevant to the situation of Africa because all Africans are indigenous to the continent.[40] The view embraced by most African countries was that all the citizens of those countries are indigenous to Africa.[41] Consequently, any conceptual construct that suggests a need to prove native attachment to the continent, or that requires an evaluation of whether some local groups are "more African" than others as a precondition for the enjoyment of certain rights, was perceived as absurd.[42]

The controversy regarding the applicability or relevance of the term *indigenous peoples* is not unique to Africa. Countries in other parts of the world have also shown reticent attitude towards the term, or indeed the notion of indigenous rights. For instance, countries like Nepal, Myanmar, India, and China have, on occasion, denied the relevance of the rubric of indigenous people to their local populations.[43] China, in particular, once asserted that there are neither indigenous people nor indigenous issues in that country, and that the question of indigenous peoples is solely the product of European countries' pursuit of colonial policies in some regions of the world.[44]

With respect to the evolution of indigenous rights in Africa, there is a disconnect between the view now held by the continent's regional human rights institutions and the governmental authorities of the constituent countries, regarding the utility of the indigenous rights framework in general, and connotation of the term *indigenous peoples* in particular. For its part, the ACHPR maintains that the term *indigenous peoples,* within the context of indigenous rights framework should be perceived in the modern analytical sense, as a *sui generis* term that is mainly intended to address serious discriminatory practices and human rights violations against certain marginalized groups within the society, as opposed to construing the term strictly to denote aboriginality.[45]

In contrast, governments of many African countries remained averse to the idea of labeling certain groups within their national territories as *indigenous* or conferring on them any special recognition, much less attempt to define the term *indigenous peoples*. By a large number, national governments across the continent have espoused the belief that embracing the concept of indigenous peoples, and its attendant collective rights such as rights to self-determination,[46] prior consultation,[47] and lands and resources,[48] could pave the way for unnecessary political unrest within the national structure, serve as a trigger for disunity, and could ultimately subvert the nation-building efforts of the national governments.[49]

This aversion stems in part from the fact that African countries are quite apprehensive about the implication of the right to self-determination, and have tended to view it along with other types of collective rights, such as rights to lands, territories, and resources, from an anti-European colonial viewpoint. This viewpoint results in a perception of indigenous peoples' rights as a platform that unduly empowers indigenous groups to either secede from preexisting national boundaries or jeopardize the territorial integrity of the various countries where they are located. Bearing in mind the sensitivity of national governments across the continent, and the need to address any encumbrance that such sensitivity might place on the path of indigenous peoples' rights advancement in Africa, the ACHPR, in its advisory opinion to the Assembly of Heads of State and Government of the African Union on the UNDRIP, made a concerted attempt to assuage any existing suspicion regarding the implication of rights to self-determination as set forth under Articles 3 and 4 of, and the preamble to the UNDRIP. The ACHPR, in evaluating the application of self-determination to the situation of Africa, reaffirms the following:

> To implicitly recognize the rights of indigenous peoples to self-determination in paragraph 13 of the preamble and in Articles 3 and 4 of the Declaration may be wrongly interpreted and understood as the granting of a unilateral right to self-determination and a possible cessation to a specific section of the national population, thus threatening the political unity and territorial integrity of any country.[50]

The ACHPR therefore counsels that

> articles 3 and 4 of the Declaration can be exercised only in the context of Article 46 of the Declaration which is in conformity with the African Commission's jurisprudence on the promotion and protection of the rights of indigenous

populations based on respect of sovereignty, the inviolability of the borders acquired at independence of the member states and respect for their territorial integrity.[51]

Overall, very few African countries incorporated the term *indigenous peoples* in their constitutions, especially within the context of collective human rights. That said, countries like Cameroon[52] and Kenya[53] did make direct and indirect references to the need to protect their indigenous populations. The Constitution of the Republic of Cameroon declares that "the State shall ensure the protection of minorities and shall preserve the rights of indigenous populations in accordance with the law."[54] The Constitution of Kenya, on its part, mainly provides a number of pathways to protect the collective rights of communities in Kenya, by securing protections for indigenous languages, culture and cultural heritage, and intellectual property, among others.[55]

In this context, Victoria Tauli-Corpuz, the UN Special Rapporteur on the Rights of Indigenous Peoples, similarly observed that the type of recognition enjoyed by indigenous groups, or the manner by which such groups is identified, may have some impact on the level of protection available to them within their national jurisdictions.[56]

> The Special Rapporteur notes with particular concern that a number of States have somewhat restrictive criteria relating to the recognition of indigenous status. That may result in approaches to land rights, socioeconomic policy and development, for example, that may fail to recognize the distinct circumstances, problems and experiences faced by indigenous peoples, including connections to land, distinct cultures and ways of life, discrimination and exclusion, and disadvantage. Approaches that do not recognize indigenous peoples or acknowledge that certain groups may face distinct challenges similar to other indigenous peoples around the world, do not allow for key tools and resources offered by the international indigenous framework to be employed—a framework that was developed precisely to respond to indigenous peoples' concerns in a way that takes into consideration their distinct contexts and experiences.[57]

For the most part, the legal frameworks existing in many African countries frequently identify indigenous groups using diverse designations, other than *indigenous peoples*. Indigenous groups in many African countries are often identified by labels such as tribes, ethnic minority, marginalized or vulnerable populations, and minorities.[58] As an example, the Tuareg people are one of the well-known indigenous groups in the Republic of Mali, a western African country. The Tuareg people present themselves as an indigenous community, and have been so recognized internationally, including by the ACHPR. Yet the government of Mali disclaimed any existence of *indigenous peoples*, such as the Tuaregs, within its national boundaries.[59]

The *Tuareg* people, and several other indigenous communities in Mali, are mainly treated as an ethnic group.[60] Similarly, the Ogoni people in southern Nigeria are recognized as an indigenous group before the UN Permanent Forum on Indigenous Issues, and several other international human rights mechanisms. More so, in their efforts to address the many human rights violations ongoing within their territory in Nigeria, they have attained notoriety as one of the foremost indigenous groups in Africa.[61] Nevertheless, neither the Nigerian Constitution nor the national government recognizes the Ogoni people, or any other local groups for that matter, as indigenous peoples who deserve some special sets of rights. They are simply treated as an ethnic group or ethnic minority.[62]

The identification by some African countries of indigenous groups within their national boundaries in this way carries some significant implications. The rights and protections afforded to minorities[63] within the framework of international law are substantially different from those afforded indigenous peoples. First, minority rights are solely individual rights that can be exercised in community with other members of the minority group, but indigenous rights are conceptually collective in nature.[64] Secondly, minority rights are not primarily targeted at enhancing the survival of the group itself, but rather developed from the recognition that, in order for these rights to be enjoyed by individuals, such rights may require protection of their collective exercise.[65] Thirdly, is the special attachment of the people to their land and territory, or to specific livelihoods, in cases of nomadic/pastoralist. While this particular feature is essential in the context of indigenous rights,[66] it is perhaps relevant to, but not a cornerstone of, minority rights.[67]

Other African countries, such as Central African Republic (CAR) and the Republic of Congo, have taken various significant steps to recognize the indigenous populations within their national boundaries, and provide protections for their collective rights. As a case in point, the CAR became the first African country to ratify ILO Convention No. 169[68] in August of 2010, and, as of March 8, 2019, the only one from the continent.[69] For its part, in 2011, the Republic of Congo promulgated a landmark legislation, the Law on the Promotion and Protection of Indigenous Populations,[70] making it the first country in Africa to enact a law with a specific focus on indigenous peoples.[71] That law conspicuously defines the term *indigenous populations* as denoting groups "who are different from the national population by their cultural identity, lifestyle and extreme vulnerability."[72] This definition, in some respects, aligns with the modern analytical view of the meaning of *indigenous peoples* held by the ACHPR, as noted above. It is noteworthy that the law passed by Congo not only mandated that the indigenous populations in that country be consulted by the government before any actions which are likely to directly or indirectly affect them, are undertaken,[73] it proscribed all forms of discriminations against the country's indigenous populations based on their social origin or indigenous identity.[74]

Factors-Based Approach to Definition of the Term *Indigenous*

As discussed above, so far, no global consensus exists on a faultless and all-embracing meaning of the term *indigenous peoples*. Considering this challenge, defining who is indigenous based on some descriptive factors has proved more acceptable to indigenous advocates and State governments in many jurisdictions, and has provided more opportunity to indigenous peoples to vindicate their claims.

Consistent with this modern approach, indigenous peoples were bestowed with the right to determine their own identity in accordance with their customs and traditions, in order to show their distinct cultural features and a collective attachment to the territory where they are located. In addition to the collective attachment to lands or ancestral territories, exemplified with the Saramaka people in Suriname and Bedouins in Palestine, self-identification as indigenous is also regarded as one of the key factors for determining who is indigenous.

The idea of providing some guidelines for identifying indigenous peoples, or defining the category that constitutes the group rather than the term *indigenous people* itself, is not unprecedented. A similar proposal was made in 1995 by Erica-Irene Daes, the founding Chairperson and former Special Rapporteur of the UN Working Group on Indigenous Populations (WGIP).[75] In the note she presented at the thirteenth session of the WGIP in 1995, Daes introduced certain criteria which might be applied when considering the concept of indigenous peoples.[76]

The Notion of Self-Identification

The UNDRIP, the principal international instrument for indigenous rights protection, does not itself offer any formal definition, but rather endorses the prerogative of indigenous groups to define their own indigenous identity, in accordance with certain criteria.[77] According to UNDRIP, indigenous peoples have the right to determine their own identity, and to belong to an indigenous community, based on their traditions and customs.[78]

Likewise, ILO Convention No. 169, the only binding international treaty concerning indigenous peoples, affirms that self-identification as *indigenous* should be considered a fundamental criterion for determining which groups qualify for protection under its provisions.[79] According to the Convention, its provision would only apply to those groups "whose social, cultural and economic conditions distinguish them from other sections of the national community, and whose status is regulated wholly or partially by their own customs or traditions or by special laws or regulations."[80]

The self-identification approach was also considered and ultimately embraced by the African Working Group of Experts on Indigenous Population/Communities in their recommendation to the ACHPR.[81] The African Working Group emphasized that the previous aboriginality-centered approach to defining indigenous peoples is inapplicable to the peculiarities of Africa's indigenous populations. On the contrary, the African Working Group recommended that a modern analytical approach should be adopted. This approach allows for self-identification based on some sets of guiding parameters, such as special attachment to a territory, distinct language, and culture, as well as experience of subjugation, marginalization, dispossession, or discrimination.[82] The African Working Group noted that, in order to ascertain those who are indigenous people within the continent, it is far more constructive to simply outline some major characteristics that can help recognize any group claiming the status of *indigenous peoples*.[83] For this reason, the African Working Group examined and endorsed the criteria already laid out by the World Bank in its Operational Policy Manual on Indigenous Peoples.[84]

The World Bank instituted the Operational Policy Manual on Indigenous Peoples (OP 4.10)[85] to ensure that development projects financed by the bank which may impact indigenous communities fully respects the communities' rights and cultures.[86] The World Bank recognizes the lack of a universally accepted definition,[87] and thereby applied the term *indigenous people* in a generic sense in the Operational Policy Manual.[88] However, in a bid to provide some criteria for identifying which groups are indigenous, the Operational Policy Manual describes indigenous people as possessing the following characteristics:

a. Self-identification as members of a distinct indigenous cultural group and recognition of this identity by others;
b. Collective attachment to geographically distinct habitats or ancestral territories in the project area and to the natural resources in these habitats and territories;
c. Customary cultural, economic, social, or political institutions that are separate from those of the dominant society and culture; and
d. An indigenous language, often different from the official language of the country or region.[89]

For the purpose of adapting the foregoing criteria to the distinctive situation of African countries, the African Working Group, through a joint initiative with the ILO, later recommended an expanded standard intended to serve

as guidance for any group identifying as *indigenous peoples* on the continent.[90] The recommendation emphasizes that any group seeking recognition
as indigenous in Africa should possess the following characteristics:

a. Socially, culturally, and economically distinctive.
b. Their cultures and ways of life differ considerably from the dominant
   society and their cultures are often under threat, in some cases to the
   extent of extinction.
c. They have a special attachment to their lands or territories. A key charac-
   teristic for most indigenous peoples is that the survival of their particular
   way of life depends on access and rights to their traditional lands and the
   natural resources thereon.
d. They suffer discrimination as they are regarded as "less developed" and
   "less advanced" than other more dominant sectors of society.
e. They often live in inaccessible regions, often geographically isolated, and
   are subjected to various forms of marginalization, both politically and
   socially.
f. They are subject to domination and exploitation within national political
   and economic structures that are commonly designed to reflect the interests and activities of the national majority.
g. The people themselves acknowledge their distinct cultural identity, way of
   life, and seek to perpetuate and retain their identity.[91]

The issue of finding a formal generally applicable definition of the term
indigenous peoples is far from being resolved. Nonetheless, the lack of such
a universal definition should by no means be allowed to constitute an obstacle
to protecting the rights of indigenous communities.[92] Besides, the WGIP has
equally made the point clear that the lack of a formal generally applicable
definition of indigenous peoples was not an imperative for the enjoyment of
rights and protections under UNDRIP.[93]

A more nuanced understanding of the concept of *indigenous peoples* has,
thus far, proven to provide a vital opportunity for indigenous groups seeking
protections for their territories, cultural values, and way of life. The term
indigenous peoples should, therefore, not be treated as a constrictive label,
but seen as a broad descriptive term that points primarily to the borderlines
within which any group may assert their indigenousness based on a com-
pound of parameters. In other words, the term should not be applied rigidly
to define who are indigenous, but to identify those groups that may fall into
the category of indigenous peoples. In this case, aboriginality may qualify a
group as indigenous but the absence of such an element should not exclude
any group that possesses other necessary attributes from enjoying the fundamental protections of the indigenous rights framework either.

NOTES

1. *See generally*: *The State of the World's Indigenous Peoples* (United Nations, 2009); Rishabh Kumar Dhir, *Indigenous Peoples in the World of Work in Asia and the Pacific* (ILO, Geneva, 2015); Richard Evans Schultes, *Where the Gods Reign: Plants and Peoples of the Colombian Amazon* (Synergetic Press, 2018); Watters Lawrence, Indigenous Peoples and the Environment: Convergence from a Nordic Perspective, *UCLA Journal of Environmental Law and Policy*, Vol. 20 (2001/2002), p. 237; Bent Ole Gram Mortensen and Ulrike Barten, The Greenland Self-Government Act: The Pitfall for the Inuit in Greenland to Remain an Indigenous People? *The Yearbook of Polar Law Online*, Vol. 8, No. 1 (2017), p. 103; Sumudu Atapattu, Climate Change, Indigenous Peoples and the Arctic: The Changing Horizon of International Law, *Michigan State International Law Review*, Vol. 22, No. 1 (2013), p. 377; *The Indigenous Peoples of Russia: Country Profile* (IBRD/World Bank, 2014); and Renee Sylvain, *Indigenous Peoples in Africa, Oxford Research Encyclopedia of African History* (Oxford University Press, 2016).

2. See Report of the Working Group on Indigenous Populations (WGIP) on its fourteenth session, E/CN.4/Sub.2/1996/21, August 16, 1996.

3. See Economic and Social Council resolution 1982/34.

4. See *Id.*, WGIP (E/CN.4/Sub.2/1996/21), para 31.

5. See *Id.*, WGIP (E/CN.4/Sub.2/1996/21), para 32.

6. See *Id.*, WGIP (E/CN.4/Sub.2/1996/21), para 34.

7. See *Id.*, WGIP (E/CN.4/Sub.2/1996/21), para 34.

8. See Jeff Corntassel, Who Is Indigenous? Peoplehood and Ethnonationalist Approaches to Rearticulating Indigenous Identity, *Nationalism & Ethnic Policies*, Vol. 9, No. 1 (Spring 2003), pp. 75–100, at 76.

9. See *Id.*, WGIP (E/CN.4/Sub.2/1996/21), paras 35 and 44.

10. See *Id.*, Jeff Corntassel, *Who Is Indigenous?* (Spring 2003), pp. 76–77.

11. See Report of the Working Group on Minorities on its first session, E/CN.4/Sub.2/1996/2, November 30, 1995, at 18.

12. See *Id.*, *The State of the World's Indigenous Peoples* (2009), p. 6. See also *Id.*, WGIP (E/CN.4/Sub.2/1996/21), paras 28, 31, 32, 33, and 44; and, Erica-Irene A Daes, An Overview of the History of Indigenous Peoples: Self-determination and the United Nations, *Cambridge Review of International Affairs*, Vol. 21, No. 1 (March 2008).

13. See *Id.*, *State of the World's Indigenous Peoples*, p. 6. See also S. James Anaya, *International Human Rights and Indigenous Peoples* (Aspen, 2009), p. 27; and Jeremie Gilbert, Indigenous Peoples' Human Rights in Africa: The Pragmatic Revolution of the African Commission on Human and Peoples' Rights, *International & Comparative Law Quarterly*, Vol. 60, No. 1 (January 2011), pp. 245–270.

14. See *Id.*, *State of the World's Indigenous Peoples*; *Id.*, James Anaya, *International Human Rights and Indigenous Peoples*; *Id.*, Gilbert, Indigenous Peoples' Human Rights in Africa; and, *Id.*, Erica-Irene A Daes, An Overview of the History of Indigenous Peoples.

15. See The Concept of Indigenous Peoples, *Workshop on Data Collection and Disaggregation for Indigenous Peoples*, New York, January 19–21, 2004,

Background Paper Prepared by the Secretariat of the Permanent Forum on Indigenous Issues (PFII/2004/WS.1/3). See also *Id.,* WGIP (E/CN.4/Sub.2/1996/21), Para 31.

16. See José R. Martínez Cobo, UN Sub-Commission on Prevention of Discrimination and Protection of Minorities, Study on the Problem of Discrimination against Indigenous Populations, E/CN.4/Sub.2/1983/21/Add. 8, September 1983.

17. *Id.* José R. Martínez Cobo (E/CN.4/Sub.2/1983/21/Add. 8), paras 379–382.

18. *Id.* José R. Martínez Cobo (E/CN.4/Sub.2/1983/21/Add. 8), para 380.

19. *Id.* José R. Martínez Cobo (E/CN.4/Sub.2/1983/21/Add. 8), para 378.

20. See, for example, Richard Price, *To Slay the Hydra: Dutch Colonial Perspectives on the Saramaka Wars* (Karoma Publishers, 1984); and Richard Price, *First-Time: The Historical Vision of an Afro-American People* (The Johns Hopkins University Press, October 1983).

21. See the application filed by the Inter-American Commission on Human Rights with the Inter-American Court of Human Rights in *Case 12.338*, 12 Saramaka Clans against the Republic of Suriname (June 2006), https://www.cidh.oas.org/demandas/1 2.338%20Saramaka%20Clans%20Suriname%2023%20junio%202006%20ENG.pdf (last accessed March 20, 2019). See also: Marcos A. Orellana, Saramaka People V. Suriname, *The American Journal of International Law*, Vol. 102, No. 4, 2008, pp. 841–847; and, *Id.*, Price, *First-Time.*

22. See *Id., 12 Saramaka Clans against the Republic of Suriname* (Case 12.338); *Id.*, Orellana, Saramaka People V. Suriname; and, *Id.*, Price, *First-Time.*

23. See Saramaka People v. Suriname, *Preliminary Objections, Merits, Reparations and Costs*, Judgment of November 28, 2008, Inter-Am. Ct. H.R. Series C No. 172.

24. This particular application originated from the petition (No. 12.338) filed by the Saramaka people with the Secretariat of the Inter-American Commission on Human Rights in October of 2000. See *Id., Saramaka People v. Suriname* (Inter-Am. Ct. H.R, 2008).

25. See generally *Id., Saramaka People v. Suriname* (Inter-Am. Ct. H.R, 2008).

26. *Id., Saramaka People v. Suriname* (Inter-Am. Ct. H.R, 2008), para 174.

27. *Id., Saramaka People v. Suriname* (Inter-Am. Ct. H.R, 2008), para 174.

28. *Id., Saramaka People v. Suriname* (Inter-Am. Ct. H.R, 2008), para 178. See also Case of the *Indigenous Community Yakye Axa v. Paraguay.* Merits, Reparations and Costs. Judgment of June 17, 2005 Series C No. 125.

29. *Id., Saramaka People v. Suriname* (Inter-Am. Ct. H.R, 2008), para 193 (C1) (b) and (d).

30. See Report by the Special Rapporteur on the Situation of Human Rights and Fundamental Freedom of Indigenous Peoples-Addendum on the Situation of Indigenous Peoples of Nepal (James Anaya), A/HRC/12/34/Add.3, July 20, 2009.

31. See, for example, Richard Burghart, The Formation of the Concept of Nation-State in Nepal, *The Journal of Asian Studies*, Vol. 44, No. 1 (1984), pp. 101–125; Tim I Gurung, Why the British Never Colonized Nepal, *Asia Times*, May 6, 2018; and, John Whelpton, *A History of Nepal* (Cambridge University Press, 2005).

32. See *Report by the Special Rapporteur*, James Anaya (Nepal: A/HRC/12/34/Add.3, July 20, 2009), p. 6.

33. See, for example, Havatzelet Yahel, Ruth Kark, and Seth J. Frantzman, Fabricating Palestinian History Are the Negev Bedouin an Indigenous People? *Middle East Quarterly* Vol. 4 (Summer, 2012); and, Mansour Nasasra, The Ongoing Judaisation of the Naqab and the Struggle for Recognizing the Indigenous Rights of the Arab Bedouin People, *Settler Colonial Studies*, Vol. 2, No. 1 (2012), 81–107, at p. 86.

34. See, for example, *Moiwana Village v Suriname*, Inter-Am. Ct. Hum. Rts., Judgment of June 15, 2005, Series C No. 124. In a technical sense, members of the *Moiwana* community are not indigenous to the region they occupy, in fact, the *Moiwana* Village was settled by N'djuka clans late in the nineteenth century. Yet, the Inter-American Court of Human Rights held that members of *Moiwana* community possess an "all-encompassing relationship" to their traditional lands, and their concept of ownership regarding that territory is not centered on the individual, but rather on the community as a whole. Thus, the Court's holdings with regard to indigenous communities and their communal rights to property under Article 21 of the American Convention must also apply to the *Moiwana* tribal community members. The traditional occupancy of *Moiwana* Village and its surrounding lands, which has been recognized and respected by other neighboring clans and indigenous communities over the years, should suffice to obtain State recognition of their ownership. *Id.* Paras 131–135. See also *Saramaka People v. Suriname* (Inter-Am. Ct. H.R, 2008): and; *Centre for Minority Rights Development (Kenya) and Minority Rights Group International on behalf of Endorois Welfare Council v. Kenya* (Endorois Case, Communication 276/2003), decision adopted by the African Commission in May 2009 and endorsed by the African Union on February 4, 2010.

35. See, for example, *Id.* James Anaya, *International Human Rights and Indigenous Peoples*, pp. 1–3.

36. See the UNDRIP, adopted by the General Assembly in September of 2007, article 33 (1) and (2).

37. See generally, Report of the African Commission's Working Group of Expert on Indigenous Population/Communities, adopted by the African Commission on Human and Peoples' Rights at its 28th ordinary session, 2005.

38. See *The Indigenous Peoples in Africa: The Forgotten Peoples?* The African Commissions' Work on Indigenous Peoples in Africa (ACHPR/IWGIA, 2006), p. 10.

39. See *Id., Report of the African Commission's Working Group of Expert* (28th ordinary session, 2005), p. 86. See also Naomi Kipuri, The UN Declaration on the Rights of Indigenous Peoples in the African Context, cited in Claire Charters and Rodolfo Stavenhagen (eds), *Making the Declaration Work: The United Nations Declaration on the Rights of Indigenous Peoples* (IWGIA, 2009), at p. 256.

40. See *The Indigenous World 2001/2002* (IWGIA, 2002), p. 453.

41. See *Id., Indigenous Peoples in Africa: The Forgotten Peoples?* pp. 11–13. See also F. Mukwiza Ndahinda, *Indigenousness in Africa: A Contested Legal Framework for Empowerment of "Marginalized" Communities* (Springer, 2011); and Kealeboga N Bojosi and George Mukundi Wachira, Protecting Indigenous Peoples in Africa: An Analysis of the Approach of the African Commission on Human and Peoples' Rights, *AHRLJ*, Vol. 2 (2006), pp. 382–406.

42. See *Id., Indigenous Peoples in Africa: The Forgotten Peoples?* (ACHPR/ IWGIA, 2006), p. 10. See also: Gilbert, Indigenous Peoples' Human Rights in Africa, p. 249; Sanders Douglas, *Indigenous Peoples: Issues of Definition* (Cambridge University Press, 1999) and; James Anaya, *International Human Rights and Indigenous Peoples*, p. 32.

43. "Unlike many other Asian countries, Nepal does not recognize any particular groups as *indigenous*, and entitled as beneficiaries of special program and affirmative action." See *Id* James Anaya, *International Human Rights and Indigenous Peoples*, p. 30. See further Christian Erni (ed.), *The Concept of Indigenous Peoples in Asia: A Resource Book* (IWGIA/AIPP, 2008), p. 105. See also Benedict Kingsbury, Indigenous Peoples in International Law: A Constructivist Approach to the Asian Controversy, *The American Journal of International Law*, Vol. 92, No. 3 (July 1998).

44. Long Xuequn, the Adviser of the Chinese delegation, made this point clear during his address to the 53rd Session of the UN Commission on Human Rights in 1997. See excerpt of this address in Christian Erni, *Tribes, States and Colonialism in Asia: The Evolution of the Concept of Indigenous Peoples and its Application in Asia* (IWGIA, 2014), p. 6. Similar comments were made by China to the Working Group of the UN Commission on Human Rights in 1995, See UN Doc. E/CN.4/1995/ WG.15/2. See further Christian Erni (ed.), *The Concept of Indigenous Peoples in Asia: A Resource Book* (IWGIA/AIPP, 2008), p. 106.

45. See *Id., Report of the African Commission's Working Group of Expert* (28th ordinary session, 2005), p. 88.

46. See *Id.,* UNDRIP (2007), articles 1–5 and 33–37.

47. See *Id*, UNDRIP (2007), articles 18–19.

48. See *Id*, UNDRIP (2007), articles 26–28.

49. See generally *Overview Report of the Research Project by the International Labour Organization and the African Commission on Human and Peoples' Rights on the Constitutional and Legislative Protection of the Rights of Indigenous Peoples in 24 African Countries* (ILO/ACHPR, 2009).

50. See Advisory Opinion of The African Commission on Human and Peoples' Rights on The United Nations Declaration on The Rights of Indigenous Peoples, adopted by the African Commission on Human and Peoples' Rights at its 41st Ordinary Session held in May 2007 in Accra, Ghana, para 16.

51. *Id.,* Advisory Opinion of The African Commission on Human and Peoples' Rights (2007), para 18.

52. See the Constitution of the Republic of Cameroon, Law No. 96-06 (1972, Rev. 2008).

53. See the Constitution of the Republic of Kenya (2010).

54. See *Id.,* the Constitution of the Republic of Cameroon (1972, Rev. 2008), *preamble.*

55. See *Id.,* the Constitution of the Republic of Kenya (2010), Chapter Two, sections 7–11.

56. See Report of the Special Rapporteur on the rights of indigenous peoples, Victoria Tauli Corpuz, A/HRC/27/52, August 11, 2014, paras 12–16.

57. See *Id.,* Report of the Special Rapporteur, Victoria Tauli Corpuz (A/ HRC/27/52), para 14.

58. See *Id.,* Overview Report of the Research Project by ILO/ACHPR (2009), pp. 17–22.

59. *Id.,* Overview Report of the Research Project by ILO/ACHPR (2009). See also *The Indigenous World 2018,* ed. Pamela Jacquelin-Andersen (IWGIA, 2018), p. 416.

60. It is worth noting that the term *indigenous people* or *indigenous* was not specifically mentioned in the Malian Constitution. See generally, The Constitution of the Republic of Mali, 1992.

61. See *Id.,* Report of the African Commission's Working Group of Expert (28th ordinary session, 2005), p. 18. See also The Adverse Impacts of Oil Pollution on the Environment and Wellbeing of a Local Indigenous Community: The Experience of the *Ogoni* People of Nigeria, International Expert Group Meeting on Indigenous Peoples and Protection of the Environment, August 2007, UNPFII/2007/WS.3/6.

62. See the Constitution of the Federal Republic of Nigeria 1999. See also *Country Report of International Labour Organization and African Commission on Human & Peoples' Rights on the Constitution and Legislative Protection of the Rights of Indigenous Peoples in Nigeria* (ILO/ACHPR, 2009).

63. There are germane conceptual differences between the concepts of *indigenous peoples* and *minorities.* Currently under international law, like the rubric of *indigenous peoples*, there is no universally applicable definition of the term *minority*; even the International Covenant on Civil and Political Rights (ICCPR) of 1966, the most prominent instrument on minority rights did not define the concept. However, some have suggested that minorities are groups numerically inferior to the rest of the population of a state, and are not in a dominant position. They possess ethnic, religious, or linguistic characteristics which differ from those of the rest of the population and maintain a sense of solidarity towards preserving their culture, tradition, religion or language. See, for example, Ulrike Barten, What's in a Name? Peoples, Minorities, Indigenous Peoples, Tribal Groups and Nations, *Journal on Ethnopolitics and Minority Issues in Europe*, Vol. 14, No. 1 (2015), pp. 1–25, at p. 6. See also, Solomon Dersso (ed.), *Perspectives on the Rights of Minorities and Indigenous Peoples in Africa* (Pretoria University Law Press, 2010).

64. See generally Dersso (ed.), *Perspectives on the Rights of Minorities and Indigenous Peoples in Africa*; and Vanessa Sedletzki, Fulfilling the Right to Education for Minority and Indigenous Children: Where We Are in International Legal Standards? Cited in *State of the World's Minorities and Indigenous Peoples 2009* (Minority Rights Group International, July 2009), p. 42.

65. *Id.,* Dersso (ed.), *Perspectives on the Rights of Minorities and Indigenous Peoples in Africa*; and *Id.,* Sedletzki, Fulfilling the Right to Education for Minority and Indigenous Children.

66. *Id.,* James Anaya, *International Human Rights and Indigenous Peoples*, p. 35.

67. *Id.,* Dersso (ed.), *Perspectives on the Rights of Minorities and Indigenous Peoples in Africa*; and *Id.,* Sedletzki, Fulfilling the Right to Education for Minority and Indigenous Children.

68. See ILO Convention No, 169 of 1989.

69. See Ratifications of ILO C-169, https://www.ilo.org/dyn/normlex/en/f?p=N ORMLEXPUB:11300:0::NO::P11300_INSTRUMENT_ID:312314 (last accessed March 08, 2019).

70. See Republic of Congo Law on the Promotion and Protection of Indigenous Populations, Act No. 5-2011 of February 25, 2011.

71. This indigenous peoples–focused law passed by the Republic of Congo was commended as a landmark legislation by both regional and international human rights institutions. See, for example, Media Statement: *UN Expert Praises New Congolese Law on Indigenous Peoples*, January 07, 2011, http://unsr.jamesanaya.org/statements/media-statement-un-expert-praises-new-congolese-law-on-indigenous-peoples (last accessed March 22, 2019). See also The Library of Congress: Congo: New Law on Rights of Indigenous Peoples: http://www.loc.gov/law/foreign-news/article/congo-new-law-on-rights-of-indigenous-peoples/ (last accessed March 22, 2019).

72. See Republic of Congo Law on the Promotion and Protection of Indigenous Populations, article 1.

73. *Id.*, Republic of Congo Law (Act No. 5-2011), article 3.

74. *Id.*, Republic of Congo Law (Act No. 5-2011), article 2.

75. See Note by the UNWGIP Chairperson-Rapporteur on criteria which might be applied when considering the concept of indigenous peoples, Erica-Irene Daes, E/CN.4/Sub.2/AC.4/1995/3.

76. See *Id.,* Erica-Irene Daes, E/CN.4/Sub.2/AC.4/1995/3. *See also* Erica-Irene Daes, Working Paper on the Concept of Indigenous People, *Australian Indigenous Law Reporter*, AUIndigLawRpr 22; *Australian Indigenous Law Reporter* Vol. 2, No. 1 (1997), 162.

77. See *Id.,* UNDRIP (2007), articles 9 and 33 (1); and, *Id.*, James Anaya, *International Human Rights and Indigenous Peoples*, pp. 29 and 35.

78. See *Id.,* UNDRIP (2007), articles 9, 12, 13, 20, 25 and 33, and preamble. See also *Id.*, James Anaya, *International Human Rights and Indigenous Peoples*, p. 29.

79. See ILO Convention No. 169, article 1 (2).

80. See ILO Convention No. 169, article 1(1)(a).

81. See *Id* Report of the African Commission's Working Group of Expert (28th ordinary session, 2005), p. 92.

82. *Id.,* Report of the African Commission's Working Group of Expert (28th ordinary session, 2005), pp. 91–93.

83. *Id.,* Report of the African Commission's Working Group of Expert (28th ordinary session, 2005), pp. 92–93.

84. *Id.,* Report of the African Commission's Working Group of Expert (28th ordinary session, 2005), p. 94.

85. See World Bank Operational Policy Manual on Indigenous Peoples, OP 4.10-Indigenous Peoples (July, 2005) (Revised, April 2013).

86. *Id.*, World Bank Operational Policy Manual, para 1.

87. *Id.*, World Bank Operational Policy Manual, paras 3 and 4.

88. *Id.*, World Bank Operational Policy Manual, para 4.

89. *Id.,* World Bank Operational Policy Manual, para 4.

90. See *Report on the Workshop Examining Constitutional, Legislative and Administrative Provisions Concerning Indigenous and Tribal Peoples in Africa* (ACHPR/ILO, Yaoundé Cameroon, September 2006), https://www.ilo.org/wcmsp5/groups/public/@ed_norm/@normes/documents/publication/wcms_100797.pdf (last accessed March 30, 2019).

91. *Id., Report on the Workshop Examining Constitutional, Legislative and Administrative Provisions Concerning Indigenous and Tribal Peoples in Africa*, p. 10.

92. See *Id., State of the World's Indigenous Peoples*, p. 6.

93. See Report of the Working Group on Indigenous Populations on its fifteenth session, E/CN.4/Sub.2/1997/14, August 13, 1997, para 129; Report of the Working Group on Indigenous Populations on its Fourteenth Session, E/CN.4/Sub.2/1996/21, August 16, 1996, paras 153–154; and *State of the World's Indigenous Peoples*, p. 5.

Chapter 3

The Scope of Corporate Responsibility for Human Rights of Indigenous Peoples

CORPORATE SOCIAL RESPÓNSIBILITY: DEVELOPMENT, MEANING, PERCEPTIONS, AND PRACTICES

Brief Historical Context of CSR

Some scholars have suggested that early formulations of practices akin to the social responsibility of businesses are traceable to the 1700s BC.[1] During this period, King Hammurabi, the then king of the First Babylonian Dynasty, introduced a code which set death penalty as punishment for any negligence on the part of builders, innkeepers, or farmers that resulted in injury or fatality to other citizens, thus influencing the concerned business people and farmers to conduct themselves responsibly.[2] Similarly, in the 1700s, Adam Smith, a Scottish economist and moral philosopher, was credited for writing several papers, including the *Theory of Moral Sentiments and Lectures in Jurisprudence*, and *The Wealth of Nations*, in which he helped to frame discussions concerning how businesses should be guided by morality in discharging their responsibility to society.[3]

Others have also discussed the connection between businesses and their moral duty to the society as emerging from practices associated with the industrial revolution in the 1800s. In this era, it became imperative for business organizations to formulate industrial welfare programs in Britain and the United States, considered then as both a business and social tool, in order to forestall labor crisis and improve workplace performance.[4] However, the modern conceptualization of CSR as we know it today began in the twentieth century, especially starting from the early 1950s,[5] as part of corporate *philanthropic* or *charity* agenda that was gaining popularity at the time.[6]

The demand for some form of socially conscious behavior on the part of corporate entities is not new.[7] The nature and scope of social responsibility that corporations owe their employees and society has been consistently debated since the early twentieth century.[8] Interestingly, the kernel of what constitutes responsible corporate behavior evolves with the times,[9] and over the years the concept of CSR has mirrored different eras of social awareness. What began as a response to labor concerns evolved into philanthropy, environmental protection, and core human rights, centered corporate practices.[10] For instance, in the 1970s and 1980s, CSR was largely driven by labor and workers' rights issues, culminating in the "sweatshops" controversy in the early 1990s that implicated Nike, a prominent global brand and one of the biggest suppliers of athletic shoes and apparel in the world.[11] Nike and several other big merchandise companies were accused of perpetrating labor rights violations by adopting substandard and unethical operational practices for their factories located in developing countries.[12] Similarly, from the 1990s onward, CSR responded to the huge public outcry over the monumental environmental degradation and human rights infractions caused by the Exxon Valdez oil spill in Alaska,[13] the Deepwater Horizon oil-drilling rig explosion in the Gulf of Mexico,[14] and the unprecedented pollution of the Niger Delta region in Nigeria.[15]

In his groundbreaking work, Howard Bowen, a pioneer of the conceptual evolution of CSR, characterizes the concept as the "obligations of business to pursue those policies, to make those decisions or to follow those lines of action which are desirable in terms of the objectives and values of our society."[16] However, as the discussions throughout this chapter will show, the concept of CSR today is as much a legal paradox as it is morally ambiguous.

Meaning and Nature of CSR

In recent times, different understandings of CSR have emerged, and descriptions such as corporate citizenship, or responsible business, were commonly used interchangeably.[17] Perhaps because of this mutability, and as with the term *indigenous peoples* discussed in the preceding chapters, there is no singular generally applicable definition of CSR. One early formulation of what CSR entails was put forward by Milton Friedman, a renowned economist and Nobel Laureate, who saw the concept as being concerned solely with the objective of corporate profit-making, and nothing more.[18] As Friedman described it:

> There is one and only one social responsibility of business—to use its resources and engage in activities designed to increase its profits so long as it stays within the rules of the game, which is to say, engages in open and free competition without deception or fraud.[19]

However, Friedman's constrictive view of the meaning of CSR has not been vindicated by domestic and global events, especially in the past two decades. Corporations are now increasingly seen as an integral part of our social institutions, and as such, in addition to making a profit for their shareholders, they must also be mindful of the interests of the community of stakeholders affected by their profit-making activities.[20]

According to the World Business Council for Sustainable Development (WBCSD), CSR is composed of a corporation's interaction with the legal and social obligations of the societies in which it operates, coupled with how it fulfills those obligations.[21] More to the point, the concept of CSR focuses on how corporate entities mindfully manage the impact of their conduct and operational activities on stakeholders and society. Given that CSR is primarily a voluntary framework, it mainly refers to the sustained commitment by a corporation to be proper, fair, and responsible above and beyond legal requirements, in a manner that contributes to the overall economic development, and improves the life of its employees and their families, as well as the local community.[22]

Archie Carroll, in one of the most prominent expositions on the concept of CSR, *The Pyramid of Corporate Social Responsibility*, proposed that the social responsibility of businesses is an aggregation of the economic, legal, ethical, and philanthropic (discretionary) expectations of a corporation, respectively, arranged in a hierarchical order.[23] In other words, the primary responsibility of a corporation is to generate profits for its shareholders and to do so within the legal framework drawn by the host government.[24] Ancillary to that is the ethical responsibility of a corporation to conduct its business in accordance with acceptable standards and avoid detriment to its stakeholders.

Figure 3.1   Pyramid of CSR. *Source*: Author, adapted from Archie Carroll's Pyramid of CSR, 1991.

And, lastly, businesses have the responsibility to adopt a philanthropic strategy that can be beneficial to both the business and society.[25]

While Carroll's pyramid model captures the basic characteristics of CSR as is known in modern business and commerce, it cannot be accurately concluded that the model scrupulously described the actual practice of CSR among corporations operating in developing countries.[26] As Hevina Dashwood noted, it is always paramount that any evaluation of the scope and nature of a corporation's social responsibility differentiates between what a corporation should be doing from what they are in fact doing.[27]

Perceptions and Practices of CSR

CSR was initially viewed as an attempt by corporations to simply reach out and interact with the communities located in the area where they operate, beyond the solitary premise of corporate profit-making.[28] Many were—and are still—skeptical about whether these corporate outreaches were intended to genuinely engage with the broader society beyond the fixation on profits, or, perhaps, geared towards creating mere appearances of such effort in order to serve the public relations utility of corporations.[29] Those who find fault with the practice of CSR in this way largely present the concept as a contraption by big businesses, motivated by a desire to enhance and maintain the image of corporations and to gain reputational assurance for positive bottom-line purposes.[30] They add that CSR was a surreptitious agenda meant to induce a more compliant workforce, to easily gain resource development leases or licenses, and develop a loyal and yielding customer base.[31]

Undeniably, the debate is still open as it concerns the true scope of the concept of CSR and the utility of its inconsistent application around the world, be it as a form of public relation or veritable outreach to the broader society by corporate entities. In addition, the question of whether or not CSR, as it is known and practiced in the western industrialized world, is different from what the concept implies in the developing countries, is in the balance. It is noteworthy, and indeed fascinating to realize, that the extent to which the protection of human rights of *indigenous peoples*, especially in developing countries, was impeded was not strictly restricted to the problem of misconception about the term *indigenous peoples*, as discussed in the preceding chapters, but also because of how CSR is understood and practiced. Efforts to ensure corporate compliance with the human rights of indigenous peoples was, in some ways, hampered by the skewed perception about what the scope of CSR entails, and the impact of its aberrant practices in different parts of the world.

It appears as though in the developed western countries, strict legal compliance, high ethical standards, and diligent environmental compliance largely constitute the core of CSR practice, as reflected in Carroll's pyramid of CSR model highlighted above. On the contrary, in most developing parts of the world, Carroll's pyramid is somewhat turned on its head. Accordingly, in these less-developed parts of the world, philanthropic endeavors of corporations, such as their contributions to community infrastructural development or provision of educational scholarships for locals, has become synonymous with CSR, and actually forms its core. For instance, philanthropic acts continue to play a central role in the practice of CSR in many African countries. As Jedrzej Frynas noted,[32] philanthropic activities are still considered the main social responsibility of business in Africa, and even so, such activities may simply be a well-calculated reputational strategy which serves the corporation much more than the community.[33] During an extensive study of CSR practices of multinational oil companies in the Gulf of Guinea region, Frynas pointed out an instance of such disparate CSR practices:

> Shell's main Nigerian affiliate Shell Petroleum Development Company (SPDC) provides its major contract managers with a development budget, so that when a new pipeline is built, the manager can initiate a new development project within a community in order to enable pipeline construction to continue unhindered. When the SPDC team finishes the construction of a particular section of the pipeline, the community development budget for the area is simply closed, which follows the logic of why the firm embarked on the project in the first instance.[34]

It is based on this contorted understanding of what CSR represents that corporations operating in developing countries formulate what their role within broader society entails, and determines the degree of responsibility they owe to the local communities. Some corporations operating in these developing countries seem to place a higher premium on discretionary philanthropic gestures toward communities than on strict adherence to existing rules and regulations or observance of ethical principles. Sadly, it is not an uncommon practice for corporations, especially multinationals, to adopt different corporate practices and ethical standards depending on the geography of their business.[35] This kind of corporate operational pattern was exposed by events leading up to the sweatshops scandal which erupted in the 1990s, as highlighted earlier. Nike and other big merchandise companies were criticized for adopting and implementing substandard ethical operational practices in their factories located in developing countries.[36]

Corporate entities tend to implement superior standards for their business operations in developed parts of the world, and then apply watered-down standards for their activities in less-developed countries.[37] In one particular case, the United Kingdom (UK)–based Thor Chemical Company was censured by the health and safety regulatory body in the UK for allowing its operation to cause excessive levels of airborne mercury beyond the allowable regulatory limits, and thereby exposing its British neighbors and workers to mercury contamination.[38] Thor was ordered to either comply with the regulation or face prosecution by the regulatory body.[39] Instead, the company's ultimate decision was simply to move its operations to KwaZulu-Natal Province in South Africa to escape the UK's regulatory requirements and scrutiny.[40] Thor later became embroiled in another compliance problem arising from the company's adverse operational activities in South Africa. A group of South African residents brought action against Thor for adopting inferior and detrimental operational practices in South Africa, which the company would not have succeeded in carrying through at its UK plants because such practice was prohibited by the UK government.[41] The group alleged that they suffered acute, often fatal, poisoning as a result of their exposure to, and inhalation of, mercury vapor and mercury compounds while working at the company's Cato Ridge plant in KwaZulu-Natal, South Africa.[42] Thor eventually settled the case with the group for about GBP 1.3 million.[43]

The decision of Thor to simply move its operation to a developing country instead of addressing the concerns raised by the UK's health and safety regulatory authority was telling. This kind of divergent practice could be attributable to the varying understanding of what CSR entails, and in terms of existing regulatory protections in both developed and developing countries.[44] The CSR practice by Thor, in this instance, is no different from those adopted by other corporate entities. In 2010, a catastrophic explosion occurred at BP's *Deepwater Horizon* drilling platform located in the Gulf of Mexico in the United States, killing 11 people and causing more than 130 million gallons of oil to spill over the Gulf, which resulted in massive damage across several states in the United States.[45] Following this massive spill, BP was both publicly apologetic for causing the tragic incident and firm in its commitment to remediate any damages that may result. BP's chief executive officer, Tony Hayward, in his address to the U.S. Congress' Energy and Commerce Sub-Committee on Oversight and Investigation, made the following statement:

Nonetheless, I am here today because I have a responsibility to the American people to do my best to explain what BP has done, is doing, and will do in the future to respond to this terrible incident. And while we can't undo these tragic events, I give you my word that we will do the right thing. We will not rest until the well is under control, and we will meet all our obligations to clean up the spill and address its environmental and economic impacts. From the moment I learned of the explosion and fire, I committed the global resources of BP to the response efforts. To be sure, neither I nor the company is perfect. But we are unwavering in our commitment to fulfil all our responsibilities. We are a strong company, and nothing is being spared. We are going to do everything in our power to address fully the economic and environmental consequences of this spill and to ensure that we use the lessons learned from this incident to make energy exploration and production safer and more reliable for everyone.[46]

In addition to BP's all-inclusive response to deal with the spill, the U.S. government also made it abundantly clear that the company must clean up the Gulf and pay compensation to anyone who incurred damages to real or personal property, lost earnings or profits, was denied subsistence use of natural resources, or suffered physical injury or death, as a result of the spill.[47] In the end, BP agreed to pay more than USD 20 billion in a settlement negotiated between the company, the U.S. government, governments of five U.S. states, and several local government authorities and other affected groups.[48]

However, the BP's Deepwater Horizon case in the United States does not appear to fully represent the practice of BP, and many other multinational extractive companies in different parts of the world, particularly as it concerns developing countries. For instance, in contrast to BP's response to the Deepwater Horizon incident in the United States, claims brought against BP-Columbia by more than 100 farmers for causing significant damage to their lands, crops, and animals, over the Ocensa Pipeline Project connecting Cusiana and Cupiagua oil-fields in Colombia, was vigorously contested by BP.[49] The claims by the farmers resulted in a long-running legal contest that ended up before the British High Court, where the farmers recently lost.[50]

Additionally, it is no secret that massive oil spills resulting from the operations of multinational oil and gas companies have, for decades, wreaked havoc on many local communities in developing parts of the world, such as the Niger Delta region of Nigeria, without any significant effort by the companies to clean up the environment or fairly compensate the local population for the damages that result.[51] For example, according to a scientific study conducted by the UNEP, petroleum hydrocarbon pollution in the Niger Delta was quite extensive and prevalent.[52] Furthermore, a report by Amnesty International also shows that Shell caused about 204 oil spills in the Niger Delta, while ENI, for its part, was responsible for about 350.[53] Conversely, only an average of ten spills a year was recorded across all of Europe during the period between 1971 and 2011.[54] Although Amnesty noted that in other countries such a sustained recurring environmental pollution would be deemed a national emergency, the organization concluded that the practice appears to be a standard operating procedure for oil companies operating in Nigeria.[55]

Even if one concedes that corporations' economic, legal, and ethical burden form the core of CSR, as Carroll and others have argued, obviously a mere declaration of commitment by corporations to be socially responsible and respect existing legal and ethical rules in places where they operate cannot adequately protect the human rights of indigenous peoples located within those places. This is especially true considering that the framework for CSR is generally discretionary and non-binding, and no obligatory international instruments on corporate accountability presently exist. In addition, fulfilling a commitment to be an upright corporate citizen who abides by legal rules, ethical, and human rights standards could be more complex in national jurisdictions where existing laws and regulations are weak or do not provide adequate protection for human rights generally, or human rights of indigenous peoples particularly. This is particularly true for smaller corporations without significant market share or power.

CONTEXTUALIZING CORPORATE RESPONSIBILITY TO RESPECT HUMAN RIGHTS OF INDIGENOUS PEOPLES

Presently, there are no direct binding legal obligations imposed on corporations to uphold international human rights standards, except those legal obligations imposed upon them through domestic laws of States. Under international law, the substantive primary duty to protect against violations of human rights lies with States, not corporations or other private actors. As the court in Kiobel *v. Royal Dutch Petroleum Co.* explained, the law of nations does not recognize corporate liability.[56] This is especially so because international law incorporates only those standards, rules, or customs affecting the relationship between States or between an individual and a foreign State.[57] A situation that, unfortunately, creates significant limitation in terms of opportunities to hold multinational corporations accountable for violations of international human rights standards, especially those committed in jurisdictions where the domestic legal framework, does not afford meaningful protection.

In *Kiobel*, the plaintiffs, who are members of the Niger Delta communities in Nigeria, brought claims under the U.S. court system against Royal Dutch Shell and its local subsidiary, Shell Petroleum Development Company (SPDC), for colluding with the Nigerian government to violate their human rights.[58] The plaintiffs sought damages under the United States' Alien Tort Statute (ATS).[59] The ATS vests federal district courts in the United States with jurisdiction to hear civil claims, brought by an alien, for a tort committed in violation of the law of nations or a treaty of the United States.[60] For almost four decades, many plaintiffs have relied heavily on the ATS as their principal legal basis to hold corporate perpetrators and foreign government officials responsible, at least in the United States, for the human rights abuses they caused in other countries.[61] The ATS claims became indispensable in this context, considering the lack of a universal binding legal instrument compelling corporate human rights compliance.

However, after a series of encouraging outcomes achieved by ATS-based claims at the lower courts,[62] the U.S. Supreme Court, in *Kiobel*, seem to close off this ATS avenue for corporate human rights accountability, by holding that the presumption against the extraterritorial application of U.S. law applies to claims under the ATS.[63] Although the apex court did not make a definitive ruling on the issue of whether or not corporations are generally shielded from tort liability for violations of international law, it, nonetheless, concluded that Shell could not be liable in U.S. courts under the ATS for the human rights abuses it committed overseas, on the grounds that all of the relevant conduct took place outside the United States, and that the case had no U.S. connection other than Shell's mere corporate presence in the country.[64] The Supreme Court reasoned in *Kiobel* that ATS may only permit federal court's jurisdiction over claims that *touches and concern* the territory of the United States with *sufficient force*, enough to displace the presumption against extraterritorial application of ATS.[65]

The Supreme Court further handed down a more categorical ruling on this issue of ATS and corporate liability in the recent case of *Jesner v. Arab Bank*, when it, unambiguously, affirms that ATS simply does not permit aliens to bring lawsuits against foreign corporations in the United States.[66]

States' Duty to Protect Human Rights

The foundational principles articulated in the UN Guiding Principles on Business and Human Rights[67] reflect the existing scope and nature of the responsibility borne by corporate entities in terms of how their conduct and operational activities align with internationally affirmed human rights standards. As the UN Guiding Principles enunciate, States possesses the primary *duty to protect* against human rights abuses by corporate entities, and corporations largely incur bare *responsibility to respect* human rights rules, while both the States and corporations share the burden to remediate any infraction or abuse that may occur therefrom.[68] (Further discussion of the UN Guiding Principles and corporate due diligence duty is below.)

As noted above, the duty to protect human rights, and to ensure corporations comply with international human rights standards, was generally attributed to States, not corporations.[69] In keeping with the consequences of statehood,[70] the primary responsibility for establishing legal and regulatory control over the activities of all persons, including corporate entities, located within the geographical confines of States, which is rightfully vested in the governments of those States as sovereign authorities. In general, States have obligations and duties under international law to promote universal respect for human rights, avoid curtailment of the enjoyment of these rights, and to collaborate with other States in order to accomplish these objectives.[71] However, much of the jurisprudence concerning the obligations of States to protect human rights has evolved through the regional human rights systems.

The *duty to protect* principle[72] requires States to safeguard the human rights and fundamental freedoms of all persons and groups within their national boundaries, as well as to shield such rights against abuses by third parties, including corporate or other private actors. As a corollary, States bear the burden of adopting legislative, administrative, or other legal measures that are necessary to ensure the full enjoyment of human rights by their citizens and residents, and to prevent corporate actors from violating those rights. As the European Court of Human Rights pointed out in the *Costello-Roberts v. United Kingdom* case,[73] the duty incurred in this respect is an abiding one, and for which States cannot be negligent in discharging.[74] In this particular case, the applicant, Jeremy Costello-Roberts, claimed that the corporal punishment inflicted on him by a private school located in North Devon, England, constituted *degrading punishment* contrary to Article 3 of the European Convention on Human Rights, which prohibits torture, inhuman, or degrading treatment or punishment.[75] Although, the court in *Costello-Roberts* ruled against the applicant, on the ground that the punishment in question did not attain the required level of severity to amount to a breach of Article 3 of the Convention, it concluded that the State has an obligation to secure the rights of every child, and indeed, every citizen.[76] The court emphasized that

> the responsibility of a State is engaged if a violation of one of the rights and freedoms defined in the Convention [for the Protection of Human Rights and Fundamental Freedoms] is the result of non-observance by that State of its obligation under Article 1 (art. 1) to secure those rights and freedoms in its domestic law to everyone within its jurisdiction.[77]

The duty of a State to protect human rights was also entrenched within the Inter-American human rights system. According to the American Declaration of the Rights and Duties of Man,[78] the principal aim of all members of the Organization of American States shall be "the protection of the essential rights of man and the creation of circumstances that will permit him to achieve spiritual and material progress and attain happiness."[79] In addition, the American Convention on Human Rights[80] provides that

> the States Parties to this Convention undertake to respect the rights and freedoms recognized herein and to ensure to all persons subject to their jurisdiction the free and full exercise of those rights and freedoms, without any discrimination for reasons of race, color, sex, language, religion, political or other opinion, national or social origin, economic status, birth, or any other social condition.[81]

As a result, should any member of the Organization of American States (OAS), who are State parties to the American Convention on Human Rights, fail to prevent violations perpetrated against any person or group of persons by a corporate actor, the member would be derogating from this duty.[82] Here, the deterring factor that activates the protective action of the State party is that the State would become liable for any inaction, not because it directly committed the violation, but because of the lack of due diligence on the part of that State in preventing the violation.[83] More specifically, in *Velásquez Rodríguez v. Honduras*,[84] where Manfredo Velasquez Rodríguez was violently detained without a warrant and tortured by members of the security apparatuses of Honduras, the Inter-American Court of Human Rights concluded on the States' liability for inaction as follows:

> [t]he State has a legal duty to take reasonable steps to prevent human rights violations and to use the means at its disposal to carry out a serious investigation of violations committed within its jurisdiction, to identify those responsible, to impose the appropriate punishment and to ensure the victim adequate compensation.[85]

As the court concluded further:

> [t]he State is obligated to investigate every situation involving a violation of the rights protected by the Convention. If the State apparatus acts in such a way that the violation goes unpunished and the victim's full enjoyment of such rights is not restored as soon as possible, the State has failed to comply with its duty to ensure the free and full exercise of those rights to the persons within its jurisdiction. The same is true when the State allows private persons or groups to act freely and with impunity to the detriment of the rights recognized by the Convention.[86]

In addition to investigating violations and vindicating the human rights of their citizens, liability is also attracted when Member States fail to adopt appropriate domestic laws to safeguard those human rights.[87]

The European human rights system implements a similar *duty to protect* principle pursuant to the Convention for the Protection of Human Rights and Fundamental Freedoms,[88] which imposes certain obligations on all Council of Europe Member States to respect and protect the human rights of their populations.[89] According to the Convention, Member States must "secure to everyone within their jurisdiction the rights and freedoms defined in Section I of [the] Convention."[90] In other words, Member States are required to shield their populations from the action(s) attributable to private persons or other entities such as corporations that are capable of infringing the populace's human rights.[91]

Unfortunately, however, the African human rights system lacks any clear and consistent jurisprudential position on the *duty to protect* principle. In contrast to the other regional human rights systems,[92] the African Charter on Human and Peoples Rights[93] does not contain any direct stipulations with regard to the duty of the State to protect. The closest operative provision in the Charter states that

> [t]he Member States of the Organization of African Unity parties to the present Charter shall recognize the rights, duties and freedoms enshrined in this Chapter and shall undertake to adopt legislative or other measures to give effect to them.[94]

The foregoing provision defines the duty of African States to protect the human rights of their populations mainly in terms of the States' burden to adopt some legislative or other similar measures for that purpose. Unlike the American Convention on Human Rights and the European Convention on Human Rights, the African Charter does not specifically impose any direct legal obligation on the African States to secure the enjoyment of human rights and fundamental freedoms to their populations by preventing violations perpetrated by third parties such as corporate entities.

Despite this, the African Commission on Human and Peoples Rights (ACHPR) has on one occasion interpreted the duty imposed on the African States under the African Charter to incorporate the broad duty of State to protect, as applicable in other parts of the world.[95] The ACHPR, in *SERAC v Nigeria*,[96] held that an African State can be held liable not only for their own acts of human rights violation, but also for failure to protect their citizens from violations inflicted by corporations or other private actors.[97] In this particular case, the Nigerian National Petroleum Company (NNPC) in conjunction with Shell Petroleum Development Corporation (SPDC) carried on oil and gas production operations within the territory of the *Ogoni* peoples in southern Nigeria, without regard for the peoples' environment and human rights. The communication before the Commission alleged, among others, that the government of Nigeria condoned and facilitated these violations by placing the legal and military powers of the State at the disposal of the oil companies.[98] The Commission concluded that the action of the Nigerian government in permissively giving a green light to the oil company to interfere with the well-being of the *Ogonis* fell short of the minimum conduct expected of governments and, thus, constituted a violation of the African Charter.[99] The Commission in its reasoning relied heavily on jurisprudence within the Inter-American and European human rights systems[100] to assert the view that a governments' duty to protect their citizens goes beyond an undertaking to adopt appropriate legislation and effective enforcement, but also requires protecting citizens from damaging acts that may be perpetrated by private parties.[101]

Notwithstanding the foregoing, an unwavering reliance on the *duty to protect* principle is not a failproof mechanism that could be relied on by human rights defenders to ensure the protection of individuals and groups against human rights abuses by corporations, in the absence of international legally binding obligation imposed on corporations themselves. This is in part due to some of the obstacles in the way of establishing meaningful corporate human rights responsibility as discussed throughout this book. In addition, the reluctance of developing countries' governments, and in many cases due to practical inability, to impose strict rules to regulate corporate conduct poses a significant barrier. Besides, the *duty to protect* principle does not equally lend itself to global application, considering the fact that it remains inoperative, without the need for additional step, in certain regions of the world. This is even so with respect to States that have not yet signed or ratified the appropriate human rights instruments but are located in regions of the world where the principle is otherwise applicable.

Corporate Responsibility to Respect Human Rights

Corporations play an important role in the socio-economic life of our society and thus incur the responsibility to respect human rights, avoid infringing those rights, and address any adverse impact they cause in the process of conducting their business.[102] Corporate responsibility to respect ethical and good practice standards generally, and human rights norms specifically, can be distilled from the numerous international and industry-focused voluntary codes of conduct such as the UN Global Compact,[103] Equator Principles,[104] Extractive Industries Transparency Initiative,[105] UN Principles for Responsible Investment,[106] Global Network Initiative,[107] Global Reporting Initiative,[108] and Voluntary Principles on Security and Human Rights.[109] As with the other corporate codes of conduct, the UN Global Compact offers important parameters meant to ensure that corporations support and respect internationally proclaimed human rights standards, and to prevent them from being complicit in human rights abuses.[110] (See further discussion on this subject in chapter 4, particularly on redefining corporate responsibility under the international systems.)

Corporate Human Rights Due Diligence Duty

Presently, the breadth of responsibility owed by corporations to respect human rights is defined by their due diligence duty to avoid violations of human rights. This due diligence duty requires corporations to identify actual or potential adverse human rights impacts their operations may cause, take appropriate steps to avoid such adverse impacts, and implement effective measures to remedy impacts where they occur.[111] An articulation of the human rights due diligence duty of corporations can be found in the Guiding Principles on Business and Human Rights.[112] These principles, endorsed by the UN Human Rights Council in the summer of 2011, were meant to effectuate the UN "Protect, Respect and Remedy" Framework, the first definitive framework on human rights expectations for corporations.[113] The development of the "Protect, Respect and Remedy" Framework itself was spearheaded by John Ruggie, the then Special Representative of the UN Secretary-General on the issue of human rights and transnational corporations and other business enterprises.[114] Pursuant to the Protect, Respect, and Remedy Framework, corporate entities, regardless of their size, sector, location, ownership, and structure, are expected to fully respect human rights.[115] That is, corporations should avoid violating the human rights of others and must address any adverse human rights impacts they may cause.[116] The nature of responsibility envisaged here relates to all internationally recognized human rights.[117] The Guiding Principles on Business and Human Rights themselves are stated to be anchored on the following underlying precepts:

(a) States' existing obligations to respect, protect, and fulfill human rights and fundamental freedoms;
(b) The role of business enterprises as specialized organs of society performing specialized functions, required to comply with all applicable laws and to respect human rights;
(c) The need for rights and obligations to be matched to appropriate and effective remedies when breached.[118]

An overview of the Guiding Principles on Business and Human Rights, and the underlying "Protect, Respect, and Remedy" Framework upon which the principles were grounded reveals that States possess the primary duty to protect against human rights abuses by corporate entities; corporations have a general duty to fully respect human rights rules, both domestic and international human rights regimes; and both states and corporations share responsibility to remediate and address adverse human rights impacts they cause.[119] For this reason, the Guiding Principles set forth the ambits of the due diligence duty incurred by corporate entities with respect to human rights as follows:

> In order to identify, prevent, mitigate and account for how they address their adverse human rights impacts, business enterprises should carry out human rights' due diligence. The process should include assessing actual and potential human rights impacts, integrating and acting upon the findings, tracking responses, and communicating how impacts are addressed. Human rights due diligence

(a) should cover adverse human rights impacts that the business enterprise may cause or contribute to through its own activities, or which may be directly linked to its operations, products, or services by its business relationships;

(b) will vary in complexity with the size of the business enterprise, the risk of severe human rights impacts, and the nature and context of its operations;

(c) should be ongoing, recognizing that the human rights risks may change over time as the business enterprise's operations and operating context evolve.[120]

It is worth noting here that while the UN Guiding Principles remain a useful international standard-setting tool,[121] they themselves do not create any binding legal obligations for either corporate entities or States, because it is, by its nature, a non-binding instrument.[122]

In addition to the UN Guiding Principles on Business and Human Rights, other international instruments have also put forward tangible due diligence standards for the purpose of regulating corporate human rights responsibility. For instance, the ILO Tripartite Declaration of Principles Concerning Multinational Enterprises and Social Policy (MNE Declaration),[123] and the OECD Due Diligence Guidance for Responsible Business Conduct (OECD Due Diligence Guidance),[124] provide some valuable guidelines with respect to corporate human rights due diligence duty. The principles introduced in the MNE Declaration are, however, focused on three parties: the governments of host countries, workers, and multinational enterprises. The MNE Declaration specifically addresses corporate conduct, recognizing that multinational enterprises can make important contributions to the enjoyment of human rights throughout the world, including freedom of association.[125] To this end, the MNE Declaration endorses the same corporate human rights responsibility outlined in the Guiding Principles on Business and Human Right, including its due diligence duty.[126] The MNE Declaration makes the point that multinational enterprises, for their part, have a clear duty to respect fundamental human rights and rights at work, and also elaborates on the content of that duty. The MNE Declaration proclaims thus:

(c) The corporate responsibility to respect human rights requires that enterprises, including multinational enterprises wherever they operate, (i) avoid causing or contributing to adverse impacts through their own activities, and address such impacts when they occur; and (ii) seek to prevent or mitigate adverse human rights impacts that are directly linked to their operations, products, or services by their business relationships, even if they have not contributed to those impacts.

(d) Enterprises, including multinational enterprises, should carry out due diligence to identify, prevent, mitigate, and account for how they address their actual and potential adverse impacts that relate to internationally recognized human rights, understood, at a minimum, as those expressed in the International Bill of Human Rights and the principles concerning fundamental rights set out in the ILO Declaration on Fundamental Principles and Rights at Work.[127]

The OECD Due Diligence Guidance, for its part, essentially elaborates on the provisions requiring multinational enterprises to respect human rights already contained in the OECD Guidelines for Multinational Enterprises (OECD Guidelines for MNEs).[128] According to the OECD Due Diligence Guidance:

> The concept of due diligence under the OECD Guidelines for MNEs involves a bundle of interrelated processes to identify adverse impacts, prevent and mitigate them, track implementation and results and communicate on how adverse impacts are addressed with respect to the enterprises' own operations, their supply chains and other business relationships. Due diligence should be an integral part of enterprise decision-making and risk management.[129]

The primary due diligence obligation of multinational enterprises, as both the OECD Guidelines for MNEs and OECD Due Diligence Guidance have emphasized, is to ensure that corporations obey domestic laws and regulations, and internationally recognized human rights in the jurisdictions where they operate or are domiciled.[130]

Corporate Due Diligence Duty for Human Rights of Indigenous Peoples

Many of the international standards regarding corporate human rights responsibility, enunciated above, generally apply to the human rights situation of *indigenous peoples*. Unlike the traditional human rights regime, indigenous rights–specific regulatory frameworks that set standards for corporate responsibility with regard to human rights of *indigenous peoples* are still gradually fledging. In this context, some preexisting human rights frameworks have incorporated indigenous rights regime into their implementation processes to bridge the gap.[131] Furthermore, certain institutional codes of conduct and policy initiatives have also either been revised, or new guidelines developed, in order to specifically addressed corporate responsibility for indigenous peoples' rights.

For instance, the World Bank was responsible for the formulation of an Operational Policy on Indigenous people (OP 4.10).[132] This policy requires that all development projects proposed for financing by the World Bank, and that affect indigenous peoples, must be fully respectful of the dignity, human rights, economies, and cultures of the indigenous peoples concerned.[133] The Performance Standard (PS7) developed by the International Financial Corporations (IFC) contains identical requirements directed at both public and private corporations to respect international indigenous rights standards in their operations.[134] Both the World Resource Institute (WRI) Principles for Effective Community Engagement,[135] and the International Council on Mining and Metals (ICMM) Position Statement[136] and Good Practice Guide,[137] similarly prescribe standards for corporate responsibility for indigenous rights as it relates to the extractive sector. To cite an example, the first commitment of the ICMM Position Statement calls for all corporations aligned with the institution to ensure that any development of mining and metals projects occurring within or near indigenous territories are respectful of the rights, interests, aspirations, culture, and natural resource–based livelihoods of indigenous peoples.[138]

There is also the aforementioned OECD Guidelines for MNEs,[139] the provisions of which apply in a comparable manner to local communities as a collective. The OECD Guidelines for MNEs demand that multinational enterprises carry out risk-based due diligence to identify, prevent, and mitigate actual and potential adverse impacts that their activity may cause to local communities.[140] It emphasized that multinational enterprises should engage with local communities and ensure that their views are taken into account with respect to the planning and decision-making concerning projects that may impact them.[141]

One other example is the Akwé: Kon Guidelines,[142] which contains comprehensive provisions for the protection of the cultural and environmental rights of indigenous peoples. The Akwé: Kon Guidelines require both private enterprises and governmental agencies proposing any project that may affect lands or waters of indigenous communities to acknowledge the rights of those communities, and engage in a process of notification and public consultation with them about the intention to carry out such project.[143] Consistent with the goal of the Akwé: Kon Guidelines to safeguard the rights of indigenous communities, all project proponents have a responsibility to implement cultural, environmental, and social impact assessment protocols before commencing any project.[144]

As noted earlier, the majority of the foregoing guidelines and standards for corporate human rights responsibility also broadly apply to the situation of *indigenous peoples*. While this is a commendable starting point, corporate entities may still encounter some difficulty in applying these existing guidelines and standards, as they were formulated on the basis of traditional, individual-oriented human rights precepts. Put differently, a corporation may fail to adequately discharge its due diligence duty by inflexibly addressing

indigenous peoples' rights issues with the same due diligence policy measures meant for its traditional human rights compliance. Even though indigenous peoples' rights may rightfully be deemed conceptually analogous to
traditional human rights precepts, the nature of the constituent rights of both
indigenous rights and traditional human rights are characteristically unique.[145]
Oftentimes, the due diligence compliance requirements for indigenous rights
are dictated by the peculiarity or distinctiveness of the indigenous groups
concerned.[146] Even John Ruggie, the architect of the UN "Protect, Respect,
and Remedy" Framework, made the point earlier that corporations may need
to consider additional standards, especially as it concerns human rights of
indigenous groups.[147]

In 2010, an indigenous rights–focused corporate due diligence duty was
articulated by the then UN Special Rapporteur on Indigenous Rights, James
Anaya, in his annual report to the UN Human Rights Council during its fifteenth session.[148] Anaya affirmed the importance of both the corporations'
duty to respect human rights and the concept of due diligence as expressed
in international guidelines and standards.[149] He further emphasized that corporate entities have a general duty to respect international human rights rules
within the framework of human rights due diligence, which must guide their
conduct and operations.[150] Anaya described the corporate due diligence duty
for indigenous peoples' rights as follows:

> In the context of indigenous peoples, the corporate responsibility to respect
> human rights means that companies must exercise due diligence by identify-
> ing, prior to commencing their activities, various matters relating to the basic
> rights of indigenous peoples, and by paying adequate attention to those matters
> as the activities are being carried out. Such matters include recognition of the
> existence of indigenous peoples and of their own social and political structures;
> indigenous possession and use of land, territory and natural resources; exercise
> by the State of its duty to consult indigenous peoples in relation to activities that
> might affect them, and the related responsibility of business; impact studies and
> mitigation measures; and benefit sharing with indigenous peoples.[151]

Likewise, Victoria Tauli-Corpuz, the current UN Special Rapporteur on
the Rights of Indigenous Peoples, in echoing the concern over widespread
instances of disregard for the rights of indigenous peoples with regard to
extractive and other development projects, emphasized in her 2018 report to
the UN Human Rights Council that

> transnational corporations and other business enterprises should respect human
> rights, as set out in the Guiding Principles on Business and Human Rights:
> Implementing the United Nations "Protect, Respect and Remedy" Framework,
> which rest on three pillars: the State duty to protect against human rights abuses

by third parties, including businesses; the corporate responsibility to respect human rights; and the need for access to an effective remedy for victims of business-related human rights abuses. Principle 18 requires that business enterprises identify and assess any actual or potential adverse human rights impacts through meaningful consultation with potentially affected groups as an integral part of their responsibility to respect human rights.[152]

Thus, considering all of the above, the responsibility of corporate entities to respect human rights may no longer be subjected to a purely discretionary philanthropic CSR rationalization. Corporations may no longer have total control over the level of respect they demonstrate for human rights. There is a building international normative consensus that corporations are now expected to exercise a higher due diligence duty to respect human rights. In order to discharge this due diligence duty, a corporation should at all instances during the conduct of its businesses avoid not only infringing upon any human rights rules, but also ensure redress of any harms when they occur.[153] Corporations, as part of their CSR approach, should not merely show respect for national laws and regulations, they also have the due diligence responsibility to go beyond national laws and ensure respect for all the applicable international standard prescriptions.[154] As outlined by the Guiding Principles on Business and Human Rights:

> The responsibility to respect human rights is a global standard of expected conduct for all business enterprises wherever they operate. It exists independently of States' abilities and/or willingness to fulfil their own human rights obligations, and does not diminish those obligations. And it exists over and above compliance with national laws and regulations protecting human rights.[155]

Accordingly, the due diligence duty of corporations, with particular regard to human rights of indigenous peoples, includes the task of identifying and acknowledging the various indigenous groups that are, or may be, affected by their operational activities. Furthermore, corporations must be cognizant and respectful of the rights of indigenous communities to the lands, territories, and natural resources that they traditionally use and occupy, as provided for under relevant international instruments like the UNDRIP and ILO Convention No.169.[156]

In discharging their duty, corporations can neither claim the non-recognition of, nor inadequate or well-defined legal protections for, indigenous peoples in the jurisdictions where they operate as a pretext for not applying the minimum international normative standards concerning human rights of *indigenous peoples*.[157] It is imperative for corporations to realize that their due diligence duty to comply with all applicable laws, and also to respect human rights of *indigenous peoples*, exists whether or not indigenous rights protections are formally provided for under the legal framework of the national jurisdictions where they operate.[158]

Overall, a corporation's due diligence duty to respect human rights norms subsist independently of the national governments' own *duty to protect* against human rights abuse within their jurisdiction.[159]

Emerging Approach to Corporate Responsibility for Human Rights of Indigenous Peoples

The full spectrum of a definitive corporate human rights responsibility is still evolving. However, there is a prevailing global consensus that corporations should no longer see their existence strictly from the shareholders' lens-view, but also from the standpoint of the society as a valuable stakeholder whose rights should be respected and concerns addressed.[160] The obligation of corporations to ensure that their conducts are respectful of international human rights standards applicable where they operate is now viewed as an integral component of a corporation's bottom-line metrics. This point of view was reflected in the following statement made by Björn Stigson, the former president of the WBCSD:

> I believe companies are realizing that a strong sustainable development and corporate social responsibility strategy makes good business sense. Companies are an integral part of the societies and communities in which they operate, and they cannot succeed if the society around them fails. Companies also have come to recognize that CSR goes beyond philanthropy and is a matter for strategic debate . . . . The companies that do not manage their social issues in the same way they manage other strategic business issues will not stay in business long-term.[161]

Besides, and as Charles Handy has emphasized, a good corporation should be a community with a purpose, not a piece of property.[162] That is, a corporation ought to consider itself a wealth-creating community consisting of members, whereby such a community can also help repair the image of the business by insisting that its purpose is not just to make a profit but to make a profit in order to do something better.[163] A broad appraisal of contemporary developments on this subject has led some to surmise that

> [a.] corporation is a creation of the society whose purpose is the production of needed goods and services, to the profit of society and itself. As an institution of society, a corporation must reflect that society's shared values—social, moral, political and legal, as well as economic. It must change as society changes. However, as a dynamic institution, it can also seek to influence the ultimate form and expression of those changes.[164]

Bottom-Line Case—The Upside of Compliance with Human Rights Standards

There are increasing indications these days suggesting that the long-term profitability of corporations, that is their economic responsibilities, cannot be reasonably detached from the quality of their corporate citizenship and the character of the social license they enjoy.[165] In other words, beyond the debate about whether *mere* profit-making along with corporate legal and ethical burdens constitute the core of CSR, it simply makes good bottom-line sense to be an upright corporate citizen. Corporate concern for human rights is now vital to long-term business success. As Mary Robinson, the former UN High Commissioner for Human Rights, noted:

> The issue of human rights is central to good corporate citizenship and to a healthy bottom line. Many companies find strength in their human rights records; others suffer the consequences of ignoring this vital part of corporate life. Today, human rights [compliance] is a key performance indicator for corporations all over the world . . . . Successfully facing the corporate human rights challenge will be crucial to business success nationally and internationally in the years ahead.[166]

When corporations abide by the law and respect human rights in the course of conducting their business activities or implementing projects, it tends to create broad support for the corporations' operations within the host communities as well as brand loyalty among their consumers.[167] Diligent compliance with human rights standards ultimately helps corporations to avoid or mitigates against potential pecuniary losses that may result from disregarding those human rights, such as costly litigation, regulatory penalties, project delays caused by community protests, and even reputational damage.[168] Essentially, by verifying if their operational conduct is consistent with human right standards, corporations are able to avoid legal and ethical challenges to their activities, build favorable and mutually beneficial community relations, and cultivate a productive business environment for its operations.[169]

The case of SPDC (Shell Petroleum Development Company) in Nigeria provides a good example here. The company's bottom line was negatively impacted not too long after the Nigerian Federal High Court ruled against SPDC in 2006,[170] ordering the company to pay the sum of US$1.5 billion in damages to the indigenous *Ijaw* people of the Niger Delta region who had been embroiled in a long battle with the company over violations of their environmental and human rights.[171] SPDC's profit slowed down during that period because its daily production level was cut back to an average of 455,000 barrels per day due to the protracted conflict with the communities.[172] Constant unrest and protests organized against the company by members of the communities caused several disruptions in the company's production schedule and, in part, the reduction in profits.[173] Conversely, in the Philippines, the Malampaya natural gas project operated by Shell Philippines Exploration (SPEX) committed about US\$6 million to conduct meaningful community engagement aimed at ensuring that the project provides adequate environmental safeguards for, and is compliant with the human rights demands of the affected host community.[174] This approach, meant to build a relationship of trust with the community, ultimately saved the project more than US\$50 million that delay or disruption of production arising from community protests could have cost the project.[175] The Newmont's Yanacocha gold mine in Peru is another illustrative example. In the Latin American country of Peru, it was reported that antipathy of members of the community against a proposed project expansion of the Newmont's Yanacocha gold mine resulted in close to US\$2 billion in lost earnings as a result of persistent project delays.[176]

What has become undeniable is that the responsibility of corporations in today's modern business environment is fast changing, and the impacts of their conduct on society are now far more momentous, to the extent that a reconsideration of their role within the societal scheme is unavoidable. The inception of new internationally recognized normative standards regarding the collective human rights of *indigenous peoples* has created some ramifications for corporate entities. These new normative standards have empowered indigenous communities to demand recognition and respect for their human rights, often with high-profile direct action on the ground that usually garners significant public support.[177] The materialization of this set of rights was lauded by the UN as crucial in order to achieve sustainable development, peace, and security, of human societies.[178] Therefore, it is very important for corporate entities to become familiar with the normative standards concerning human rights of *indigenous peoples* because neglecting them can ultimately be costly to their bottom line. It is becoming increasingly manifest that how well corporations respect the rights of the host communities can shape a corporation's project success.[179] Thus:

> [I]n order to be socially responsible, firms must firstly abide by the laws of the land as the laws set the minimum standard of practice. At the same time, in doing their business, firms must also consider the impact they have on the wider society they operate in, particularly on economic, social, environmental and human rights issues.[180]

Accordingly, dialogue about the practice of CSR ought to be pragmatic, and move beyond the question of whether or not corporations *should* become socially responsible; the point of convergence has to be on the plain question of *how* they can do so.[181]

While it might not always be the case that trade and businesses are good for human rights, it most certainly is the case that a good human rights environment is always good for business. Businesses are acting in their own self-interest when they actively promote respect for human rights in countries where they operate.[182]

The social responsibility of corporations can, therefore, be characterized as their fidelity to conduct business uprightly, respect applicable laws and ethical limitations, and contribute to the socio-economic improvement of the local communities where they operate in ways that are both good for the corporations' bottom line and for society at large.[183] It is essential for corporations to ensure that their operational activities are responsive to the legal and moral expectations of the communities that host, or are impacted by, their operational activities.

NOTES

1. See, for example, Abhishek Tripathi and Anupama Bains, Evolution of Corporate Social Responsibility: A Journey from 1700 BC till 21st Century, *International Journal of Advanced Research*, Vol. 1, No. 8 (2013), pp. 788–796.

2. See Marina Nehme and Claudia Wee, Tracing the Historical Development of Corporate Social Responsibility and Corporate Social Reporting, *James Cook University Law Review*, Vol. 15 (2008), pp. 129–168; and, *Id.*, Tripathi and Bains, Evolution of Corporate Social Responsibility, pp. 788–796.

3. See Jill A. Brown and William R. Forster, CSR and Stakeholder Theory: A Tale of Adam Smith, *Journal of Business Ethics*, Vol. 112, No. 2 (January, 2013), pp. 301–312. *See also Id.*, Marina Nehme and Claudia Wee, *Tracing the Historical Development of Corporate Social Responsibility and Corporate Social Reporting* (2008); and, *Id.*, Tripathi and Bains, Evolution of Corporate Social Responsibility.

4. See Archie B. Carroll, A History of Corporate Social Responsibility: Concepts and Practices, in *The Oxford Handbook of Corporate Social Responsibility* (Oxford University Press, 2008), pp. 19–46.

5. See *Id.*, Nehme and Wee, *Tracing the Historical Development of Corporate Social Responsibility and Corporate Social Reporting*; and, *Id.*, Tripathi and Bains, Evolution of Corporate Social Responsibility. See also Firuza S. Madrakhimova, Evolution of the Concept and Definition of Corporate Social Responsibility, *Global Conference on Business and Finance Proceedings*, Vol. 8, No. 2 (2013), pp. 113–118, p. 113.

6. See *Id.,* Carroll, A History of Corporate Social Responsibility, p. 25.

7. See *Id.,* Carroll, A History of Corporate Social Responsibility, pp. 19 and 25. See also Jide James-Eluyode, The Notion of Collective Human Rights and Corporate Social Responsibility: Issues and Trends in International Law, *International Company and Commercial Law Review*, ICCLR, No. 5 (2013), p. 209, pp. 209–2010.

8. See, for example, Harwell Wells, The Cycles of Corporate Social Responsibility: An Historical Retrospective for the Twenty-First Century, *The University of Kansas Law Review*, Vol. 51 (2002) p. 77; Rosamaria C. Moura-Leite and Robert C. Padgett, Historical Background of Corporate Social Responsibility, *Social Responsibility Journal*, Vol. 7, No. 4 (2011), pp. 528–539, at p. 528; and *Id.*, James-Eluyode, The Notion of Collective Human Rights and Corporate Social Responsibility, p. 210.

9. See generally, Paul B. Lewis, *Corporate Ethics in the 21st Century: Social Responsibility, International Trade and Human Rights*, CLE Conference Paper, Center for International Law—John Marshall Law School, November 2008.

10. *Id.*, James-Eluyode, The Notion of Collective Human Rights and Corporate Social Responsibility, p. 210.

11. See Naomi Klein, *No Logo* (Picador, 2002). *See also* Lance A. Compa, Corporate Social Responsibility and Workers' Rights, *Comparative Labor Law and Policy Journal*, Vol. 30, No. 1 (2008).

12. *Id.*, Klein, *No Logo*. See also *Id.*, Compa, Corporate Social Responsibility and Workers' Rights.

13. See Stephen Haycox, Fetched Up: Unlearned Lessons from the Exxon Valdez, *Journal of American History*, Vol. 99, No. 1 (June 2012), pp. 219–228; Miriam Cherry and Judd Sneirson, Beyond Profit: Rethinking Corporate Social Responsibility and Greenwashing After the BP Oil Disaster, *Tulane Law Review*, Vol. 85 (2011), p. 983.

14. See *Id.*, Haycox, Fetched Up; and *Id.*, Cherry and Sneirson, Beyond Profit.

15. See United Nations Environment Programme, *Environmental Assessment of Ogoniland* (UNEP, 2011), p. 9; Jonathan Brown, Niger Delta Bears Brunt After 50 Years of Oil Spills, *The Independent (UK)*, October 26, 2006; Human Rights Watch, *The Price of Oil: Corporate Responsibility and Human Rights Violations in Nigeria's Oil Producing Communities* (1999).

16. See Howard Rothmann Bowen, *Social Responsibilities of the Businessman* (Harper, 1953).

17. See D. Logan, Corporate Citizenship in a Global Age, *RSA Journal*, No. 3/4 (1998), pp. 65–71. *See also* Natalia Yakovleva, *Corporate Social Responsibility in the Mining Industries* (Ashgate, 2005), p. 12.

18. See Milton Friedman, The Social Responsibility of Business is to Increase its Profits, *New York Times Magazine*, September 13, 1970, reprinted in Thomas Donaldson and Patricia Werhane, *Ethical Issues in Business: A Philosophical Approach*, 2nd Ed. (Englewood Cliffs, N.J/Prentice-Hall, 1983).

19. See *Id.*, Friedman, The Social Responsibility of Business is to Increase its Profits.

20. See William Shaw, *Business Ethics*, 7th Ed. (Wadsworth/Cengage, 2010), p. 179; Chris Myers, The New "Rules of The Game": Balancing Profits and Social Responsibility in the 21st Century, *Forbes*, August 30, 2016; John Friedman, Milton Friedman Was Wrong About Corporate Social Responsibility, *Huffington Post*, June 12, 2013.

21. See *Corporate Social Responsibility: The WBCSD's Journey* (The World Business Council for Sustainable Development, January 2002).

22. See, for example, Michael Fontaine, Corporate Social Responsibility and Sustainability: The New Bottom Line? *International Journal of Business and Social Science*, Vol. 4, No. 4 (April 2013), p. 112.

23. Archie B. Carroll, *The Pyramid of Corporate Social Responsibility: Toward the Moral Management of Organizational Stakeholders* (Business Horizons, 1991).

24. *Id.*, Carroll, *The Pyramid of Corporate Social Responsibility*.

25. *Id.*, Carroll, *The Pyramid of Corporate Social Responsibility*. See also William B Werther Jr. and David Chandler, *Strategic Corporate Social Responsibility: Stakeholders in a Global Environment* (Sage Publications, 2006), p. 6.

26. See Wayne Visser, Malcolm McIntosh and Charlotte Middleton, *Corporate Citizenship in Africa: Lessons from the Past – Paths to the Future* (Greenleaf, 2006).

27. See Hevina S. Dashwood, Corporate Social Responsibility and the Evolution of International Norms, in John Kirton (ed.), *Hard Choices, Soft Law: Voluntary Standards in Global Trade, Environment and Social Governance* (Ashgate, 2004), p. 191.

28. See *Id., Corporate Social Responsibility: The WBCSD's Journey*.

29. See, for example, C. B. Bhattacharya, Corporate Social Responsibility: It's All About Marketing, *Forbes Media*, November 20, 2009, https://www.forbes.com/2009/11/20/corporate-social-responsibility-leadership-citizenship-marketing.html#45f621552795 (last accessed April 07, 2019).

30. See, for example, Peter Frankental, Corporate Social Responsibility – A PR Invention? *Corporate Communications: An International Journal*, Vol. 6, No. 1 (2001), pp. 18–23; and *Id.*, Bhattacharya, Corporate Social Responsibility.

31. See *Id.,* Frankental, Corporate Social Responsibility – A PR Invention? pp. 18–23; Bhattacharya, Corporate Social Responsibility.

32. See generally Jedrzej George Frynas, *Beyond Corporate Responsibility: Oil Multinationals and Social Challenges* (Cambridge, 2009). See also Jedrzej George Frynas, The False Developmental Promise of Corporate Social Responsibility: Evidence from Multinational oil Companies, *International Affairs*, Vol. 81, No. 3 (2005), pp. 581–598.

33. See, for example, *Id.*, Frynas, *Beyond Corporate Responsibility*; and, *Id.,* Frynas, The False Developmental Promise of Corporate Social Responsibility.

34. See *Id.,* Frynas, The False Developmental Promise of Corporate Social Responsibility, p. 584.

35. See generally Stephen Tully (ed.), *Research Handbook on Corporate Legal Responsibility* (Edward Elgar, 2005).

36. See generally *Id.,* Klein, *No Logo*. See also Burhan Wazir, Nike Accused of Tolerating Sweatshops, *Guardian News*, May 19, 2001, https://www.theguardian.com/world/2001/may/20/burhanwazir.theobserver (last accessed April 08, 2019).

37. *Id.,* Tully (ed.), *Research Handbook on Corporate Legal Responsibility*.

38. See Lael Bethlehem and Michael Goldblat (eds.), *The Bottom Line: Industry and the Environment in South Africa* (International Development Research Centre, 1997), p. 195.

39. *Id.,* Bethlehem and Goldblat (eds.), *The Bottom Line*, p. 195.

40. See Ian Burrell, Mercury Poisoning Victims Win Pounds 1.3m in Landmark Case, *The Independent*, April 12, 1997, https://www.independent.co.uk/news/mercu ry-poisoning-victims-win-pounds-13m-in-landmark-case-1266578.html (last accessed April 08, 2019). *See also Id.,* Bethlehem and Goldblat (eds.), *The Bottom Line*; *Id.,* Tully (ed.), *Research Handbook on Corporate Legal Responsibility* (2005); Michael Anderson, Transnational Corporations and Environmental Damage: Is Tort Law the Answer? *Washburn Law Journal*, Vol. 3, No. 41 (2002); and Llewellyn Leonard and Bobby Peek, *Technical and Financial Report for European Environmental Bureau: Advising and Monitoring the Clean Up and Disposal of Mercury Waste in Kwazulu-Natal, South Africa – The Case of Thor Chemicals* (EEB Report, December 2005).

41. See *Sithole & Others v. Thor Chemical Holdings Ltd.* (1999) 96 (9) L.S.G 32. See also *Id., See* Burrell, *Mercury Poisoning Victims Win Pounds 1.3m in Land-mark Case*; Ann Eveleth, New Claim Against Chemical Giant Thor, *Mail & Guard-ian Online*, February 20, 1998, https://mg.co.za/article/1998-02-20-new-claim-agai nst-chemical-giant-thor (last accessed February 09, 2019); *Id.*, Tully (ed.), *Research Handbook on Corporate Legal Responsibility*; *Id.*, Anderson, *Transnational Cor-porations and Environmental Damage*; and *Id.*, Leonard and Peek, *Technical and Financial Report for European Environmental Bureau.*

42. *Id., Sithole & Others v. Thor Chemical Holdings Ltd.* (1999); and *Id.*, Tully (ed.), *Research Handbook on Corporate Legal Responsibility.*

43. See Thor-20 Win Appeal in UK, 09-29-2000, *News 24*, https://www.news24. com/xArchive/Archive/Thor-20-win-appeal-in-UK-20000929 (last accessed April 08, 2019). See also *Id.*, Burrell, *Mercury Poisoning Victims Win Pounds 1.3m in Landmark Case.*

44. Reports show that Thor, rather than deal with the scrutiny from government agencies in the UK, not only moved to South Africa, where environment regulation was lax, the company also hired many untrained and unskilled community members, who later became exposed to contaminants. See Environmental Justice Case Study, *Thor Chemicals and Mercury Exposure in Cato-Ridge, South Africa*, University of Michigan, http://umich.edu/~snre492/Jones/thorchem.htm#Table%20of%20Content s (last accessed March 17, 2019); and, James Clarke, *Coming Back to Earth: South Africa's Changing Environment*, 1st edition (Jacana, 2002), p. 156.

45. See *Deep Water: The Gulf Oil Disaster and the Future of Offshore Drill-ing*, Report of the National Commission on the BP Deepwater Horizon Oil Spill and Offshore Drilling, January 2011, https://www.nrt.org/sites/2/files/GPO-OILCOMM ISSION.pdf (last accessed March 17, 2019). See also Alex Susskind, Mark Bonn, & Benjamin Lawrence, How the Deepwater Horizon Oil Spill Damaged the Environ-ment, the Travel Industry, and Corporate Reputations, *Cornell Hospitality Report*, Vol. 15, No. 14 (2015), pp. 3–13.

46. See BP and the Gulf of Mexico Oil Spill, Opening Statements, *C-Span*, June 17, 2010, https://www.c-span.org/video/?294112-1/bp-gulf-mexico-oil-spill-o pening-statements&start=3114 (last accessed March 17, 2019). *See also*, BP Boss's Full Statement to Congressional Committee on the Deepwater Horizon Oil Spill, the Causes, Clean-up Operation, and BP's Actions and Responsibilities, *The Guard-ian*, June 17, 2010, https://www.theguardian.com/business/2010/jun/17/bp-tony-hay ward-oil-spill-statement (last accessed March 11, 2019).

47. See, for example, *Deepwater BP Oil Spill*, The White House, https://ob amawhitehouse.archives.gov/deepwater-bp-oil-spill (last accessed March 12, 2019).

48. See Jim Malewitz, Federal Judge Approves $20.8 Billion BP Spill Settlement, *The Texas Tribune*, April 4, 2016, https://www.texastribune.org/2016/04/04/judge-approves-208-billion-bp-settlement/ (last accessed March 11, 2019).

49. See *Pedro Emiro Florez Arroyo and others v. Equion Energia Limited* (formerly known as BP Exploration Company (Colombia) Limited) [2016] EWHC 1699 (TCC), http://www.bailii.org/ew/cases/EWHC/TCC/2016/1699.html#para1 (last accessed March 09, 2019).

50. See *Id., Pedro Emiro Florez Arroyo and others v Equion Energia Limited* (2016). See also Diane Taylor, Colombian Farmers Sue BP in British Court, *The Guardian*, October 15, 2014; Brianna Lee, Colombia Farmers Take BP to Court Over Oil Pipeline, *International Business Times*, October 17, 2014; and Greg Muttitt and James Marriott, How 12 Meters Became 200: BP Fails to Compensate Landowners in Colombia for Land Taken for the OCENSA Pipeline, in *Some Common Concerns* (Platform, 2002), http://www.platformlondon.org/carbonweb/documents/chapter9.pdf (last accessed March 09, 2019).

51. See, for example, Enegide Chinedu and Chukwuma K. Chukwuemeka, Oil Spillage and Heavy Metals Toxicity Risk in the Niger Delta, Nigeria, *Journal of Health and Pollution*, Vol. 8, No. 19 (September 2018). See also, John Vidal, Niger Delta Oil Spills Clean-up Will Take 30 Years, Says UN, *The Guardian*, August 4, 2011; Sarah Kent, Shell Oil Spills Led to "Astonishingly High" Pollution in Nigeria, *The Wall Street Journal*, March 23, 2017; and, Kate Hodal, Absolutely Shocking: Niger Delta Oil Spills Linked with Infant Deaths, *The Guardian*, November 6, 2017.

52. See *Id.,* UNEP, *Environmental Assessment of Ogoniland*, p. 8. See also, Earl Ofari Hutchinson, BP and the Niger Delta: A Horrendous Tale of Two Oil Spills, *HuffPost*, June 23, 2010, https://www.huffingtonpost.com/earl-ofari-hutchinson/bp -and-the-nigeria-delta_b_622631.html (last accessed March 13, 2019).

53. See Nigeria: Hundreds of Oil Spills Continue to Blight Niger Delta, *Amnesty International*, March 19, 2015, https://www.amnesty.org/en/latest/news/2015/03/hun dreds-of-oil-spills-continue-to-blight-niger-delta/ (last accessed March 11, 2019).

54. See *Id.,* Nigeria: Hundreds of Oil Spills Continue to Blight Niger Delta.

55. See *Id.,* Nigeria: Hundreds of Oil Spills Continue to Blight Niger Delta.

56. See *Kiobel v. Royal Dutch Petroleum Co.,* 621 F.3d 111 (2d Cir. 2010); 80 U.S.L.W. 3237 (U.S. Oct. 17, 2011) (No. 10-1491). *See also Kiobel v. Royal Dutch Petroleum Co.,* 569 U. S. __ (2013), at p. 3.

57. See *Id., Kiobel,* (2d Cir. 2010); and, *Id., Kiobel,* 569 U. S. __ (2013).

58. See *Id., Kiobel,* (2d Cir. 2010); and, *Id., Kiobel,* 569 U. S. __ (2013).

59. See the Alien Tort Statute, 28 U.S. Code § 1350 (Alien's action for tort). This legislation, which was part of the Judiciary Act of 1789, is also referred to as the Alien Tort Claims Act (ATCA). See also *Id., Kiobel,* 569 U. S. __ (2013).

60. See *Id.,* ATS 28 U.S. Code § 1350.

61. See, for example, Kevin R. Carter, Amending the Alien Tort Claims Act: Protecting Human Rights or Closing off Corporate Accountability, *Case Western Reserve Journal of International Law*, Vol. 38 (2007), p. 629; and, Ross J. Corbett,

Kiobel, Bauman, and the Presumption Against the Extraterritorial Application of the Alien Tort Statute, *Northwestern Journal of Human Rights*, Vol. 13 (2015), p. 50.

62. See, for example, *Filartiga v. Pena-Irala*, 630 F.2d 876, 1980 U.S. App. LEXIS 16111 (2d Cir. N.Y. June 30, 1980); *Sosa v. Alvarez-Machain*, 542 U.S. 692 (2004); *Doe v. Unocal*, 395 F.3d 932 (9th Cir. 2002); and *Wiwa v. Royal Dutch Petroleum Co.*, 226 F.3d 88 (2d Cir. 2000).

63. See *Id., Kiobel,* 569 U. S. __ (2013).

64. See *Id., Kiobel,* 569 U. S. __ (2013).

65. See *Id., Kiobel,* 569 U. S. __ (2013). *See further,* David P. Stewart and Ingrid Wuerth, Kiobel v. Royal Dutch Petroleum Co.: The Supreme court and the Alien Tort Statute, *American Journal of International Law*, Vol. 107, No. 3 (2013), pp. 601–621.

66. See *Jesner v. Arab Bank, PLC,* 584 U.S. ___ (2018). See further Rebecca J. Hamilton, Jesner v. Arab Bank, *American Journal of International Law*, Vol. 112, No. 4, (2018), pp. 720–727. See generally Stephen P. Mulligan, The Rise and Decline of the Alien Tort Statute, *Congressional Research Service-Legal Sidebar*, June 6, 2018.

67. See *Guiding Principles on Business and Human Rights: Implementing the United Nations "Protect, Respect and Remedy" Framework* (United Nations, 2011), https://www.ohchr.org/Documents/Publications/GuidingPrinciplesBusinessHR_EN .pdf (last accessed March 14, 2019).

68. *Id., Guiding Principles on Business and Human Rights,* para 1, p. 3; para 11, p. 13; para 25, p. 27. See also Report of the Special Representative of the Secretary General on the Issue of Human Rights and Transnational Corporations and other Business Enterprises, John Ruggie, A/HRC/17/31, March 21, 2011, Annex, paras 1, 11, and 25.

69. See generally, Emeka Duruigbo, Corporate Accountability and Liability for International Human Rights Abuses: Recent Changes and Recurring Challenges, *Northwestern Journal of Human Rights*, Vol. 6 (2008), p. 222.

70. See Montevideo Convention on Rights and Duties of States, 1933. See also Patrick O'Niel, *Essentials of Comparative Politics*, 5th Ed. (W. W Norton & Company, 2015), p. 33.

71. See the Universal Declaration of Human Rights (UDHR), 1948, *preamble*, and articles 29–30. See also Malcolm Shaw, *International Law*, 5th Ed. (Cambridge, 2003), p. 250.

72. The *duty to protect* principle as discussed in this chapter is distinguished from the *responsibility to protect* doctrine that has been developed recently as a universal commitment by Member States of the UN to protect all populations from genocides, ethnic cleansing, crimes against humanity, and other mass atrocities. Here, the *duty to protect* principle relates to the obligation of States to protect and secure human rights within their national boundaries, as opposed to the more controversial *responsibility to protect* doctrine, which some have argued provides a new backdoor way to legally justify the use of force.

73. See *Costello-Roberts v United Kingdom*, European Court of Human Rights, (13134/87) [1993] ECHR 16 (Judgment of March 25, 1993).

74. See *Costello-Roberts v United Kingdom* (1993), paras 27–28.

75. See the European Convention on Human Rights (ECHR) (formally the Convention for the Protection of Human Rights and Fundamental Freedoms) of 1950, art. 3; and *Id., Costello-Roberts v. United Kingdom* (1993).

76. See *Id., Costello-Roberts v. United Kingdom* (1993), paras 25–28.

77. See *Id., Costello-Roberts v. United Kingdom* (1993), para 26.

78. See the American Declaration of the Rights and Duties of Man of 1948, Adopted by the Ninth International Conference of American States, Bogotá, Colombia, 1948.

79. See *Id.,* the American Declaration of the Rights and Duties of Man (1948), *preamble.*

80. See the American Convention on Human Rights of 1969, also known as *Pact of San Jose.*

81. See *Id.,* American Convention on Human Rights (1969), article 1.

82. See, for example, Daniel Aguirre, *The Human Rights to Development in Globalized World* (Ashgate, 2008). See also *Velasquez Rodriguez v. Honduras*, Inter-Am. Court on Human Rights, (Ser. C) No4, P 172 (July 29, 1988).

83. See *Id., Velasquez Rodriguez v. Honduras*, (1988). See further *Id.,* Daniel Aguirre, *The Human Rights to Development in Globalized World* (2008).

84. See *Id., Velasquez Rodriguez v. Honduras* (1988), paras 1–12.

85. See *Id., Velasquez Rodriguez v. Honduras* (1988), para 174.

86. See *Id., Velasquez Rodriguez v. Honduras* (1988), para 176.

87. See *Maya indigenous community of the Toledo District v. Belize*, Case 12.053, Report No. 40/04, Inter-Am. C.H.R., OEA/Ser.L/V/II.122 Doc. 5 rev. 1 at 727 (2004).

88. See generally *Id.,* the European Convention on Human Rights (1950).

89. See *Id.,* the European Convention on Human Rights (1950), article 1.

90. See *Id.,* the European Convention on Human Rights (1950), article 1, & Section I – articles 2–18).

91. See, for example,; *Id., Costello-Roberts v. United Kingdom* (1993), paras 2–28; *Mahmut Kaya v. Turkey*, European Court of Human Rights, 2000-III, 129, para 87; and, *X and Y v. Netherlands*, (Application no. 8978/80) Judgment – Strasbourg, March 26, 1985.

92. See particularly the following operative instruments: *Id.,* American Convention on Human Rights (1969), article 1; and, *Id.,* the European Convention on Human Rights (1950), article 1.

93. See the African Charter on Human and Peoples' Rights of 1981 (a.k.a. the Banjul Charter). The Charter was adopted by the then Organization of African Unity (OAU) on June 01, 1981, and entered into force on October 21, 1986.

94. See *Id.,* African Charter on Human and Peoples Rights (1981), article 1.

95. See *Social and Economic Rights Action Centre (SERAC) & Another v. Nigeria,* (2001) AHRLR 60 (ACHPR 2001). Communication 155/96, Decided at the 30th ordinary session, Oct. 2001. See also *Union of Young Lawyers v Chad* (Union des Jeunes Avocats c/Chad), Communication 74/92 National Commission for Human Rights and Freedoms/Chad (Commission Nationale des Droits de l'Homme et des Libertes/Chad), http://caselaw.ihrda.org/doc/74.92/view/en/ (last accessed February 06, 2019).

96. *Id., SERAC & Another v. Nigeria* (2001).
97. *Id., SERAC & Another v. Nigeria* (2001), para 57.
98. *Id., SERAC & Another v. Nigeria* (2001), para 3.
99. *Id., SERAC & Another v. Nigeria* (2001), para 58.
100. The African Commission, in formulating its conclusion, specifically cited the cases of *Id. Velàsquez Rodríguez v. Honduras* (1988), and *Id., X and Y v. Netherlands* (1985).
101. *Id., SERAC & Another v. Nigeria* (2001), para 57.
102. See Claire Methven O'Brien and Dhanarajan, Sumithra. The Corporate Responsibility to Respect Human Rights: A Status Review, *Accounting, Auditing and Accountability Journal*, Vol. 29, No. 4 (April 2016), pp. 542–567; and, *Id., Guiding Principles on Business and Human Rights*.
103. See UN Global Compact (July 2000).
104. See the Equator Principles (June 2013).
105. See Extractive Industries Transparency Initiative Standards – The EITI STANDARD 2016.
106. See Principles for Responsible Investment, https://www.unpri.org/pri/what -are-the-principles-for-responsible-investment (last accessed March 12, 2019).
107. See GNI Principles on Freedom of Expression and Privacy, 2017, https://gl obalnetworkinitiative.org/gin_tnetnoc/uploads/2018/04/GNI-Principles-on-Freedom-of-Expression-and-Privacy.pdf (last accessed March 12, 2019).
108. See the GRI Standards, available at https://www.globalreporting.org/standard s/gri-standards-download-center/ (last accessed March 12, 2019).
109. See Voluntary Principles on Security and Human Rights (2000).
110. See, for example, *Id.*, UN Global Compact (2000), principles 1 & 2.
111. See Tineke Lambooy, Corporate Due Diligence as a Tool to Respect Human Rights, *Netherland Quarterly of Human Rights*, Vol. 28, No. 3 (2010), pp. 404–448. See also *Id., Guiding Principles on Business and Human Rights*, principle 17, p. 31.
112. See generally *Id., Guiding Principles on Business and Human Rights*.
113. See Resolution adopted by the Human Rights Council, Human Rights and Transnational Corporations and Other Business Enterprises, A/HRC/RES/17/4, July 6, 2011.
114. See *Id.*, Report of the Special Representative of the Secretary General, John Ruggie, (A/HRC/17/31, March 21, 2011), Annex.
115. *Id., Guiding Principles on Business and Human Rights*, p. 1 and p. 13 (pt. II).
116. *Id., Guiding Principles on Business and Human Rights*, para 11, p. 13.
117. *Id., Guiding Principles on Business and Human Rights*, para 12, pp. 13–14.
118. *Id., Guiding Principles on Business and Human Rights*, p. 1.
119. *Id., Guiding Principles on Business and Human Rights*, para 1, p. 3; para 11, pp. 13; para 25, p. 27. See also *Id.*, Report of the Special Representative of the Secretary General, John Ruggie (A/HRC/17/31, March 21, 2011), Annex, paras 1, 11, and 25.
120. *Id., Guiding Principles on Business and Human Rights*, para 17, pp. 17–18. See also *Id.*, Report of the Special Representative of the Secretary General, John Ruggie (A/HRC/17/31, March 21, 2011), Annex, para 17.
121. This is so because, first, they were built through a long process of consultation and consensus-building. Second, they arise out of a comprehensive review of

existing standards and norms. And, third, they have the potential of decreasing human rights violations by corporations, if followed in good faith.

122. *Id., Guiding Principles on Business and Human Rights, General Principles,* p. 1.

123. See *Tripartite Declaration of Principles Concerning Multinational Enterprises and Social Policy,* 5th Ed. (MNE Declaration, 2017). This Declaration was adopted by the Governing Body of the International Labour Office at its 204th Session (Geneva, November 1977) and amended at its 279th (November 2000), 295th (March 2006), and 329th (March 2017) Sessions.

124. See *OECD Due Diligence Guidance for Responsible Business Conduct* (2018).

125. See *Id., Tripartite Declaration of Principles,* para 1, p. 2.

126. See *Id., Tripartite Declaration of Principles,* para 10 (a)–(e), pp. 4–5.

127. See *Id., Tripartite Declaration of Principles,* para 10 (c) & (d), pp. 4–5.

128. See *OECD Guidelines for Multinational Enterprises* (2011 ed.), part I (IV), p. 31.

129. See *Id., OECD Due Diligence Guidance,* pp 16 and 21.

130. See *Id., OECD Guidelines for Multinational Enterprises,* part I (IV), p. 31; and *Id., OECD Due Diligence Guidance,* p. 18.

131. For example, article 27 of the International Covenant on Civil and Political Rights has been notoriously applied to indigenous issues. See General Comment 23—UN Human Rights Committee, U.N. Doc. CCPR/C/21/Rev.1/Add.5. Similarly, the UN Committee on the Elimination of Racial Discrimination (CERD) has also considered indigenous rights issues within the general framework of the rights to non-discrimination normative standards of the Convention on the Elimination of All Forms of Racial Discrimination. See CERD, General Recommendation 23: Indigenous Peoples, U.N. Doc. A/52/18, Annex V.

132. See *World Bank Operational Manual on Indigenous Peoples, OP 4.10* (Indigenous Peoples) 2005.

133. *Id., World Bank Operational Manual on Indigenous Peoples.*

134. See IFC Policy and Performance Standards on Social and Environmental Sustainability: Performance Standard 7-Indigenous Peoples, *PS7* (January 2012).

135. See *WRI Principles for Effective Community Engagement, Enunciated in Breaking Ground: Engaging Communities in Extractive and Infrastructure Projects* (WRI, 2009), section III, p. 15.

136. See *ICMM Position Statement on Indigenous Peoples and Mining* (May 2013).

137. See *ICMM Good Practice Guide: Indigenous Peoples and Mining,* 2nd Ed.

138. See *Id.,* ICMM Position Statement (2013), Commitment 1, p. 5.

139. See generally *Id., OECD Guidelines for Multinational Enterprises.*

140. See *Id., OECD Guidelines for Multinational Enterprises,* part II-General Policy, para 10.

141. See *Id., OECD Guidelines for Multinational Enterprises,* part II-General Policy, para 14.

142. The long name for this document is *Akwé: Kon Voluntary Guidelines for the Conduct of Cultural, Environmental and Social Impact Assessment regarding*

Developments Proposed to Take Place on, or which are Likely to Impact on, Sacred Sites and on Lands and Waters Traditionally Occupied or Used by Indigenous and Local Communities. This Voluntary Guideline was published by the Secretariat of the Convention on Biological Diversity in 2004, and adopted on February 2004.

143. See *Akwé: Kon Guidelines* (2004), Part III, para. 10.

144. See *Akwé: Kon Guidelines* (2004), Part III, para. 8.

145. See, for example, Karen Engle, On Fragile Architecture: The UN Declaration on the Rights of Indigenous Peoples in the Context of Human Rights, *European Journal of International Law*, Vol. 22, No. 1 (February 1, 2011), pp. 141–163. See also *Id.*, James-Eluyode, *The Notion of Collective Human Rights and Corporate Social Responsibility.*

146. See, for example, IWGIA Report 16, *Business and Human Rights: Interpreting the UN Guiding Principles for Indigenous Peoples* (IWGIA, 2014), p. 27. [T]he interpretation and operationalization of the Guiding Principles must be firmly grounded in full recognition of the human rights of indigenous peoples in their most comprehensive and up-to-date form. *Id.*, at p. 44.

147. See *Id.*, Report of the Special Representative of the Secretary General, John Ruggie, (A/HRC/17/31, March 21, 2011), Annex, para 12, p. 13–14.

148. See *Reports of Special Rapporteur on the Situation of Human Rights and Fundamental Freedoms of Indigenous Peoples*, James Anaya, A/HRC/15/37, July 19, 2010.

149. *Id.*, *Reports of Special Rapporteur*, James Anaya (A/HRC/15/37, July 19, 2010), paras 38–39.

150. *Id.*, *Reports of Special Rapporteur*, James Anaya (A/HRC/15/37, July 19, 2010), paras 39, and 46–48.

151. *Id.*, *Reports of Special Rapporteur*, James Anaya (A/HRC/15/37, July 19, 2010), para 46.

152. See *Report of the Special Rapporteur on the Rights of Indigenous Peoples, Victoria Tauli-Corpuz*, A/HRC/39/17, August 10, 2018, para 26.

153. See *Id.*, *Guiding Principles on Business and Human Rights*, para 17, pp. 17–19; James-Eluyode, *The Notion of Collective Human Rights and Corporate Social Responsibility.*

154. *Id.*, *Guiding Principles on Business and Human Rights*, para 11, pp. 13–16.

155. *Id.*, *Guiding Principles on Business and Human Rights*, para 11, p. 13.

156. The due diligence duty to respect the rights of peoples to their land, territories, and natural resources requires that companies should conduct an independent assessment of the rights to which indigenous people may lay claim in accordance with the criteria laid down in international rules, especially where such criteria are not fully applicable under domestic law. *Id.*, *Reports of Special Rapporteur*, James Anaya (A/HRC/15/37, July 19, 2010), paras 53–59.

157. See *Id.*, *Reports of Special Rapporteur*, James Anaya (A/HRC/15/37, July 19, 2010), para 50.

158. *Id.*, *Reports of Special Rapporteur*, James Anaya (A/HRC/15/37, July 19, 2010), para 47; and *Id.*, *Guiding Principles on Business and Human Rights*, para 11, p. 13.

159. *Id., Reports of Special Rapporteur,* James Anaya (A/HRC/15/37, July 19, 2010), para 55; and *Id., Guiding Principles on Business and Human Rights,* para 23, pp. 25–26.

160. See generally Elisa Morgera, *Corporate Accountability in International Environmental Law* (Oxford, 2009); See *Id.* James-Eluyode, The Notion of Collective Human Rights and Corporate Social Responsibility, p. 209; and Ian Wilson, *The New Rules of Corporate Conduct: Rewriting the Social Charter* (Quorum Books, 2000), p. 37.

161. See Interview with Björn Stigson, President of the World Business Council for Sustainable Development (WBCSD), *EURACTIV Network,* January 26, 2004, https://www.euractiv.com/section/sustainable-dev/interview/interview-with-bjorn-stigson-president-of-the-world-business-council-for-sustainable-development-w/ (last accessed February 23, 2019).

162. See Charles Handy, *What's a Business For? Harvard Business Review on Corporate Social Responsibility* (Harvard, 2003), p. 66.

163. *Id.,* Handy, *What's a Business For?*

164. See *Id.,* Wilson, *The New Rules of Corporate Conduct,* p. 37.

165. See Kathleen Wilburn and Ralph Wilburn, Achieving Social License to Operate Using Stakeholder Theory, Journal of International Business Ethics, Vol. 4 (2011), pp. 3–16. See also, Kieren Moffat, Justine Lacey, Airong Zhang, and Sina Leipold, The Social License to Operate: A Critical Review, *Forestry [An International Journal of Forest Research],* (2016), pp. 89, 477–488.

166. See *Business and Human Rights: A Progress Report, Office of the UN High Commissioner for Human Rights* (OHCHR-Geneva, 2000), pp. 1–2, https://www.ohchr.org/Documents/Publications/BusinessHRen.pdf (last accessed June 11, 2019).

167. See generally, Steven Herz, Antonio La Vina and Jonathan Sohn, *Development Without Conflict: The Business Case for Community Consent* (World Resources Institute, 2007).

168. See *Id.,* Herz, Vina and Sohn, *Development Without Conflict.* See also *Id., Business and Human Rights: A Progress Report* (OHCHR-Geneva, 2000), pp. 3–4.

169. See *Id., Business and Human Rights: A Progress Report,* p. 4.

170. See *Shell v. Ijaw Aborigines of Bayelsa State* (February 24, 2006) F.H.C. Port Harcourt, Rivers State, Nigeria.

171. *Id., Shell v. Ijaw Aborigines of Bayelsa State. See also* Rory Carroll, Shell Told to Pay Nigerians $1.5bn Pollution Damages, *The Guardian,* February 24, 2006, https://www.theguardian.com/world/2006/feb/25/oil.business (last accessed February 28, 2019).

172. See, for example, Niger Delta Unrest Dampens Shell, *BBC News,* May 4, 2006, http://news.bbc.co.uk/2/hi/business/4971340.stm (last accessed 2/28/2019).

173. *Id.,* Carroll, Shell Told to Pay Nigerians $1.5bn Pollution Damages; *Id., Niger Delta Unrest Dampens Shell* (BBC, 2006); and *Shell v. Ijaw Aborigines of Bayelsa State* (2006). Reports further show that persistent raids and attacks on oil infrastructure and personnel stultified production capacity of corporations operating in the Niger Delta, and ultimately slashed Nigeria's total oil output from around 2.2 million barrels a day to 1.6 million barrels a day. This drop-in production was said

to be instrumental in helping to push up international oil prices to record highs of near US$150 in 2008. See, for example, Sarah Simpson, Nigeria Tries to Settle Oil Protests, *Global Post*, April 14, 2009.

174. See Kirk Herbertson, Athena R. Ballesteros, Robert Goodland and Isabel Munilla, *Breaking Ground: Engaging Communities in Extractive and Infrastructure Projects* (World Resources Institute Report, 2009), pp. 3–14.

175. *Id.*, See Herbertson, Ballesteros, Goodland and Munilla, *Breaking Ground*, p. 7.

176. See *Id.*, Herz, Vina, and Sohn, *Development Without Conflict*, pp. 40–46, at p. 43.

177. See generally The ILO Convention (No. 169) Concerning Indigenous and Tribal Peoples in Independent Countries of 1989; and the UN Declaration on the Rights of Indigenous Peoples (UNDRIP) of 2007.

178. See *State of the World's Indigenous Peoples* (UN Publication, 2009), p. 1.

179. See, for example, *Id.*, Herz, La Vina, and Sohn, *Development Without Conflict*, p. 12. See also, *Id.*, Carroll, Shell Told to Pay Nigerians $1.5bn Pollution Damages.

180. See, for example, Wan Saiful Wan-Jan, Defining Corporate Social Responsibility, *Journal of Public Affairs* Vol. 6 (2006), pp. 176–184, p. 181.

181. *Id.*, Wan-Jan, *Defining Corporate Social Responsibility*, p. 181.

182. See John Kamm, The Role of Businesses in Promoting Respect for Human Rights in China, *Business Ethics in China*, Vol. 1, No. 1 (1997); and International Business Ethics Review, November 1 (1997). See particularly Ralph G. Steinhartdt, Soft Law, Hard Markets: Competitive Self-Interest and the Emergence of Human Rights Responsibilities for Multinational Corporations, *Brooklyn Journal of International Law*, Vol. 33, No. 3 (2008), p. 933, at 943.

183. See generally H. Ward, *Public Sector Roles in Strengthening Corporate Social Responsibility: Taking Stock*, Report prepared for the World Bank (2004).

Chapter 4

Obstacles in the Pathway to Establishing Binding Corporate Code of Conduct for Human Rights

THE TRADE-OFF EFFECT: NATIONAL DEVELOPMENT VERSUS CORPORATE REGULATION

As noted in earlier chapters of this book, there is currently no legally binding international treaty to regulate corporate activities, particularly with respect to their human rights obligations. The primary responsibility for instituting legal and regulatory control over the activities of all persons, including corporations, within the boundaries of States, is vested in the governments of those States as sovereign authorities. However, efforts to ensure proper accountability for corporate conduct can be more tasking in developing parts of the world where domestic regulatory frameworks may be weak or inadequate. For varying reasons, governmental authorities in developing countries may lack the desire or practical capacity to impose strict regulatory limitations on corporations.

This lack of political will is not uncommon; it was, for instance, reflected in the promotional campaign strategy once adopted by the government of the Philippines in the 1970s.[1] As part of a campaign, which was meant to steer foreign direct investment to the Philippines, the country's government proudly and publicly stated conclusively that it had "felled mountains, razed jungles, filled swamps, moved rivers, [and] relocated towns."[2] According to the advertisement, such sweeping actions were taken simply for the purpose of eliminating perceived barriers to make it easier for corporations to invest in the Philippines.[3] Unfortunately, the underlying rationale that motivated the kind of campaign strategy pursued by the Philippines' government back in the 1970s still influences the attitude of some national governments today. The prevalence of this type of challenging situation was reflected in the 2018 report of Victoria Tauli-Corpuz, the Special Rapporteur on the Rights of Indigenous Peoples, to the UN Human Rights Council.[4] Tauli-Corpuz, in

91

highlighting the challenges currently faced by indigenous peoples who seek to protect their traditional lands and natural resources in connection with commercial development by corporations, observed that

> the escalation of attacks against indigenous peoples is occurring in the context of a skewed power structure whereby private companies wield significant influence over States and ensure that regulations, policies and investment agreements are tailored to promote the profitability of their business.[5]

In essence, when countries are compelled by economic development expediency, they often put off enactment of strict laws and regulations (mostly perceived as barriers by corporations), or fail to enforce existing rules, to pursue economic development and national prosperity.[6] Governments of many developing countries, and even developed countries,[7] are oftentimes disinclined to implement any aggressive corporate accountability measures in exchange for foreign investments by multinational corporations and, perhaps, to foster favorable relationships with the home-state governments of multinational corporations.[8] On top of that, the impact of globalization of the world's economy, which created expansive markets beyond national borders and spurred exponential growth that increases business profitability, enabled corporations to become tremendously powerful and influential enough to rival, if not overwhelm, the authority of some host States.[9] Many have called attention to the perils of the unbridled pursuit of power and influence by large corporate entities.[10] One commentator has this to say about corporations:

> They have moved like poltergeists through the international community, dominating and affecting the lives of people the world over but especially in the Third World. MNCs [multinational corporations] own and control the majority of production, distribution and exchange, and control other webs of complicated activities with varying complexities. As a result, they wield immense powers that enable them to literally bestride our "global neighborhood."[11]

The foregoing situation, oftentimes, forces State governments to perform a delicate balancing act between the exercise of their powers to the fullest extent as sovereign authority to protect their population's human rights and securing portions of the huge investment resources possessed by corporations, along with the potential impact of the immense influence and wealth those corporations hold. In many cases, the devotion of efforts by developing countries to find the right balance gets in the way of the government's ability to attain effective control over imprudent corporate behavior. The imbalance in economic power and influence between some host States and big corporations, as some have observed, tends to trigger a so-called *race to the bottom*, whereby cash-strapped States pursue economic development at any cost, including proactively creating a favorable climate for foreign investors, even if it opens the door to possible violations of those States' human rights commitments.[12]

Corporations, especially big multinational companies, have not been shy in wielding their economic power and influence to shift the internal socio-political dynamics of States, or lobby to make legal rules in these places favorable to their bottom-line agenda.[13] This is almost always borne out of the desire by these corporations to advance their profits, share value, and to protect both existing and projected investments in those States.[14] The *ChevronTexaco*[15] and *Chiquita*[16] cases are two classic examples illustrating the possible implications of unrestrained corporate power and influence over governments in developing parts of the world.

In the *ChevronTexaco* case, which was first brought in 1999 before the U.S. District Court of Northern California in San Francisco, the plaintiffs allege that the U.S. defendants, ChevronTexaco Corporation, and Chevron-Texaco Overseas Petroleum, Inc., its wholly owned Delaware-based subsidiary, are directly and indirectly liable for the acts of the companies' Nigerian subsidiary, Chevron Nigeria Limited (CNL), in the commission of human rights abuses that occurred in Nigeria.[17] The plaintiffs alleged that the U.S defendants and CNL acted unlawfully and committed human rights abuses. The plaintiffs assert that ChevronTexaco Corporation through CNL exerted influence over various apparatuses of the Nigerian government in planning and carrying out attacks on the local communities in the Niger Delta region of the country.[18] According to the allegations, CNL co-opted the Nigerian military and police, providing them with monetary and logistical support to facilitate the use of lethal force in order to suppress mounting protests by members of the communities against the company's oil production activities at the *Parabe* oil platform located in the area.[19] Two protesters were killed in the process.[20]

Although the trial court ultimately finds that the defendants cannot be held directly liable for the human rights violations, on the basis that the plaintiffs fail to provide sufficient evidence that the U.S. defendants directly commissioned the acts that are the subject of plaintiffs' complaint, but the court noted that whether indirect liability may be imposed is a closer question.[21] The court did not, however, rule as to whether CNL, on its part, was liable.[22] Nevertheless, this case clearly shows the possible consequences of unchecked corporate power and influence over governmental authorities, especially in developing countries.

In a similar way, in 2007, the Ohio-U.S.-based Chiquita Brands International Inc., one of the world's biggest produce companies, pleaded guilty in the United States to a federal charge for knowingly providing material support to a Columbian right-wing paramilitary group *Autodefensas Unidas de Colombia* (AUC) and the left-wing Revolutionary Armed Forces of Colombia (FARC).[23] Chiquita paid the groups more than US$1.7 million in security payments, through its subsidiary Banadex, to secure the company's continuing access to and control of Colombia's banana growing regions.[24]

The types of pernicious power plays and interferences by corporations in the affairs of States, as highlighted above, did not just suddenly happen, it was bound to happen. This is because, for several decades, the international community brushed off persistent calls for an adoption of some sort of binding normative standards pertaining to corporate human rights responsibilities. As it turns out, as far back as almost half a century ago, Salvador Allende Gossens, the then president of Chile, in his address delivered at the inaugural ceremony for the third session of the United Nations Conference on Trade and Development (UNCTAD) in 1972, forewarned the international community about the peril of unrestrained corporate power across national boundaries, and their brazen interference in the domestic affairs of States.[25] According to Allende Gossens:

> This flagrant intervention in the internal affairs of States is more serious, more subtle and more dangerous than that of Governments themselves, which is condemned in the Charter of the United Nations. The corporations actually seek to upset the normal functioning of the government and institutions of other nations, to start world-wide campaigns against the prestige of a Government, to make it the victim of an international boycott and to sabotage its economic relations with the rest of the world. Recent and well-known cases, which have shocked the world, and by which we are directly affected, sound the alarm for the international community, which is under an imperative obligation to react with the utmost vigor.[26]

Considering that the necessity for some form of meaningful regulation had become very glaring to the global community for more than half a century, the pertinent question then is why, at this present time, no international legally binding instrument has been put in place to address corporations and how they account for their behaviors around the world, beyond the many non-binding voluntary codes of conduct or self-regulation efforts? In light of this pressing need, some have suggested that, at the minimum, core issues like human rights, environmental pollution, and corrupt practices should not be confined to the realm of self-regulation or non-binding codes, which is the current practice, but to the scrutiny of a substantive set of binding standards.[27]

REDEFINING CORPORATE RESPONSIBILITY UNDER THE INTERNATIONAL SYSTEMS

Lack of support for the effort to adopt binding international regulation for corporate human rights responsibilities by a majority of the home-state governments of big multinational corporations, mainly from developed countries, has been attributed as the root cause of this present predicament.[28] Some have suggested that this lack of support may have been motivated, in part, by the immense economic and market control benefits accruable to the home-state governments.[29]

Endorsement by an overwhelming number of State governments across the world, especially those of influential countries in North America and Europe, of any global initiative to impose binding legal obligations on multinational corporations is critical. States have a crucial role to play in the global effort to regulate corporate conduct and in ensuring corporate accountability for human rights violations.[30] More so, most international human rights legal frameworks only address State responsibilities. Thus, States were, and still are, customarily viewed as the primary direct duty-holders under most human rights legal frameworks.[31]

Efforts to subject corporations to firm regulations by means of an international obligatory instrument have largely been unsuccessful.[32] For instance, the United States and the European Union were once reported to have bluntly indicated that they would not provide any meaningful support to an open-ended intergovernmental working group on transnational corporations and other business enterprises with respect to human rights, which was recently established by the UN Human Rights Council,[33] to develop an international legally binding instrument to regulate corporate conduct in accordance with international human rights law.[34]

The general thinking among those who loathe the idea of establishing a universal legally binding code of conduct that prevents human rights violations by corporations is that such an endeavor would constitute a clog in the wheel of global free trade and will amount to a needless interference with private business enterprise.[35] This type of thinking seems paradoxical, as it appears to suggest that protection of human rights and pursuit of economic development are at odds with each other. However, the viewpoint shared by some is that any effort to hold corporations accountable under international law is not only likely to face constant resistance, but will also continue to be an uphill battle, simply because the international governance structure is, to a great extent, too overly corporate-led.[36]

Efforts to Find a Workable Binding Code of Conduct for Corporations

The First Round

Corporations have demonstrated the inclination to influence socioeconomic and political events worldwide, whether pertaining to developed or developing parts of the world.[37] But they have caused a greater impact in developing countries. A concerted effort to explore ways to institute some form of internationally binding normative standards to regulate conduct of corporations began in the early 1970s, when issues concerning the business practices of multinational corporations in developing countries became a central topic of discussion during the UNCTAD's third session, held in Santiago, Chile, between April and May of 1972.[38] Other integral components of the early efforts to hold corporations accountable also included the following important events: the unanimous adoption by the UN Economic and Social Council of Resolution 1721 (LIII) in July 1972 (ECOSOC Res. 1721),[39] and the subsequent 1974 report of the UN Secretary-General on the impact of multinational corporations on development and on international relations;[40] there is also Resolution 3202 (S-VI) on Programme of Action on the Establishment of a New International Economic Order, adopted by the UN General Assembly in May of 1974 (UN GA Res. 3202);[41] and the Economic and Social Council Resolution 1913 (LVII) adopted in December of 1974 (ECOSOC Res. 1913).[42]

The ECOSOC Res. 1721 calls on the UN Secretary-General to appoint a "group of eminent persons" for the purpose of studying the role of multinational corporations and their impact, especially in developing countries.[43] Pursuant to ECOSOC Res. 1721, a group of twenty eminent persons, chaired by Lakshmi Kant Jha, a former ambassador of India to the United States, was inaugurated to conduct the study. The group, as part of their deliberations, conducted a general analysis of the role and impact of multinational corporations on development and on international relations, as well as a detailed examination of some specific issues regarding corporate conduct.[44] Although the group's final report could not provide any concrete pathway to resolve the many underlying issues, it recommended that the Economic and Social Council establish a dedicated commission on multinational corporations to advance the issues.[45]

For its part, the UN GA Res. 3202 articulated the need to establish some form of standards to prevent corporations from interfering in the internal affairs of the countries where they operate. Thus, the UN GA Res. 3202 declares that "all efforts should be made to formulate, adopt and implement an international code of conduct for transnational corporations."[46] Ultimately, in December of 1974, by way of ECOSOC Res. 1913, the Economic and Social Council established an intergovernmental commission on transnational corporations, otherwise known as Commission on Transnational Corporations (CTC), and a UN Centre on Transnational Corporations (UNCTC), to assist the Council with the development of some recommendations upon which a formal code of conduct for transnational corporations could be grounded.[47] The UNCTC, in particular, was mandated to, among others, conduct research with respect to the political, legal, economic, and social aspects of transnational corporations, in order to facilitate the development of an appropriate code of conduct to guide transnational corporations.[48]

Following its establishment, the UNCTC made commendable progress in fulfilling many aspects of its mandates, including the production of document detailing the global activities of transnational corporations along with information about legislative policies applicable to these corporations under both national and regional jurisdictions, as well as completion of research on economic, social, and legal matters and how they impact various aspects of economic development and international relations.[49] However, due to persistent corporate pressure, the body was unable to finalize any work leading to an elaboration of a meaningful binding code of conduct for transnational corporations.[50]

Dishearteningly, by the late 1980s, the global effort to establish internationally binding normative standards to regulate the conduct of transnational corporations had already lost steam. The intense pressure from powerful corporations, and changing global priorities, resulted in the international community treating the issue of developing a universal code of conduct coldly at the time.[51] During this period, Iraqi armed forces had invaded Iran igniting the first Persian Gulf War,[52] there was the Tiananmen Square Massacre in China,[53] the strength of the cold war had begun to abate across Europe leading to the collapse of the Berlin wall,[54] and international attention had moved towards the globalization of national economies and reduction of transboundary trade barriers, as the *Uruguay Round* of multilateral trade negotiations involving more than 120 countries, intensified.[55]

By 1992, it became apparent that a consensus on a workable framework for a universal binding corporate regulation is unlikely. This is because, throughout the work of UNCTC, the division of opinion between representatives from developing States, who pressed for the establishment of a legally binding code of conduct for transnational corporations, and those from developed States, who preferred a voluntary code of conduct, not only persisted but widened.[56] The UNCTC was eventually dissolved in 1993, and its existing work became absorbed by the UNCTAD, a permanent intergovernmental body of the UN that handles trade, investment, and development issues.[57]

The Second Round

Another serious attempt to create a binding corporate code of conduct began in 1996, when the UN Commission on Human Rights (now Human Rights Council), concerned about the prevalence of transnational corporations around the world and the impact of their activities on human rights, published a commissioned[58] report on the impact of the activities and working methods of transnational corporations on the full enjoyment of all human rights.[59]

The report noted that the rapid transboundary spread of corporate business activities, along with the increasing globalization of national economies, demonstrated the importance of establishing an international legal framework to ensure responsible corporate behavior.[60] The report called for the development of "a new comprehensive set of rules" that prescribed "standards of conduct for TNCs [transnational corporations] and set out economic and social duties for them with a view to maximizing their contribution to economic and social development."[61] In this regard, the Sub-Commission, in 1998, established a working group to examine the connection between the enjoyment of human rights and the working methods and activities of transnational corporations.[62]

The deliberations of the working group were initially intended to be concluded within a fixed three-year period.[63] However, in 2001, the Sub-Commission extended the mandate of the working group for another three-year period to facilitate the drafting of a binding corporate code of conduct.[64] In the end, the activities of the Working Group culminated in a presentation to the Sub-Commission of the 2003 draft *Norms on the Responsibilities of Transnational Corporations and Other Business Enterprises with regard to Human Rights* (UN Norms).[65] At the time, the draft was the clearest and most tangible attempt by the international community to establish a substantive and binding code of conduct for corporate entities.[66] As a result, the UN Norms took into consideration the current trends in the areas of international human rights law and corporate accountability.[67] An essential part of the UN Norms is the requirement that all transnational corporations and other business enterprises respect human rights and the national sovereignty of States.[68] As the UN Norms provided:

> Transnational corporations and other business enterprises shall recognize and respect applicable norms of international law, national laws and regulations, as well as administrative practices, the rule of law, the public interest, development objectives, social, economic and cultural policies including transparency, accountability and prohibition of corruption, and authority of the countries in which the enterprises operate.[69]

On August 13, 2013, the Sub-Commission approved the draft UN Norms,[70] and also made the decision to forward it to the Commission on Human Rights for consideration and adoption.[71] But, unfortunately, the Commission flatly declined to consider or approve the UN Norms.[72] As the Commission stated:

> [the] document E/CN.4/Sub.2/2003/12/Rev.2 [draft UN Norms] has not been requested by the Commission and, as a draft proposal, has no legal standing, and that the Sub-Commission should not perform any monitoring function in this regard.[73]

Towards the end of the decade-long process, the UN Norms met its unfortunate demise due to strong opposition from powerful transnational corporations and lack of support for a binding code of conduct by their home governments (who perceived this novel instrument as burdensome and unnecessary meddling with private business pursuits).[74] In addition, because the UN Norms allocated a major role to, and placed substantial obligations on, transnational corporations and other business enterprises, those who opposed the instrument painted it as a backdoor effort to disrupt the global order by overturning the fragile framework of international law, which traditionally designated only States as the legal subject and duty-bearer in the context of international relations and politics.[75]

The Third Round

The present process aims to establish a legally binding corporate code of conduct. It was kick-started in the fall of 2013 during the 24th session of the Human Rights Council held in Geneva, Switzerland, when the representative for the Republic of Ecuador, on behalf other developing countries concern about increasing corporate power and human rights violations, called on the Council to renew its efforts concerning the development of a legally binding international instrument to clarify the obligations of transnational corporations with respect to human rights.[76] An overwhelming number of developing countries across Africa, Asia-Pacific, Middle-East, and Latin America, as well as more than 100 regional and international human rights organizations and social movements, strongly backed the call made by Ecuador.[77]

Subsequently, in July 2014, the Council adopted Resolution 26/9, creating an Open-ended Intergovernmental Working Group on Transnational Corporations and other Business Enterprises with respect to Human Rights.[78] The central mandate of the Open-ended Intergovernmental Working Group was to "elaborate an international legally binding instrument to regulate, in international human rights law, the activities of transnational corporations and other business enterprises."[79] The inaugural session of the Open-ended Intergovernmental Working Group, chaired by María Fernanda Espinosa,[80] the former Permanent Representative of Ecuador to the UN, was held in July of 2015.[81]

It is important to note that the Open-ended Intergovernmental Working Group benefited from progressive development of the issue concerning transnational corporations and human rights accountability within the UN system, including previous work done by the erstwhile UN Commission on Human Rights, and the current Human Rights Council.[82] In addition, the proceedings of the Open-ended Intergovernmental Working Group was also strengthened by the fact that the Human Rights Council, via resolution, mandated that the first two sessions[83] of the Working Group be focused on conducting constructive deliberations to define what the content, scope, and form of a binding legal framework concerning corporate human rights obligations would look like.[84]

The fourth,[85]and the latest, session of the Open-ended Intergovernmental Working Group was recently concluded in October of 2018, in Geneva, Switzerland.[86] One notable breakthrough, a landmark accomplishment, was the completion and presentation to the Human Rights Council of the Draft *Legally Binding Instrument* and an accompanying Draft *Optional Protocol,* meant to regulate, in international human rights law, the activities of transnational corporations and other business enterprises.[87] The essential features of the Draft *Legally Binding Instrument,* which provisions are intended to apply mainly to human rights violations in the context of business activities of a transnational character, are reflected in its four interconnected pillars, namely: (i) prevention of human rights violations in the context of business activities; (ii) securement of effective access to justice and remedy for victims of human rights violations in the context of business activities, (iii) advancement of international cooperation with a view to prevent, and remedy, human rights violations in the context of business activities, and (iv) establishment of monitoring mechanisms.[88]

The Draft *Legally Binding Instrument* and the accompanying *Optional Protocol* are still steadily moving through the UN bureaucratic system, even as States and other relevant stakeholders continue to provide comments and suggested edits to the drafts. However, one cannot safely assume that a binding universal corporate code of conduct would be finalized at the end of the process this time around, if the outcomes of previous attempts are anything to go by. As before, crucial support from some governments of developed countries has not been forthcoming. For instance, activities throughout the sessions indicate that "most of the 22 EU Member-States in attendance did not actively contribute to the debates and were, in many instances, represented only by interns."[89]

Nevertheless, if the rigor and pace of proceedings at the Open-ended Intergovernmental Working Group persists, and meaningful support from home governments of transnational corporations is forthcoming, it is very likely that this present effort by the Open-ended Intergovernmental Working Group could succeed. Besides, establishing some form of binding human rights normative standards for corporate conduct has now become imperative, and inescapable.

Non-binding Regulatory Initiatives Regarding Corporate Codes of Conduct

While attempts to establish internationally binding codes of conduct for corporations have been dispiritedly unsuccessful at the international level for more than four decades, the notion of self-regulation or voluntary codes as a means to regulate corporate conduct rapidly gained substantial ground. This rapid expansion must be viewed in the light of two pertinent factors: the vigorous pushback from powerful transnational corporations against the global efforts to establish a binding corporate code of conduct; and the resentment expressed by their home governments, most of whom perceived these efforts as unnecessary meddling with private business pursuit, as discussed earlier in this chapter.[90]

Powerful transnational corporations were concerned that the international efforts indeed *might* result in binding codes, and as part of their opposition to that, steadfastly promoted voluntary codes as an acceptable alternative. An effort by these powerful transnational corporations to push discussions concerning the development of a binding corporate code of conduct towards their preferred non-binding voluntary codes began to gather momentum in the early 1990s. By the beginning of that decade, it was apparent that the activities of CTC and UNCTC were unlikely to result in the establishment of a meaningful internationally binding corporate code of conduct.[91]

Those advocating for corporate accountability, however, had a renewed opportunity, during the 1992 Rio Earth Summit, to reinvigorate support for the plan of the UN Economic and Social Council. During that period, the global community had the opportunity to formulate universally applicable and binding rules for transnational corporations but was overlooked.[92] The Rio Earth Summit, often referred to as the UNCED, held in Rio de Janeiro, Brazil, from June 3 to 14, 1992, made environmental responsibilities of States and non-State entities a central part of discussions at the conference.

However, the Rio Earth Summit shied away from serious discussion about, much less providing support for, binding international rules to regulate corporate activities.[93] This standpoint shaped deliberations concerning transnational corporations during the Summit, and was influenced by intense lobbying by corporate interest groups including, most prominently, the International Chambers of Commerce (ICC). These corporate interest groups were against any attempt to impose binding obligations on corporations.[94] As a case in point, due to the vigorous lobbying by corporations, and in some cases working in alliance with their home governments, discussion relating to the introduction of universal binding corporate regulation via the UN was removed from the Summit agenda, and substituted with a discussion about the development of a draft recommendation.[95]

Ultimately, the Rio Earth Summit elected to simply encourage corporations to operate responsibly and efficiently in carrying out their activities and call for further collaborations between governments and corporations.[96] This position was reflected in the complimentary language of *Agenda 21*,[97] a final outcome document produced at the end of the Summit, which stated that business and industry, including transnational corporations, play a crucial role in the social and economic development of a country. A stable policy regime enables and encourages business and industry to operate responsibly and efficiently and to implement longer-term policies. Increasing prosperity, a major goal of the development process, is contributed primarily by the activities of business and industry. Business enterprises, large and small, formal and informal, provide major trading, employment and livelihood opportunities. Business opportunities available to women are contributing towards their professional development, strengthening their economic role and transforming social systems. Business and industry, including transnational corporations, and their representative organizations should be full participants in the implementation and evaluation of activities related to Agenda 21 . . . Through more efficient production processes, preventive strategies, cleaner production technologies and procedures throughout the product life cycle, hence minimizing or avoiding wastes, the policies and operations of business and industry, including transnational corporations, can play a major role in reducing impacts on resource use and the environment.[98]

Since 1992, many non-binding instruments dealing with corporate conduct and human rights, as well as industry-specific regulatory standards, have emerged. Numerous international and regional organizations, along with industry associations, have shifted their focus towards the development and adoption of various types of non-binding voluntary corporate codes of conduct or industry-specific operational standards, in order to address corporate human rights infractions. Presently, the handful of influential non-binding instruments dealing with corporate conduct and human rights include the following:

- *The UN Global Compact (2000):*[99] This is often referred to as the world's largest corporate citizenship initiative.[100] The groundwork for the Global Compact began in February of 1998, with the meeting of the UN Secretary-General Kofi Annan with corporate interest groups under the auspices of the International Chamber of Commerce (ICC) in Geneva, and his subsequent January 1999 address delivered during the World Economic Forum meetings held in Davos, Switzerland.[101] The Secretary-General encouraged businesses and governments around the world to embrace new business models and social responsibility that is based on strong human rights values.[102] The World Economic Forum is an international organization dedicated to fostering public-private cooperation, by creating deliberative and interactive space for top leaders in politics, business, and other aspects of society, to influence various spheres of global agenda.[103]

  The development of the global compact framework was spearheaded by John Ruggie, former Special Advisor to the UN Secretary-General, and

Georg Kell, former Executive Director of the UN Global Compact. The Global Compact was launched in June 2000 and later adopted by the UN Secretary-General Kofi Annan in August 2005. There are presently over ten thousand participating corporations and other non-business entities that have endorsed and declared their commitments to abide by the Global Compact and its principles.[104]

The UN Global Compact is a voluntary initiative that mainly reflects the commitments made by chief executive officers of top corporations and other private and public stakeholders around the world, to adopt sustainable and socially responsible policies, and to align their operational activities and business strategies with ten principles in the areas of human rights, labor, environment, and anti-corruption.[105] The first two principles require businesses to support and respect internationally proclaimed human rights, and also to make sure they are not complicit in human rights abuses.[106]

It is, however, important to point out that the groundwork for the Global Compact began within the broader context of renewed pressure, by human rights advocates, prominently from developing countries, for another attempt by the UN to establish a working group to explore ways to formulate an enforceable corporate code of conduct. This is also coupled with increasing corporate pressure on the UN systems to move away from corporate regulation towards some kind of UN-Business sector partnership.[107]

- *The UN Protect, Respect, and Remedy Framework (2011).*[108] Although this instrument does not create any internationally binding obligations, it remains the first clearly articulated and definitive framework on human rights expectations for corporations.[109] The fundamental principle established by the Framework is that corporations must respect all internationally recognized human rights, avoid violating such human rights, and must remedy any adverse human rights impacts they may cause.[110] The Protect, Respect, and Remedy Framework applies to all business entities regardless of their size, sector, location, ownership, and structure.[111] (See the earlier discussion about the UN Protect, Respect, and Remedy Framework in chapter 3, particularly on corporate human rights due diligence duty.)
- *Akwé:Kon Voluntary Guidelines (2004):*[112] These guidelines were published by the Secretariat of the Convention on Biological Diversity, and adopted in February 2004. The Akwé: Kon Voluntary Guidelines are comprehensive provisions that require proponents of projects to be mindful of the cultural and environmental rights of the communities where they operate.[113] These Guidelines were developed by parties to the Convention on Biological Diversity (currently composed of over 190 member countries), in collaboration with indigenous and local communities, and with the objective of ensuring that all project proponents conduct adequate cultural,

environmental, and social impact assessments regarding any proposed developments.[114] The expectation is that

> impact assessment procedures and methodologies embodied in the Voluntary Guidelines will play a key role in providing information on the cultural, environmental and social impacts of proposed developments and, thereby, help to prevent their potential adverse impacts on the livelihoods of indigenous and local communities concerned.[115]

> Consequently, all project proponents are expected to undertake cultural, environmental, and social impact assessments with respect to any proposed project that will occur on, or likely to impact, lands and waters traditionally occupied or used by indigenous and local communities.[116]

- *The OECD Guidelines for Multinational Enterprises (2011):*[117] In accordance with these guidelines, multinational enterprises are expected to observe certain principles and standards of good practices which are consistent with applicable internationally recognized rules in conducting their operations. That is, they are required to obey domestic laws and regulations, and internationally recognized human rights, in the jurisdictions where they operate.[118] At the core of the OECD Guidelines for MNEs is the enunciation of corporate due diligence responsibility, which includes set of connected processes that multinational enterprises should undertake to identify adverse impacts of their own operations, prevent and mitigate them, track implementation and results, and communicate on how the adverse impacts are addressed.[119]
- *The ILO Tripartite Declaration of Principles Concerning Multinational Enterprises and Social Policy (MNE Declaration, 5th ed 2017):*[120] This declaration is unique in that its principles are directed at three parties: multinational enterprises, their workers, and the government of project host countries.[121] The MNE Declaration establishes guiding standards for multinational enterprises regarding their labor and human rights responsibilities.[122] In this regard, the MNE Declaration prescribes that multinational enterprises should, wherever they operate, avoid causing or contributing to adverse impacts through their own activities, and must remedy such impacts when they occur.[123]

In addition to the foregoing non-binding codes of conduct, there are several other standards or guidelines proposed by certain international institutions and industry associations. They include

- UN Principles for Responsible Investment;[124]
- The World Bank Operational Policy on Indigenous People (OP 4.10);[125]

- International Financial Corporations Performance Standards (PS7);[126]
- World Resource Institute (WRI) Principles for Effective Community Engagement;[127]
- International Council on Mining and Metals (ICMM) Position Statement[128] and Good Practice Guide;[129]
- Extractive Industries Transparency Initiative;[130]
- Equator Principles;[131]
- Global Network Initiative;[132]
- Global Reporting Initiative;[133] and
- Voluntary Principles on Security and Human Rights.[134]

The objectives proclaimed by these non-binding voluntary codes and industry initiatives are laudable; they are helpful in filling existing regulatory lacuna, in terms of a universal binding standard for corporate conduct. Nonetheless, their practical utility remains questionable. Many of these non-binding voluntary codes have been derided for lacking any meaningful "sign-on" or adherence procedures, such that specific actions can be taken against participating corporations if they fail to comply.[135] For instance, the UN Global Compact lacks any direct consequential sanction against corporations who fail to comply with any of its principles.[136] Similarly, the OECD Guidelines for Multinational Enterprises makes it very clear that its provisions are merely advisory in nature, with no binding effect:

> The OECD Guidelines for Multinational Enterprises are recommendations addressed by governments to multinational enterprises operating in or from adhering countries. They provide non-binding principles and standards for responsible business conduct in a global context consistent with applicable laws and internationally recognized standards.[137]

In reality, the standards promoted by these various international codes of conduct and industry guidelines have become more of platitudinous statements than consequential conduct-regulating provisions. This, of course, is probably why an overwhelming number of corporations have consistently advocated for a non-binding and self-regulation approach. Since there are no legal obligations involved, corporate entities may easily, and publicly, endorse these kinds of non-binding standards mainly for public relation purposes, in order to divert focus from their actual operational practices, while facing no serious jeopardy for failing to comply with them. Some have suggested that the underlying reason why many corporations quickly lined up to support the UN Global Compact initiative was because it provides a good opportunity to hide a myriad of social and environmental sins under the blue cover of the UN logo.[138]

Considering the above developments, if the human rights of individuals and groups are to be protected from corporate power and influence, which in some cases exceeds that of States, it is imperative that corporations have a binding duty to ensure compliance with applicable national laws and regulations, and to verify that their conduct is respectful of all relevant international normative prescriptions concerning human rights. Besides, doing so is especially prudent in terms of a corporation's reputational capital and bottom line.

NOTES

1. See, for example, Advertisement by the Ferdinand Marcos Government in the Philippines, which was reproduced in *Fortune Magazine*, 1975. See excerpts in David C. Korten, *When Corporations Rule the World*, 2nd Ed. (Kumarian/Barrett-Koehler, 2001), p. 293.

2. *Id.*, Korten, *When Corporations Rule the World*, p. 293.

3. *Id.*, Korten, *When Corporations Rule the World*, p. 293.

4. See *Report of the Special Rapporteur on the Rights of Indigenous Peoples, Victoria Tauli-Corpuz*, A/HRC/39/17, August 10, 2018.

5. *Id., Report of the Special Rapporteur, Victoria Tauli-Corpuz* (A/HRC/39/17–2018), paras 31–36, at 35.

6. See, for example, Shedrack C. Agbakwa, A Line in the Sand: International (Dis)Order and the Impunity of Non-State Corporate Actors in the Developing World, in Antony Anghie et al. (eds.), *Third World and International Order, Law Politics and Globalization* (Martinus Nijhoff Publishers, 2003), p. 1–18.

7. With respect to developed countries, the Dakota Access pipeline Project in the United States and the following Standing Rock protests is a good example. See, for example, Sam Levin, Dakota Access Pipeline: The Who, What and Why of the Standing Rock Protests, *The Guardian* (November 3, 2016); Stephen Young, The Sioux's Suits: Global Law and the Dakota Access Pipeline, *American Indian Law Journal*, Vol. 6, No. 1 (2017), Article 4; Kate Harris and Michael Gonchar, Battle Over an Oil Pipeline: Teaching About the Standing Rock Sioux Protests, *New York Times* (November 30, 2016); and Steven Mufson, A Dakota Pipeline's Last Stand, *The Washington Post* (November 25, 2016).

8. See *Id.*, Agbakwa, A Line in the Sand, pp. 1–18.

9. See Donald K. Anton and Dinah L. Shelton, *Environmental Protection and Human Rights* (Cambridge, 2011), p. 865.

10. See, for example, *Id.*, Korten, *When Corporations Rule the World*; *Id.*, Anton and Shelton, *Environmental Protection and Human Rights*; and *Id.*, Agbakwa, A Line in the Sand.

11. See *Id.*, Agbakwa, A Line in the Sand, pp. 3–4. See also Okafor, The Status and Effect of the Right to Development in Contemporary International Law: Towards a South-North "Entente," *African Journal of International & Comparative Law*, Vol. 7 (1995), p. 865.

12. See Elena Blanco and Jona Razzaque, *Globalization and Natural Resources Law: Challenges, Key Issues and Perspectives* (Edward Elgar, 2011), pp. 212–217. See also Elisa Morgera, *Corporate Accountability in International Environmental Law* (Oxford, 2009), p. 25.

13. See Niamh Garvey and Peter Newell, Corporate Accountability to the Poor? Assessing the Effectiveness of Community-based Strategies, *Development in Practice*, Vol. 15, Nos. 3 and 4 (June 2005).

14. See, for example, Juliette Bennett, Multinational Corporations, Social Responsibility and Conflict, *Journal of International Affairs*, Vol. 55, No. 2 (Spring 2002), p. 393.

15. See *Larry Bowoto, et al. v. Chevron Texaco Corp., et al.*, 312 F.Supp.2d 1229 (2004), U.S. District Court, N.D. California, March 2004. *See also Larry Bowoto, et al v. Chevron Texaco Corp., et al,* Superior Court for the State of California, Case No. CGC-03-417580, (2008). See further Richard C. Paddock, Jury Urged to find Chevron Liable in Oil Platform Assault, *LA Times* (November 26, 2008).

16. See *Doe v. Chiquita Brands International Inc.*, Case 0:08-md-01916-KAM (FLSD, 2008). See also Jason Ryan, Chiquita Pleads Guilty to Paying Terrorists, *ABC News* (March 19, 2007).

17. See *Id., Larry Bowoto v. Chevron Texaco Corp.* (2004); *Id., Larry Bowoto v. Chevron Texaco Corp.* (2008).

18. See *Id., Larry Bowoto v. Chevron Texaco Corp.* (2004); *Id., Larry Bowoto v. Chevron Texaco Corp.* (2008); and *Id.,* Richard C. Paddock, *Jury Urged to find Chevron Liable in Oil Platform Assault* (2008).

19. *Id.,* See *Larry Bowoto v. Chevron Texaco Corp.* (2004); *Id., Larry Bowoto v. Chevron Texaco Corp.* (2008); and *Id.,* Richard C. Paddock, *Jury Urged to find Chevron Liable in Oil Platform Assault* (2008).

20. See *Id., Larry Bowoto v. Chevron Texaco Corp.* (2004); *Id., Larry Bowoto v. Chevron Texaco Corp.* (2008); and *Id.,* Richard C. Paddock, *Jury Urged to find Chevron Liable in Oil Platform* Assault (2008).

21. See *Id., Larry Bowoto v. Chevron Texaco Corp.* (2004). The holdings of this trial court were subsequently upheld on appeal. See *Id., Larry Bowoto v. Chevron Texaco Corp.* (2008); and *Bowoto* v. ChevronTexaco Corp., 621 F.3d 1116 (9th Cir. 2010). As John Ruggie also noted, "The 'parent company' enjoys limited liability even if it wholly owns all of its subsidiaries. This means that the corporate parent is generally not liable for risks incurred by a subsidiary, or monetary damages imposed on a subsidiary, beyond the extent of its investment in it." See John G. Ruggie, Multinationals as Global Institution: Power, Authority and Relative Autonomy, *Regulation & Governance*, Vol. 12, No. 3 (2018), 317–333.

22. See *Id., Larry Bowoto v. Chevron Texaco Corp.* (2004); *Id., Larry Bowoto v. Chevron Texaco Corp.* (2008); and *Id., Bowoto v. ChevronTexaco Corp.* (2010).

23. See *Doe v. Chiquita Brands International Inc.* (2008). See also *Id.,* Jason Ryan, *Chiquita Pleads Guilty to Paying Terrorists* (2007).

24. See *Id., Doe v. Chiquita Brands International Inc.* (2008); *Id.,* Jason Ryan, *Chiquita Pleads Guilty to Paying Terrorists* (2007); and, Juliette Bennett, *Business in Zones of Conflict: The Role of the Multinationals in Promoting Regional Stability*, Report Prepared for the UN Global Compact Policy Dialogues (January 2001).

25. See Address Delivered by Mr. Salvador Allende Gossens, President of Chile at the Inaugural Ceremony on April 13, 1972, Proceedings of the United Nations Conference on Trade and Development, third session Santiago de Chile, April 13 to May 21, 1972, U.N. Doc. TD/180 (Vol. 1), Annex VIII (1973), p. 349, https://unctad.org/en/Docs/td180vol1_en.pdf (last accessed February 05, 2019).

26. *Id.*, Address Delivered by Mr. Salvador Allende Gossens, U.N. Doc. TD/180 (Vol. 1), Annex VIII (1973), p. 353, para 62.

27. See Bede Nwete, Corporate Social Responsibility and Transparency in the Development of Energy and Mining Projects in Emerging Markets: Is Soft Law the Answer? *German Law Journal*, Vol. 8, No. 4 (2007), 312 at 339.

28. See *Id.,* Blanco and Razzaque, *Globalization and Natural Resources Law*; Anup Shah, Corporations' Social Responsibility, *Global Issues* (July 7, 2007).

29. See, for example, M. Sornarajah, The Liability of Multinational Corporations and Home State Measures, in *The International Law on Foreign Investment*, 4th Ed. (Cambridge University Press, 2017), pp. 172–203; Theodore H. Moran, Multinational Corporations and The Political Economy Of U.S-European Relations, *Journal of International Affairs*, Vol. 30, No. 1, (Spring/Summer 1976), pp. 65–79; Matthew Davis, Effects of Multinational Company Investments, *National Bureau of Economic Research*, June 2019, https://www.nber.org/digest/may03/w9293.html (last accessed June 22, 2019); and Lúcia Ortiz and Anne van Schaik, Why Does the European Union Fear a Binding Human Rights Treaty on Transnational Corporations? *Friends of the Earth International* (July 11, 2018).

30. See, for example, Camilla Wee, Regulating the Human Rights Impact of State-owned Enterprises: Tendencies of Corporate Accountability and State Responsibility, *International Commission of Jurists-Danish Section* (October 2008).

31. See Larissa van den Herik and Jernej Letnar Cernic, Regulating Corporations under International Law: From Human Rights to International Criminal Law and Back Again, *Journal of International Criminal Justice, JICJ*, Vol. 8 (2010), pp. 725–743.

32. See *Id.*, Agbakwa, A Line in the Sand, p. 4.

33. See Resolution 26/9, Elaboration of an international legally binding instrument on transnational corporations and other business enterprises with respect to human rights, Human Rights Council, A/HRC/RES/26/9, July 14, 2014.

34. Stephen Townley, the U.S. representative in the Human Rights Council was reported to have informed delegates that "[t]he United States will not participate in this IGWG, and we encourage others to do the same." See, for example, Thalif Deen, After Losing Vote, US-EU Threaten to Undermine Treaty, *Helsinki Times* (July 3, 2014), http://www.helsinkitimes.fi/world-int/world-news/international-news/11077-after-losing-vote-us-eu-threaten-to-undermine-treaty.html (last accessed July 15, 2019).

35. See generally Upendra Baxi, Market Fundamentalisms: Business Ethics at the Altar of Human Rights, *Human Rights Law Review*, Vol. 5, No. 1 (2005), pp. 1–26; *Id.,* Blanco and Razzaque, *Globalization and Natural Resources Law*; and Emeka Duruigbo, Corporate Accountability and Liability for International Human Rights Abuses: Recent Changes and Recurring Challenges, *Northwestern University Journal of International Human Rights*, Vol. 6 (2008), p. 222.

36. See *Id.*, Korten, *When Corporations Rule the World*; and *Id.*, Shah, Corporations' Social Responsibility.

37. See, for example, Clarke N. Ellis, United States Multinational Corporations: The Impact of Foreign Direct Investment on United States Foreign Relations, *San Diego Law Review*, Vol. 11 (1973–1974), p. 1; Rebeca Jasso-Aguilar, Howard Waitzkin, and Angela Landwehr, Multinational Corporations and Health Care in the United States and Latin America: Strategies, Actions, and Effects, *Journal of Health and Social Behavior* , Vol. 45 (Suppl; 2004), pp. 136–157; D. Coen, The Evolution of the Large Firm as a Political Actor in the European Union, *Journal of European Public Policy*, Vol. 4, No. 1 (2011), pp. 91–108; Sorcha Macleod and Douglas Lewis, Transnational Corporations: Power, Influence and Responsibility, *Global Social Policy*, Vol. 4, no. 1 (April 2004), pp. 77–98; Brian Roach, Corporate Power in a Global Economy, *Global Development and Environment Institute* (Tufts University, 2007); and Leonard, H. Jeffrey, Multinational Corporations and Politics in Developing Countries, *World Politics*, Vol. 32, No. 3 (1980).

38. See UNCTAD Resolution 73 (III), Restrictive business practice, 118th plenary meeting May 19, 1972. See especially, *Id.*, Address Delivered by Mr. Salvador Allende Gossens, U.N. Doc. TD/180 (Vol. 1), Annex VIII (1973), p. 349.

39. See Economic and Social Council Resolution 1721 (LIII) of July 28, 1972. See also Report of the UN Secretary-General on the impact of multinational corporations on development and on international relations (E/5500/Rev.1 ST/ESA/6), produced pursuant to Economic and Social Council Resolution 1721 (LIII) of July 28, 1972.

40. See *Id.*, Report of the UN Secretary-General (E/5500/Rev.1 ST/ESA/6: 1972).

41. See Resolution adopted by the General Assembly, 3202 (S-VI). Programme of Action on the Establishment of a New International Economic Order, A/RES/S-6/3202, May 1, 1974.

42. See Resolution adopted on the Report of the Special Intersessional Committee Convened under Council Resolution 1908 LVII: 1913 (LVII), 1931st Plenary Meeting, December 5, 1974.

43. See Economic and Social Council Resolution 1721 (LIII) of July 28, 1972. See also *Id.*, Report of the UN Secretary-General on the impact of multinational corporations on development and on international relations (E/5500/Rev.1 ST/ESA/6), p. 3.

44. See *Id.*, Report of the UN Secretary-General (E/5500/Rev.1 ST/ESA/6: 1972), pp. 25 and 59.

45. See *Id.*, Report of the UN Secretary-General (E/5500/Rev.1 ST/ESA/6: 1972), p. 14.

46. See, *Id.* Resolution adopted by the General Assembly (A/RES/S-6/3202, May 1, 1974), para V-Regulation and Control over the Activities of Transnational Corporations.

47. See, *Id.* Resolution adopted on the Report of the Special Intersessional Committee (1931st Plenary Meeting, December 5, 1974), paras 1 and 4.

48. *Id.* Resolution adopted on the Report of the Special Intersessional Committee (1931st Plenary Meeting, December 5, 1974), para 4 (d).

49. See UN Intellectual History Project, *The UN and Transnational Corporations* (Briefing Note Number 17, July 2009), p. 2.

50. See *Id.,* UN Intellectual History Project (Briefing Note Number 17, July 2009), p. 2. See also Jens Martens, *Corporate Influence on the Business and Human Rights Agenda of the United Nations* (Bischöfliches Hilfswerk MISEREOR e.V, June 2014), p. 6.

51. See *Id.* Martens, *Corporate Influence on the Business and Human Rights Agenda of the United Nations*, p. 6.

52. See Roger Hardy, The Iran-Iraq War: 25 Years On, *BBC News* (September 22, 2005). See also, Iran-Iraq War, Encyclopedia Britannica, https://www.britanni ca.com/event/Iran-Iraq-War (last accessed March 12, 2019).

53. During this unfortunate incident, the governing Chinese Communist Party ordered the use of brutal military force against thousands of students protesting over-bearing restrictions on their individual rights and freedoms, sparking global outcry. See Nicholas D. Kristof, Crackdown in Beijing; Troops Attack and Crush Beijing Protest; Thousands Fight Back, Scores Are Killed, *The New York Times* (June 4, 1989). See also, *Tiananmen Square Incident*, Encyclopaedia Britannica, https://ww w.britannica.com/event/Tiananmen-Square-incident (last accessed March 12, 2019).

54. Robert Snyder and Timothy White, The Fall of the Berlin Wall: The Counter-revolution in Soviet Foreign Policy and the End of Communism, in K. Gerstenberger and J.E. Braziel (eds), *After the Berlin Wall* (Palgrave Macmillan, New York, 2011).

55. The Uruguay Rounds of multilateral trade negotiations, held from 1986 to 1993, resulted in the establishment of the World Trade Organization (WTO). See Matt Schaefer, Thomas Singer, Multilateral Trade Agreements and U.S. States-An Analysis of Potential GATT Uruguay Round Agreements, *Journal of World Trade*, Vol. 26, No. 6 (1992), pp. 31–59; Ernest H. Preeg, The Uruguay Round Negotiations and the Creation of the WTO, in *The Oxford Handbook on The World Trade Organization* (Oxford University Press, 2012).

56. Theodore H. Moran, The United Nations and Transnational Corporations: A Review and a Perspective, *Transnational Corporations*, Vol. 18, No. 2 (August 2009), p. 91 at 93. See also *Id.*, UN Intellectual History Project (Briefing Note Number 17, July 2009), p. 2. See also, Khalil Hamdani, Lorraine Ruffing, *United Nations Centre on Transnational Corporations: Corporate Conduct and the Public Interest*, 1st Ed. (Routledge, 2017).

57. *Id.*, UN Intellectual History Project (Briefing Note Number 17, July 2009), p. 2. See also, *Id.*, Hamdani and Ruffing, *United Nations Centre on Transnational Corporations*.

58. See the Realization of Economic, Social and Cultural Rights, Sub-Commission on Prevention of Discrimination and Protection of Minorities Forty-Seventh Session, E/CN.4/Sub.2/1995//11 July 24, 1995.

59. See *Id.,* The Realization of Economic, Social and Cultural Rights, (E/CN.4/ Sub.2/1995//11 July 24, 1995).

60. *Id.*, E/CN.4/Sub.2/1996/12, July 2, 1996, paras 77–79.

61. *Id.*, E/CN.4/Sub.2/1996/12, July 2, 1996, para 74.

62. See Sub-Commission on the Promotion and Protection of Human Rights Resolution 1998/8: E/CN.4/SUB.2/RES/1998/8, August 20, 1998.

63. *Id.*, E/CN.4/SUB.2/RES/1998/8, August 20, 1998.

64. See Sub-Commission on the Promotion and Protection of Human Rights Resolution 2001/3: E/CN.4/Sub.2/Res/2001/3, August 15, 2001.

65. See Sub-Commission on the Promotion and Protection of Human Rights Fifty-Fifth Session: E/CN.4/Sub.2/2003/12/Rev.2, August 26, 2003.

66. For further exposition on the UN Norms, See David Weissbrodt and Muria Kruger, Norms on the Responsibilities of Transnational Corporations and Other Business Enterprises with Regard to Human Rights, *The American Journal of International Law*, Vol. 97, No. 4 (October 2003), pp. 901–922. See also Surya Deva, UN's Human Rights Norms for Transnational Corporations and Other Business Enterprises: An Imperfect Step in Right Direction? *Bepress Legal Series, Working Paper 112* (January 14, 2004).

67. *Id.*, E/CN.4/Sub.2/2003/12/Rev.2, August 26, 2003, *preamble.*

68. *Id.*, E/CN.4/Sub.2/2003/12/Rev.2, August 26, 2003, part E, paras 10–12.

69. *Id.*, E/CN.4/Sub.2/2003/12/Rev.2, August 26, 2003, para 10.

70. See Sub-Commission on the Promotion and Protection of Human Rights Resolution 2003/16: U.N. Doc. E/CN.4/Sub.2/2003/L.11 at 52 (2003), August 13, 2003, para 1.

71. *Id.*, U.N. Doc. E/CN.4/Sub.2/2003/L.11 at 52 (2003), August 13, 2003, para 2.

72. See Commission on Human Rights *Decision 2004/116*, Responsibilities of Transnational Corporations and Related Business Enterprises with regard to Human Rights, 60th Session, April 22, 2004.

73. *Id.*, Commission on Human Rights Decision 2004/116, para c.

74. See *Id.*, Baxi, Market Fundamentalisms; *Id.*, Blanco and Razzaque, *Globalization and Natural Resources Law*; *Id.*, Duruigbo, Corporate Accountability and Liability for International Human Rights Abuses; and Pini Pavel Miretski and Sascha-Dominik Bachmann, *Global Business and Human Rights - The UN Norms on the Responsibility of Transnational Corporations and Other Business Enterprises with Regard to Human Rights - A Requiem*, Deakin Law Review, Vol. 17, No. 1 (2012).

75. See *Id.*, Pini Pavel Miretski and Sascha-Dominik Bachmann, *Global Business and Human Rights* (2012), pp. 6–10. See also *Id.*, Baxi, Market Fundamentalisms; *Id.*, Blanco and Razzaque, *Globalization and Natural Resources Law*; *Id.*, Duruigbo, Corporate Accountability and Liability for International Human Rights Abuses.

76. See *Statement on behalf of a Group of Countries at the 24th Session of the Human Rights Council*, delivered on September 13, 2013, General Debate Item No 3, https://www.business-humanrights.org/sites/default/files/media/documents/statement-unhrc-legally-binding.pdf (last accessed March 21,2019).

77. See UN Human Rights Council Sessions, at https://www.business-humanrights.org/en/binding-treaty/un-human-rights-council-sessions#twenty_four_session (last accessed July 12, 2019).

78. See Human Rights Council Resolution 26/9: A/HRC/RES/26/9, July 14, 2014.

79. *Id.*, Human Rights Council Resolution 26/9, para 1.

80. It should be noted that, Luis Gallegos, another Permanent Representative of Ecuador, was elected to take over as Chair-Rapporteur, during the Fourth Session

held from October 15 to 19, 2018. See Draft Report on the Fourth Session of the open-ended intergovernmental working group on transnational corporations and other business enterprises with respect to human rights, available at https://www.business -humanrights.org/en/binding-treaty/intergovernmental-working-group-sessions (last accessed July 12, 2019).

81. The first session was held from July 6 to 10, 2015. See Report on the first session of the open-ended intergovernmental working group on transnational corporations and other business enterprises with respect to human rights, with the mandate of elaborating an international legally binding instrument: A/HRC/31/50, February 5, 2016.

82. See *Id.*, Human Rights Council Resolution 26/9, *preamble.*

83. The second session was held between October 24 and 28, 2016. See Report on the second session of the open-ended intergovernmental working group on transnational corporations and other business enterprises with respect to human rights: A/ HRC/34/47, January 4, 2017.

84. See *Id.*, Human Rights Council Resolution 26/9, para 2.

85. An earlier event, the third session, took place between October 23 and 27, 2017. See Report on the third session of the open-ended intergovernmental working group on transnational corporations and other business enterprises with respect to human rights: A/HRC/37/67, January 24, 2018.

86. A formal report on the fourth session has not been adopted by the Human Rights Council at this time. But see the Draft report on the fourth session of the open-ended intergovernmental working group on transnational corporations and other business enterprises with respect to human rights, available at https://www.business -humanrights.org/en/binding-treaty/intergovernmental-working-group-sessions (last accessed April 21, 2019).

87. *Id.*, the Draft Report on the Fourth Session of the open-ended intergovernmental working group, paras 25 and 114.

88. *Id.*, the Draft Report on the Fourth Session of the open-ended intergovernmental working group, para 25. See also Zero Draft 16.7.2018: Legally Binding Instrument to Regulate, in International Human Rights Law, The Activities of Transnational Corporations and Other Business Enterprises. Available at https://www.ohc hr.org/Documents/HRBodies/HRCouncil/WGTransCorp/Session3/DraftLBI.pdf (last accessed April 22, 2019).

89. See Karolin Seitz, One Step further towards Global Regulation of Business, *Global Policy Forum*, Briefing of January 2018, p. 3.

90. See *Id.*, Karolin Seitz, *One Step Further Towards Global Regulation of Business* (2018); *Id.*, Pini Pavel Miretski and Sascha-Dominik Bachmann, *Global Business and Human Rights* (2012), pp. 6–10; *Id.*, Baxi, Market Fundamentalisms; *Id.*, Blanco and Razzaque, *Globalization and Natural Resources Law*; and *Id.*, Duruigbo, Corporate Accountability and Liability for International Human Rights Abuses.

91. See *Id.*, Martens, *Corporate Influence on the Business and Human Rights Agenda of the United Nations*, pp. 6–9.

92. See, for example, Richard Welford, *Hijacking Environmentalism: Corporate Responses to Sustainable Development* (Taylor & Francis/Earthscan, 1997). See also

Id. Martens, *Corporate Influence on the Business and Human Rights Agenda of the United Nations*, p. 8; and Kenny Bruno, The Corporate Capture of the Earth Summit, *Multinational Monitor* (1992), https://www.multinationalmonitor.org/hyper/issues/1992/07/mm0792_07.html (last accessed March 29, 2019).

93. See, for example, *Id.*, Martens, *Corporate Influence on the Business and Human Rights Agenda of the United Nations*, pp. 7–9; and *Id.* Bruno, The Corporate Capture of the Earth Summit.

94. See generally, *Id.* Richard Welford, *Hijacking Environmentalism* (1997); *Id.*, Martens, *Corporate Influence on the Business and Human Rights Agenda of the United Nations*; and *Id.* Bruno, The Corporate Capture of the Earth Summit.

95. See *Id.*, Martens, *Corporate Influence on the Business and Human Rights Agenda of the United Nations*, pp. 7–9. See also *Id.*, Richard Welford, *Hijacking Environmentalism* (1997); and *Id.* Bruno, The Corporate Capture of the Earth Summit.

96. See Rio Declaration on Environment and Development (UN, 1992), principles 11–17; and Agenda 21 Programme of Action for Sustainable Development (UN, 1992), chapter 30.

97. Agenda 21 is the comprehensive plan of action to be taken at both international and domestic levels by the UN Systems, UN Members-States, and other stakeholders, concerning human impacts on the environment. It was adopted by over 178 UN Members-States at the Rio earth Summit in June 1992.

98. See *Id.*, Agenda 21 (UN 1992), chapter 30(1)–30(2).

99. Launched in July 2000, the Global Compact is a strategic policy initiative meant to ensure that businesses are committed to aligning their operations and strategies with ten universal principles in the areas of human rights, labor, environment, and anti-corruption. See the UN Global Compact, available at https://www.unglobalcompact.org/ (last accessed July 11, 2019).

100. See, for example, *Id.*, John G. Ruggie, *Multinationals as Global Institution* (2018), p. 317.

101. See *Id.*, Martens, *Corporate Influence on the Business and Human Rights Agenda of the United Nations*, p. 8; Gonzalez-Perez, Maria-Alejandra and Leonard Liam, The UN Global Compact, in Alice de Jonge and Roman Tomasic (eds.), *Research Handbook on Transnational Companies* (Edward Elgards, 2017), pp. 117–138, at p. 124; and the UN Global Compact, https://www.unglobalcompact.org/ (last accessed July 11, 2019).

102. See *Id.* Martens, *Corporate Influence on the Business and Human Rights Agenda of the United Nations*, p. 9; and *Id.*, Gonzalez-Perez, Maria-Alejandra and Liam, *The UN Global Compact* (2017), p. 124.

103. See The World Economic Forum at https://www.weforum.org/about/world-economic-forum (last accessed June 22, 2019).

104. See UN Global Compact, https://www.unglobalcompact.org/participation/join/commitment (last accessed June 23, 2019). *See also* The Global Compact: What It Is – and Isn't, *CorpWatch*, https://corpwatch.org/article/global-compact-what-it-and-isnt (last accessed June 23, 2019).

105. See the Ten Principles of the UN Global Compact, https://www.unglobalcompact.org/what-is-gc/mission/principles (last accessed June 23, 2019).

106. UN Global Compact (2000), principles 1 and 2, https://www.unglobalcompa ct.org/what-is-gc/mission/principles (last accessed February 01, 2019).

107. See *Id.* Martens, *Corporate Influence on the Business and Human Rights Agenda of the United Nations*, pp. 8–11; *Id.*, Gonzalez-Perez, Maria-Alejandra and Liam, *The UN Global Compact*, p. 124; and Sub-Commission on the Promotion and Protection of Human Rights Resolution 1998/8: E/CN.4/SUB.2/RES/1998/8, August 20, 1998.

108. See Resolution adopted by the Human Rights Council, Human rights and transnational corporations and other business enterprises, A/HRC/RES/17/4, July 6, 2011. See also *Id.,* Guiding Principles on Business and Human Rights (2011).

109. The development of the "Protect, Respect, and Remedy" Framework was spearheaded by Prof. John Ruggie, the former Special Representative of the UN Secretary-General on the issue of human rights and transnational corporations and other business enterprises. See Report of the Special Representative of the Secretary General on the issue of human rights and transnational corporations and other business enterprises, John Ruggie, A/HRC/17/31, March 21, 2011.

110. *Id.*, Guiding Principles on Business and Human Rights (2011), para 11, p. 13.

111. *Id.*, Guiding Principles on Business and Human Rights (2011), p. 1 and p. 13 (pt. II).

112. The Guidelines are formally cited as Secretariat of the Convention on Biological Diversity (2004)—Akwé: Kon Voluntary Guidelines for the Conduct of Cultural, Environmental and Social Impact Assessment regarding Developments Proposed to Take Place on, or which are Likely to Impact on, Sacred Sites and on Lands and Waters Traditionally Occupied or Used by Indigenous and Local Communities, 2004.

113. See *Id.,* Akwé: Kon Guidelines (2004), Part III, para.10.

114. See Convention on Biological Diversity, https://www.cbd.int/information/ parties.shtml (last accessed June 24, 2019); and *Id.,* Akwé: Kon Guidelines (2004), *foreword* to Guidelines, p. 1.

115. See *Id.,* Akwé: Kon Guidelines (2004), *foreword* to Guidelines, p. 1.

116. See *Id* Akwé: Kon Guidelines (2004), Part III, para.8.

117. The Organization for Economic Cooperation and Development (OECD) Guidelines was first adopted in 1976 and revised in 2011. This updated OECD Guidelines form part of the OECD Declaration on International Investment and Multinational Enterprises, adopted by the 42 OECD adhering governments on May 25, 2011.

118. See OECD Guidelines for Multinational Enterprises, 2011, part I (IV), p. 31; OECD Due Diligence Guidance for Responsible Business Conduct, 2018, p. 18.

119. See *Id.,* OECD Guidelines for Multinational Enterprises, 2011, part II General Policies & Commentary on General Policies. See also *Id.,* OECD Due Diligence Guidance for Responsible Business Conduct, 2018, pp. 16 and 21.

120. See Tripartite Declaration of Principles Concerning Multinational Enterprises and Social Policy (MNE Declaration)—5th Edition (2017). Adopted by the Governing Body of the International Labour Office at its 204th Session (Geneva, November 1977) and amended at its 279th (November 2000), 295th (March 2006), and 329th (March 2017) Sessions.

121. *Id.,* MNE Declaration (2017), para 1, p. 2.

122. *Id.,* MNE Declaration (2017), para 10 (a)–(e), pp. 4–5.

123. *Id.*, MNE Declaration (2017), para 10 (c) and (d), pp. 4–5.

124. These voluntary principles provide guidance on how corporations can ensure that proper actions are taken in resolving environmental, social, and corporate governance (ESG) issues that may arise in their investment practice. See Principles for Responsible Investment, available at https://www.unpri.org/pri/what-are-the-principles-for-responsible-investment (last accessed June 15, 2019).

125. This policy requires that all development projects that are proposed for financing by the World Bank, and which affect indigenous peoples, must be fully respectful of the dignity, human rights, economies, and cultures, of the indigenous peoples concerned. See World Bank Operational Manual on Indigenous Peoples, OP 4.10 (Indigenous Peoples) 2005, Revised April 2013.

126. This policy was developed by the International Financial Corporations (IFC) to ensure that business activities supported by the institution minimize negative impacts, and respect human rights, dignity, and culture of indigenous peoples in their operations. See IFC Policy and Performance Standards on Social and Environmental Sustainability: Performance Standard 7-Indigenous Peoples (PS7, January 2012).

127. These standards were developed by WRI to define the corporate responsibility for human rights of indigenous peoples with respect to corporations operating in the extractive sector. See WRI Principles for Effective Community Engagement, enunciated in Breaking Ground: Engaging Communities in Extractive and Infrastructure Projects (WRI, 2009), section III, p. 15.

128. This Position Statement requires all corporations aligned with the ICMM to ensure that any development of mining and metals projects occurring within or near indigenous territories are respectful of the rights, interests, aspirations, culture, and natural resource-based livelihoods of indigenous peoples. See ICMM Position Statement on indigenous peoples and mining (May 2013), Commitment 1, p. 5.

129. See ICMM Good Practice Guide: Indigenous Peoples and Mining (Second edition).

130. The EITI set forth standards that are applicable worldwide and focuses on ensuring good governance of oil, gas, and mineral resources. See Extractive Industries Transparency Initiative Standards—the EITI STANDARD 2016.

131. The Equator Principles (EPs) is a risk management framework, adopted by financial institutions, in order to ensure that the Projects they finance are developed in a manner that is socially responsible and reflects sound environmental management practices. See the Equator Principles, June 2013.

132. The GNI Principles were developed to ensure that companies are accountable, and that they respect laws and policies that protect free expression and privacy rights, worldwide. These Principles are grounded on internationally recognized laws and standards relating to human rights, including the Universal Declaration of Human Rights ("UDHR"), and all the other core human rights instrument. See GNI Principles on Freedom of Expression and Privacy, 2017. Available at https://globalnetworkinitiative.org/gin_tnetnoc/uploads/2018/04/GNI-Principles-on-Freedom-of-Expression-and-Privacy.pdf (last accessed June 15, 2019).

133. The GRI creates the global best practice for reporting concerning a range of economic, environmental, and social impacts. See the GRI Standards, available

at https://www.globalreporting.org/standards/gri-standards-download-center/ (last accessed June 15, 2019).

134. The Voluntary Principles were developed to provide guidance to companies, especially those in in the extractive and energy sectors, in maintaining the safety and security of their operations within an operating framework that encourages respect for human rights. See Voluntary Principles on Security and Human Rights, 2000.

135. See *Id.*, Bede Nwete, *Corporate Social Responsibility and Transparency in the Development of Energy and Mining Projects in Emerging Markets* (2007). See also Daniel I. Márquez and Beatriz F. Pérez, *Corporate Social Responsibility: The Role of Codes of Conduct in Fostering Environmental Sustainability in Latin America*. Publication based on research conducted in the context of the project "Del desarrollo sostenible a la justicia ambiental: Hacia una matriz conceptual para la gobernanza global" (DER2013-44009-P) funded by the Spanish Ministry of Economy and Competitiveness (JEL classification: K32, M14), file:///C:/Users/Jay%20Jay/Downloads/03_Marquez_Perez%20(1).pdf (last accessed June 14, 2019).

136. See Jem Bendell, *Flags of Inconvenience? The Global Compact and the Future of the United Nations,* International Centre for Corporate Social Responsibility (ICCSR), Nottingham University Business School (ICCSR Research Paper Series No. 22-2004 – ISSN 1479-5124); Christian Voegtlin and Nicola M. Pless, Global Governance: CSR and the Role of the UN Global Compact, *Journal of Business Ethics*, Vol. 122, No. 2 (June 2014), pp. 179–191; and, Gustavo Capdevila, UN: Global Compact with Business "Lacks Teeth" – NGOs, *Inter Press News Service (IPS)*, Friday, July 6, 2007.

137. *See* OECD Guidelines for Multinational Enterprises, 2011, *preface*.

138. See *Id.*, Nwete, *Corporate Social Responsibility and Transparency in the Development of Energy and Mining Projects in Emerging Markets*, p. 313. See also *Id.*, Ruggie, *Multinationals as Global Institution*, p. 317.

Chapter 5

Corporate Responsibility and Indigenous Peoples' Right to Consultation

One of the most common problems facing indigenous communities through-out the world today is the lack of adequate implementation of a good faith consultation process before governmental authorities make decisions about policies, measures, or projects that may affect indigenous communities and their territories. This problem is particularly acute with respect to situations where governmental authorities permit, or acquiesce to, corporate entities' execution of projects within or near territories of *indigenous peoples*.[1]

The right of *indigenous peoples* to consultation is cardinal and has been described as vital to the realization of all other human rights guaranteed to *indigenous peoples* as a unit,[2] whether relating to land rights, environmental protection, natural resources, cultural traditions, or governance.[3] Lack of meaningful consultation by States and corporations is exceedingly prevalent with respect to indigenous communities located in developing countries.

Many African governments, for instance, have relentlessly scoffed at the notion that certain groups within their national boundaries ought to be entitled to any form of special treatment, simply by claiming *indigenous*, or be bestowed with prior consultation privileges, before decisions are made on matters usually considered by those governments as falling within the pur-view of regular national governmental powers.[4]

NORMATIVE STANDARDS

Right to Consultation under International Law

The current international normative standards on rights of *indigenous peoples* to consultation were laid out in the UNDRIP,[5] and ILO Convention (No. 169) concerning Indigenous and Tribal Peoples in Independent Countries.[6]

The foundational basis for the normative standards concerning right to consultation as expressed in the UNDRIP and ILO Convention (No. 169) were themselves traceable to the self-determination principle established by a number of traditional human rights instruments such as the UN Charter of 1945,[7] the International Covenant on Civil and Political Rights (ICCPR) of 1966,[8] and the International Covenant on Economic, Social, and Cultural Rights (ICESCR) of 1966.[9] For example, both the ICCPR and ICESCR guarantee that

1. All peoples have the right of self-determination. By virtue of that right they freely determine their political status and freely pursue their economic, social, and cultural development.
2. All peoples may, for their own ends, freely dispose of their natural wealth and resources without prejudice to any obligations arising out of international economic co-operation, based upon the principle of mutual benefit, and international law. In no case may a people be deprived of its own means of subsistence.[10]

Nevertheless, the cornerstones for the rights of indigenous peoples to consultation, as is now evolved today, remain the ILO Convention No. 169 and UNDRIP. With respect to the ILO Convention No. 169, Articles 6 and 7 launched the global legal framework for the right to consultation. The Convention's Article 7 enunciated the obligation of State governments to ensure that indigenous peoples participate in the formulation, implementation, and evaluation of measures or projects that may affect them and their territories directly.[11] Article 6, particularly, mandated governments to

(a) consult the peoples concerned, through appropriate procedures and in particular through their representative institutions, whenever consideration is being given to legislative or administrative measures which may affect them directly;
(b) establish means by which these peoples can freely participate, to at least the same extent as other sectors of the population, at all levels of decision-making in elective institutions and administrative and other bodies responsible for policies and programs which concern them;
(c) establish means for the full development of these peoples' own institutions and initiatives, and in appropriate cases provide the resources necessary for this purpose.[12]

Furthermore, and perhaps most importantly, the Convention requires that any such consultation must be carried out "in good faith and in a form appropriate to the circumstances, with the objective of achieving agreement or consent to the proposed measures."[13]

The UNDRIP similarly establishes a baseline for securing the rights of indigenous peoples to consultation and participation.[14] In accordance with the provisions of UNDRIP, *indigenous peoples* possess the right to participate, through their own freely chosen representatives, in the decision-making process concerning matters that affect them.[15] In this regard, state governments are required to

> consult and cooperate in good faith with the indigenous peoples concerned through their own representative institutions in order to obtain their free, prior and informed consent before adopting and implementing legislative or administrative measures that may affect them.[16]

In light of the foregoing provision, it is safe to say that the fundamental character of rights of *indigenous peoples* to consultation was manifestly made more specific through the principle of *free, prior, and informed consent* (FPIC). On that account, for any consultation undertaken pursuant to UNDRIP to be considered meaningful, the entire consultation process must patently be

(a) *free* from of any form of browbeating, manipulation, or coercion;
(b) initiated *prior* to the commencement of the impactful activity or project;
(c) fully and adequately *inform* the affected indigenous peoples of both the negative and positive impacts of the proposed activity or project;
(d) conducted in an atmosphere of mutual respect and good faith, and with the objective of arriving at an amicable *consensual* agreement.[17]

Consequently, any information provided as part of the process of consultation must sufficiently and objectively describe the impactful activity or project.[18] Such information must cover areas including nature, locality, size, duration, and scope of the impactful activity or project. Also relevant to the process of good faith and meaningful consultation is information concerning any likely sociocultural, economic, and environmental impact, including potential risks and fair and equitable benefits that may arise.[19]

Regional Framework for Right to Consultation

In addition to the general consultation normative standards established by the ILO No. 169 and UNDRIP, consultation obligation at the regional level is largely based on the provisions of the respective regional human rights instruments. In the Americas, the *right to participate* under Article 23 of the American Convention on Human Rights of 1969[20] may be described as the overarching basis upon which the right to consultation has been grounded.[21] Thus, in keeping with the jurisprudence of the Inter-American human rights system, formulated through several landmark cases decided by its adjudicative bodies, the consultation right of *indigenous peoples* in the Americas was, for the most part, anchored upon the combined provisions of Article 23, along with those of Articles 1, 2, 21, and 24 of the American Convention on Human Rights.[22] These foregoing articles are, however, in addition to corresponding rights concerning property, culture, and non-discrimination already established under respective provisions contained in the American Declaration on the Rights and Duties of Man.[23]

For its part, Article 23 guarantees to every citizen the right to take part in the conduct of public affairs, directly or indirectly through their own freely chosen representatives.[24] Whereas Article 21 secures the right of every citizen to the use and enjoyment of their property without unlawful deprivation,[25] Article 24 provides every citizen with the equal protection of the law without discrimination,[26] and lastly, Articles 1 and 2 mandate governments to protect all the rights established under the convention by taking action to adopt legislative or other measures necessary to secure those rights.[27]

By way of illustration, in the *Saramaka v. Suriname* case,[28] the Inter-American Court of Human Rights evaluated the safeguards established by the American Convention, especially with regard to the right to participation and security of property, within the context of the governmental obligation to protect these rights.[29] The Court succinctly articulated the essential elements of the right to consultation as follows:

> In ensuring the effective participation of members of the *Saramaka* people in development or investment plans within their territory, the State has a duty to actively consult with said community according to their customs and traditions [ ]. This duty requires the State to both accept and disseminate information, and entails constant communication between the parties. These consultations must be in good faith, through culturally appropriate procedures and with the objective of reaching an agreement. Furthermore, the *Saramakas* must be consulted, in accordance with their own traditions, at the early stages of a development or investment plan, not only when the need arises to obtain approval from the community, if such is the case. Early notice provides time for internal discussion within communities and for proper feedback to the State. The State must also ensure that members of the *Saramaka* people are aware of possible risks, including environmental and health risks, in order that the proposed development or investment plan is accepted knowingly and voluntarily. Finally, consultation should take account of the *Saramaka* people's traditional methods of decision-making.[30]

The foregoing articulation is very much identical to the description provided by the Inter-American Commission of Human Rights (IACHR), in the case of the *Maya Indigenous Communities of the Toledo District Belize*.[31] The IACHR evaluated the ambits of rights to consultation and stated that one of the central elements to the protection of indigenous property rights is the requirement that states undertake effective and fully informed consultations with indigenous communities regarding acts or decisions that may affect their traditional territories. As the Commission has previously noted, Articles XVIII and XXIII of the American Declaration [of the Rights and Duties of Man] specially oblige a member state to ensure that any determination of the extent to which indigenous claimants maintain interests in the lands to which they have traditionally held title and have occupied and used is based upon a process of fully informed consent on the part of the indigenous community as a whole. This requires, at a minimum, that all of the members of the community are fully and accurately informed of the nature and consequences of the process and provided with an effective opportunity to participate individually or as collectives. In the Commission's view, these requirements are equally applicable to decisions by the State that will have an impact upon indigenous lands and their communities, such as the granting of concessions to exploit the natural resources of indigenous territories.[32]

In contrast, unlike the inter-American human rights system, the African human rights system lacks a well-developed jurisprudence concerning the rights of *indigenous peoples* generally, and consultation rights particularly. One plausible justification for this disparity is that the African Charter on Human and Peoples' Rights (African Charter)[33] neither contains clear provisions addressing the obligation of African States to protect human rights (that is, lacks the *duty to protect* provision),[34] nor includes any direct and unequivocal provision defining the right to the use and enjoyment of property, other than merely stating that the "right to property shall be guaranteed."[35]

Nevertheless, one may soundly argue that the provisions of Articles 20 and 21 of the African Charter should be viewed as establishing the regional framework for the consultation rights of *indigenous peoples* in Africa. This is so because these two articles essentially mirror the self-determination provisions contained in many of the traditional human rights instruments. More so, as noted earlier in this chapter, the right to consultation, as conceptualized under the standards established by the ILO No. 169 and UNDRIP, was linked to the self-determination principle outlined in major international human rights instruments.[36] According to Article 20 of the African Charter:

All peoples shall have the right to existence. They shall have the unquestionable and inalienable right to self-determination. They shall freely determine their political status and shall pursue their economic and social development according to the policy they have freely chosen.[37]

Article 21 reinforces the above provision by adding the following:

All peoples shall freely dispose of their wealth and natural resources. This right shall be exercised in the exclusive interest of the people. In no case shall a people be deprived of it. In case of spoilation, the dispossessed people shall have the right to the lawful recovery of its property as well as to an adequate compensation.[38]

The African Commission on Human and Peoples Rights (African Commission), in considering the question of how to locate the foundational basis for the duty to consult with *indigenous peoples* within the African regional human rights system, asserted that the right to consultation should be considered a subset of the self-determination or self-management provisions of the African Charter, especially when held in the light of UNDRIP and ILO No. 169. The African Commission, therefore, concluded that

the right to self-determination in its application to indigenous populations and communities, both at the UN and regional levels, should be understood as encompassing a series of rights relative to the full participation in national affairs, the right to local self-government, the right to recognition so as to be consulted in the drafting of laws and programs concerning them, to a recognition of their structures and traditional ways of living as well as the freedom to preserve and promote their culture. It is therefore a collection of variations in the exercise of the right to self-determination, which are entirely compatible with the unity, and territorial integrity of State parties.[39]

Certainly, the African human rights system is not comparable to the Inter-American system in terms of a clearly defined and fully developed jurisprudence on indigenous peoples' rights. Having said that, the regional system has taken significant strides in recent years, in articulating the contours of the consultation right of Africa's indigenous population, especially within the context of existing international normative standards.

Early signs that the African human rights system was willing to embrace, and tackle head-on, the challenge of lack of clarity on protections for indigenous peoples under the African Charter, became glaring in the 2001 case of *SERAC v. Nigeria*.[40] In that case, the African Commission found the Nigerian government liable for not living up to the minimum expectations of the African Charter[41] on the basis that the government, among others, denied the *Ogoni* people the opportunity to partake in the decision-making process concerning issues affecting the development of *Ogoniland*.[42] Particularly because the Nigerian government withheld vital information from Ogoni people by failing to relate the dangers posed by oil exploration activities occurring within their territory. In addition, the government failed to ensure that the oil companies operating within *Ogoniland* consulted with the people prior to beginning such operations.[43]

In addition to that, almost a decade later, the African Commission provided a well-disposed enunciation on the right to consultation in the landmark *Endorois Case*.[44] Relying heavily on the *Saramaka Case* along with other case laws of the Inter-American human rights system, the African Commission explained that the right to consultation could only be characterized as sufficiently protected if undertaken to obtain the prior informed consent of *indigenous peoples*.[45] As the African Commission elaborated, with respect to development or investment projects that would have a major impact within the territory of the *Endorois* people, the government of Kenya is obligated "not only to consult with the community, but also to obtain their free, prior, and informed consent, according to their customs and traditions."[46]

Without question, the African Commission made it abundantly clear that the principle of self-determination, as the foundational basis for the consultation right, is entirely compatible with the unity, and territorial integrity of African States.[47] Yet, in a paradox, many African States remained unenthusiastic about providing legal recognition for, and/or adopting measures to secure, the consultation right of their indigenous populations, even where the underlying normative framework for this right was declared compatible with the territorial integrity of the continent.

REGULATORY FRAMEWORK FOR CORPORATE RESPONSIBILITY TO CONSULT

Admittedly, none of the foregoing international and regional schemes directly or automatically impose a binding consultation duty on non-state entities such as corporations, except by indirect implication. However, a majority of the non-binding regulatory initiatives on corporate conduct discussed earlier in chapters 3 and 4 of this book contain useful explicit consultation mandates that directly apply to corporations. For instance, as part of the corporate human rights' due diligence duty articulated in the UN Guiding Principles on Business and Human Rights,[48] corporate entities are enjoined to conduct meaningful consultation with groups and other stakeholders that may be impacted by their operational activities.[49] Principle 18 of the UN Guiding Principles reiterated that

> in order to gauge human rights risks, business enterprises should identify and assess any actual or potential adverse human rights impacts with which they may be involved either through their own activities or as a result of their business relationships. This process should
>
> (a) draw on internal and/or independent external human rights expertise; and

  (b) involve meaningful consultation with potentially affected groups and other
       relevant stakeholders, as appropriate to the size of the business enterprise
       and the nature and context of the operation.[50]

The nature of consultation responsibility contemplated by the UN Guiding
Principles does not appear to be narrowly tailored towards mere identification of adverse impact and information exchange. But it encompasses a corporation's responsibility to take proactive steps in order to remedy any such
potential impact. As stated by Principles 19 and 22:

> In order to prevent and mitigate adverse human rights impacts, business enter-
> prises should integrate the findings from their impact assessments across rel-
> evant internal functions and processes, and take appropriate action.[51]
> Where business enterprises identify that they have caused or contributed
> to adverse impacts, they should provide for or cooperate in their remediation
> through legitimate processes.[52]

Undeniably, a fundamental underlying element of the "Protect, Respect,
and Remedy" Framework, elaborated in the UN Guiding Principles, is the
emphasis that corporate due diligence duty incorporates not only the responsibility to respect both national laws and internationally recognized human
rights norms,[53] but that the corporate duty to respect international human
rights norms subsist independently of the national governments' own duty to
protect against human rights abuse within their jurisdiction.[54] In this regard,
internationally recognized human rights norms would include those standards
concerning rights to consultation and participation set out in the ILO No. 169
and UNDRIP.

In addition to the UN Guiding Principles, several other non-binding
regulatory initiatives have prescribed standards on corporate codes of conduct concerning indigenous peoples' right to consultation. One of these
initiatives is the World Bank Operational Policy on Indigenous People
(OP 4.10).[55] According to this operational manual, whenever any project
financed by the World Bank is likely to affect indigenous peoples, the borrower must implement a process of free, prior, and informed consultation
in carrying out such project.[56] The expectation here is that any consultation
process carried out by the borrower should, ultimately, result in securing
the broad community support, by the concerned indigenous people, for the
project; otherwise, the borrower may lose the bank's financing as penalty
for non-compliance.[57]

Similar provisions were also contained in the International Financial
Corporation (IFC) Performance Standard on Environmental and Social
Sustainability (PS-7),[58] which mandated every client associated with the
financial institution to implement a community engagement process with the

indigenous peoples that may be affected by a proposed project, based on the principle of FPIC.[59] The requirement, as specified by the PS-7, is that

> this engagement process includes stakeholder analysis and engagement planning, disclosure of information, consultation, and participation, in a culturally appropriate manner. In addition, this process will
>
> - involve Indigenous Peoples' representative bodies and organizations (e.g., councils of elders or village councils), as well as members of the Affected Communities of Indigenous Peoples; and
> - provide sufficient time for Indigenous Peoples' decision-making processes.[60]

According to PS-7, the process of engaging with affected communities must be carried out in a culturally appropriate manner with the goal of obtaining their FPIC.[61]

The International Council on Mining and Metals (ICMM) Good Practice Guide[62] and Position Statement,[63] and the World Resource Institute (WRI) Principles for Effective Community Engagement,[64] also prescribes consultation responsibility for corporations operating in the extractive industry. The ICMM Good Practice Guide, for example, recognizes the importance of ensuring that indigenous peoples participate meaningfully in the decision-making process regarding their lands and resources.[65] The ICMM, therefore, recommended that its member's operational approach should be focused on consulting with, and obtaining consent from, *indigenous peoples* in order to conduct any resource development project on their lands.[66]

There is also the OECD Guidelines for Multinational Enterprises,[67] which enjoins multinational enterprises operating in OECD countries to conduct "adequate and timely communication and consultation with the communities directly affected by the environmental, health and safety policies of the enterprise and by their implementation."[68] The Akwé: Kon Voluntary Guidelines is another example of a non-binding regulatory initiative that addresses corporate responsibility to consult.[69] The Akwé: Kon Voluntary Guidelines outlines the consultation responsibility incumbent upon private enterprises and governmental agencies proposing any project that may affect lands or waters of indigenous communities.[70] As the Guidelines explain:

> In any development proposed to take place on, or likely to have an impact on, sacred sites and lands and waters traditionally occupied or used by them, indigenous and local communities should be invited to participate in and are to be accorded full respect at all stages of the assessment and development process, including planning and implementation. A formal process to identify the indigenous and local community members, experts and organizations, and relevant stakeholders should be engaged, including local and open consultations.[71]

Essentially, the process of participation and consultation under the Akwé: Kon Voluntary Guidelines encompasses important aspects such as notification and public consultation; identification of indigenous and local communities and relevant stakeholders that may be affected by a proposed project; establishment of effective mechanisms for indigenous and local community participation; establishment of an environmental management or monitoring plan, development of contingency plans regarding possible adverse cultural, environmental, and social impacts resulting from a proposed project; and, crucially, establishment of a process whereby local and indigenous communities may have the option to accept or oppose a proposed project that may impact their community.[72]

Although virtually all the institutional codes of conducts discussed here are non-binding, it is imperative that corporate entities accept them in good faith as the fundamental rules of the trade—that is, as the minimum best practice standards, particularly as the superior benchmark for how well they comply with their legal, ethical, and moral obligations.

To this end, corporate entities must ensure that their operational conduct aligns with applicable international human rights normative standards, including those relating to consultation right of indigenous peoples, even if the government of the national jurisdiction where they operate, fails to do so.[73] The exigency of embracing this approach is borne out of the reality that, for indigenous communities likely to be affected by corporate activities, the implementation of meaningful consultation based on the principle of FPIC is an inviolable bulwark that helps protect their human rights.[74]

Under international law, corporate entities now owe indigenous communities substantive human rights due diligence duty to ensure that their operational activities do not contravene international human rights standards.[75] Consequently, the efficient and judicious course of action would be for corporations to ensure that they are conversant with the nature and scope of the right of indigenous peoples to consultation, especially as it pertains to the particularities of the indigenous group(s) that may be impacted by their activities. Consultation in this context should be approached as a crucial process which demands respectful dialogue, and good faith participatory negotiation, and with the objective of achieving a mutual accord with the *indigenous peoples* concerned.

NOTES

1. See generally, *Report of the Special Rapporteur on the Situation of Human Rights and Fundamental Freedom of Indigenous Peoples*, James Anaya, A/HRC/12/34, July 15, 2009. *See also* Tara Ward, The Right to Free, Prior, and

Informed Consent: Indigenous Peoples' Participation Rights Within International Law, *Northwestern University Journal of International Human Rights*. Vol. 10 (Autumn 2011), 54.

2. See the ILO Convention (No. 169) Concerning Indigenous and Tribal Peoples in Independent Countries, adopted by the General Conference of the International Labour Organization in June 1989, articles 6–7; and, UNDRIP, adopted by the UN General Assembly in September 2007, particularly articles 18–24, and generally articles 10–11, 15–17, 28–32, and 36–38.

3. See *Guiding Principles for Effective Participation by Indigenous Peoples: Training Module on Indigenous Peoples' Issues* (UNPFII, 2010), 19. See also *Id. Report of the Special Rapporteur*, James Anaya (A/HRC/12/34–2009), paras 36–45.

4. See *Report of the African Commission's Working Group of Expert on Indigenous Population/Communities*, adopted by the African Commission on Human and Peoples' Rights at its 28th ordinary session, 2005, particularly pp. 11, 45, 46 and 47.

5. See, for example, *Id.* UNDRIP of 2007, articles 18–24.

6. See, for example, *Id.* ILO Convention (No. 169) of 1989, articles 6–7.

7. See UN Charter 1945, Articles 1(2) and 55.

8. See International Covenant on Civil and Political Rights (ICCPR) 1966, adopted by General Assembly resolution 2200A (XXI) of December 16, 1966, and entered into force on March 23, 1976.

9. See International Covenant on Economic, Social and Cultural Rights (ICESCR) 1966, adopted by General Assembly resolution 2200A (XXI) of December 16, 1966, and entered into force on January 3, 1976.

10. See Id. ICCPR of 1966, articles 1(1) and (2); and, ICESCR of 1966 articles 1(1) and (2).

11. See, for example, *Id.* ILO Convention (No. 169) of 1989, article 7(1).

12. See, for example, *Id.* ILO Convention (No. 169) of 1989, article 6(1).

13. See *Id.* ILO Convention (No. 169) of 1989, article 6(2).

14. See generally *Id.* UNDRIP of 2007, articles 10–11, 15, 17–19, 28–30, 32, 36, & 38.

15. See *Id.* UNDRIP of 2007, article 18.

16. See *Id.* UNDRIP of 2007, article 19.

17. See *Id., Report of the Special Rapporteur*, James Anaya (A/HRC/12/34–2009), paras 36–53; Cathal Doyle, The Content of Free Prior and Informed Consent, in Cathal Doyle, Helen Tugendhat, and Robeliza Halip (eds.) *Mining, the Aluminium Industry, and Indigenous Peoples: Enhancing Corporate Respect for Indigenous Peoples' Rights* (AIPP/FPP/IUCN, 2015), p. 34; *Id.* Tara Ward, *The Right to Free, Prior, and Informed Consent* (2011).

18. See *Id. Report of the Special Rapporteur*, James Anaya (A/HRC/12/34–2009), para 53; *Indigenous and Tribal Peoples Rights in Practice: A Guide to ILO Convention No. 169* (ILO Geneva, 2009), p. 63; and *Id.* Cathal Doyle, *The Content of Free Prior and Informed Consent* (2015), p. 37.

19. See *Id. Report of the Special Rapporteur*, James Anaya (A/HRC/12/34–2009), para 53; *Id. Indigenous and Tribal Peoples Rights in Practice* (2009); and *Id.* Cathal Doyle, *The Content of Free Prior and Informed Consent* (2015), p. 37.

20. See the American Convention on Human Rights of 1969, adopted at the Inter-American Specialized Conference on Human Rights held in San José, Costa Rica, on November 22, 1969.

21. See *Yatama v Nicaragua, Inter-Am Court/ H.R. Preliminary Objections, Merits, Reparations and Costs*, Judgment of June 23, 2005, Series C. No. 127. See further, Maia S. Campbell, The Right of Indigenous Peoples to Political Participation and the Case of Yatama v Nicaragua, *Arizona Journal of International and Comparative Law*, Vol. 24 (2007), p. 499.

22. See, for example, *Saramaka People v. Suriname*, Preliminary Objections, Merits, Reparations, and Cost, Inter-Am. Ct. H.R. (ser. C) No. 174 (Nov. 28, 2007), paras, 129, 131–136; and *Maya Indigenous Communities of the Toledo Dist. v. Belize*, Case 12.053, Inter-Am. Comm'n H.R., Report No. 40/04, OEA/Ser.L/V/II.122 doc. 5 rev. 1 (2004), paras 142–144, and 194.

23. See American Declaration on the Rights and Duties of Man of 1948, adopted by the Ninth International Conference of American States, Bogotá, Colombia, 1948.

24. See *Id*. American Convention on Human Rights (1969), article 23(1).

25. See *Id*. American Convention on Human Rights (1969), article 21 (1) and (3).

26. See *Id*. American Convention on Human Rights (1969), article 24.

27. See *Id*. American Convention on Human Rights (1969), article 2.

28. See *Id*. *Saramaka People v. Suriname* (2007).

29. See *Id*. *Saramaka People v. Suriname* (2007), paras 129 and 133.

30. See *Id*. *Saramaka People v. Suriname* (2007), para 133. *See further Case of the Kichwa Indigenous People of Sarayaku v. Ecuador*, Merits and Reparations, Inter-Am. Ct. H.R (Judgment of June 27, 2012), paras 127–133.

31. See *Id*. *Maya Indigenous Communities of the Toledo Dist. v. Belize* (2004), paras 142–144.

32. See *Id*. *Maya Indigenous Communities of the Toledo Dist. v. Belize* (2004), paras 142.

33. See the African Charter on Human and Peoples' Rights of 1986, adopted on June 27, 1981, OAU Doc. CAB/LEG/67/3 rev. 5, 21 I.L.M. 58 (1982), and entered into force October 21, 1986.

34. See *Id*. American Convention on Human Rights (1969), articles 1 and 2 for comparison. See generally discussion in chapter 3.

35. See *Id*. African Charter on Human and Peoples' Rights (1986), article 14. But see *Id*. American Convention on Human Rights (1969), article 21.

36. See further *Id*. Tara Ward, *The Right to Free, Prior, and Informed Consent* (2011), p. 55.

37. See *Id*. African Charter on Human and Peoples' Rights (1986), article 20(1).

38. See *Id*. African Charter on Human and Peoples' Rights (1986), articles 21(1) and (2).

39. See Advisory Opinion of the African Commission on Human and Peoples' Rights on the United Nations Declaration on the Rights of Indigenous Peoples, adopted by the African Commission on Human and Peoples' Rights at its 41st Ordinary Session held in May 2007 in Accra, Ghana, para 27.

40. See *Social and Economic Rights Action Centre (SERAC) & Another v Nigeria*, Communication 155/96, Decided at the 30th ordinary session (October 2001).

41. See *Id. SERAC v. Nigeria* (2001), paras 68–69.

42. See *Id. SERAC v. Nigeria* (2001), paras 1–9 and 68–69.

43. See *Id. SERAC v. Nigeria* (2001), paras 1–9, 54–48, and 68–69.

44. See *Centre for Minority Rights Development (Kenya) and Minority Rights Group International on behalf of Endorois Welfare Council v. Kenya*, (Communication 276/2003), decision adopted by the African Commission in May 2009 and endorsed by the African Union on February 4, 2010 (*Endorois Case*).

45. See *Id. Endorois Case* (2010), para 290.

46. See *Id. Endorois Case* (2010), para 291.

47. See *Id.* Advisory Opinion of the African Commission on Human and Peoples' Rights (May 2007), para 27.

48. See *UN Guiding Principles on Business and Human Rights: Implementing the United Nations "Protect, Respect and Remedy" Framework* (United Nations, 2011).

49. See *Id. UN Guiding Principles on Business and Human Rights*, para 18(b), p. 19.

50. See *Id. UN Guiding Principles on Business and Human Rights*, para 18(a) and (b), p. 19.

51. See *Id. UN Guiding Principles on Business and Human Rights*, para 19, p. 20.

52. See *Id. UN Guiding Principles on Business and Human Rights*, para 22, p. 24.

53. See *Id., UN Guiding Principles on Business and Human Rights*, para 11, pp. 13–16.

54. See *Reports of Special Rapporteur on the Situation of Human Rights and Fundamental Freedoms of Indigenous Peoples*, James Anaya (A/HRC/15/37, July 19, 2010), para 55; *Id. UN Guiding Principles on Business and Human Rights*, para 23, pp. 25–26.

55. See *World Bank Operational Manual on Indigenous Peoples*, OP 4.10 (Indigenous Peoples) 2005, Revised April 2013.

56. See *Id. World Bank Operational Manual* (OP 4.10), para 1.

57. See *Id. World Bank Operational Manual* (OP 4.10), para 1.

58. See *IFC Policy and Performance Standards on Social and Environmental Sustainability: Performance Standard 7-Indigenous Peoples* (PS7, 2012).

59. See *Id. IFC Policy and Performance Standards* (PS7, 2012), paras 9–12.

60. See *Id. IFC Policy and Performance Standards* (PS7, 2012), paras 10, and 12–17.

61. See *Id. IFC Policy and Performance Standards* (PS7, 2012), paras 12–17. Note that free, prior, and informed consent (FPIC) "does not necessarily require unanimity and may be achieved even when individuals or groups within the community explicitly disagree." *Id* (PS7, 2012), Para 12.

62. See *ICMM Good Practice Guide: Indigenous Peoples and Mining*, 2nd Ed.

63. See ICMM Position Statement on Indigenous Peoples and Mining (May 2013).

64. See *WRI Principles for Effective Community Engagement, Enunciated in Breaking Ground: Engaging Communities in Extractive and Infrastructure Projects* (WRI, 2009), section III, pp. 15–24.

65. See *Id. ICMM Good Practice Guide*, 2nd Ed., para 2.4, pp. 24–25.

66. See *Id. ICMM Good Practice Guide*, 2nd Ed., paras 2.4 and 2.5, pp. 24–29.

67. See *OECD Guidelines for Multinational Enterprises*, 2011.

68. See *Id. OECD Guidelines*, part 1, section V, pp. 19–20.

69. See *The Akwé: Kon Voluntary Guidelines*, 2004. Otherwise referred to by its long name, Akwé: Kon Voluntary Guidelines for the Conduct of Cultural, Environmental and Social Impact Assessment regarding Developments Proposed to Take Place on, or which are Likely to Impact on, Sacred Sites and on Lands and Waters Traditionally Occupied or Used by Indigenous and Local Communities. This Voluntary Guidelines were published by Secretariat of the Convention on Biological Diversity in 2004, and adopted on February 2004. "Akwé: Kon" is a term identified with the *Mohawk* tribe, meaning "everything in creation." The term was provided by the *Kahnawake* community located near Montreal Canada, where the guidelines were negotiated.

70. See *Id. The Akwé: Kon Voluntary Guidelines*, paras 7–18.

71. See *Id. The Akwé: Kon Voluntary Guidelines*, paras 12–13.

72. See *Id. The Akwé: Kon Voluntary Guidelines*, para 8.

73. See *Id. Reports of Special Rapporteur*, James Anaya (A/HRC/15/37 – 2010), paras 55–56; *Id. UN Guiding Principles on Business and Human Rights*, para 23, pp. 25–26.

74. See *Id. Report of the Special Rapporteur,* James Anaya (A/HRC/12/34 – 2009), paras 36–45.

75. See *Id., UN Guiding Principles on Business and Human Rights*, para 11, pp. 13–16.

Chapter 6

Operationalization of Right to Consultation

CONSTITUTIONAL AND REGULATORY CHALLENGES TO FULFILLING RIGHT TO CONSULTATION IN DEVELOPING COUNTRIES

Africa

Legislative and constitutional frameworks in many African countries provide limited protection for the right to consultation. The generic "rights to participate in the political affairs of the state" or "right to vote," as well as "right to free speech" under the traditional human rights legal schemes, have generally served as the indirect legal basis for indigenous peoples' right to consultation in many African States.[1] The Eritrean Constitution, for example, simply states that it is a fundamental principle of the State of Eritrea to guarantee its citizens broad and active participation in all political, economic, social, and cultural life of the country.[2] The Nigerian Constitution similarly stipulates that participation by the people in their government shall be ensured in accordance with the provisions of the Constitution.[3]

Besides constitutional provisions, domestic regulations have also been adopted in a bid to offer indigenous groups limited opportunities to participate in governmental affairs and decision-making process. As an illustration, in Botswana, the *Bogosi* Act of 2008 was enacted in order to provide certain local groups with recognition as indigenous/tribal communities.[4] The Act empowers tribal communities to appoint a government recognized tribal leader (Kgosi),[5] who then becomes the official liaison between the tribes and the governmental structures established by the State.[6] The objective of official recognition for the Kgosi is to encourage some form of local participation in the socio-political and developmental decision-making process.[7]

The challenge associated with the implementation of indigenous peoples' right to consultation in Africa is multi-dimensional. First, violation of this right is most rampant in situations involving lands and natural resources claimed by *indigenous peoples*, and the extractive and infrastructural projects impacting these lands and resources.[8] Second, the fact that most indigenous groups in Africa lack State recognition compounded this predicament. Even where such recognition has been accorded, it is largely circumscribed.[9] Third, *indigenous peoples* generally do not possess meaningful ownership rights either in the land upon which they use and occupy, or the natural resource found on the land.[10] Fourth, the relationship between *indigenous peoples* and their lands and resources goes far beyond commercial or economic rationalization; it is more precisely in the realm of collective spiritual and cultural attachment, coupled with the sacred obligation to protect those lands and natural resources.[11] However, the constitutional and regulatory frameworks in many African countries tend to treat lands and natural resources as objects of national treasure meant only for national benefit, rather than belonging to the communities who have traditionally used and occupied the lands.[12]

The implication of the foregoing is that there is a strong presumption on the part of governmental authorities in many African countries that indigenous communities need not, as a matter of right, be consulted regarding planning, permitting, and other contracting procedures dealing with the commercial exploitation of the natural resources considered by the government as belonging to the State, even if located in areas occupied by *indigenous peoples*. John Ghazvinian,[13] in his account about the politics of oil and gas exploitation in Africa, chronicled this kind of challenging predicament as follows:

> The problem is that the only thing the federal government ever did was to give the oil companies a map of Nigeria and say, "Go and find oil there." In the local communities, they knew nothing of this. All they knew is that one day they see a white man come. They see him come with three black men, and start digging. And they ask them what they are doing, and the white man shows them a piece of paper from Abuja [the capital city] . . . the white man says it's a piece of paper that says he is allowed to dig in the backyard of my house. It says nothing about whether this might be our ancestral home.[14]

Existing legislations in several African countries also aptly reflect the plight highlighted by Ghazviniah. As a case in point, in the Republic of Ghana, the law governing natural resources management declares that

> every mineral in its natural state in, under or upon land in Ghana, rivers, streams, water-courses throughout the country, the exclusive economic zone and an area covered by the territorial sea or continental shelf is the property of the Republic and is vested in the President in trust for the people of Ghana.[15]

The effect of the above-cited provision is that whenever any land is required to secure the development of a mineral resource in Ghana, the state may assertively acquire such land and authorize a third party to occupy and use the land.[16] In other words, the state may compulsorily take over any lands occupied by indigenous groups for the purpose of extracting the natural resources therein, and may also transfer such lands to private business entities for the same reason.[17] The government may take this particular action without necessarily engaging in prior consultation with the indigenous group for the purpose of securing their informed consent.

Like Ghana, comparable provisions are also present in the Constitution of the Democratic Republic of Congo (2005),[18] the Mines and Minerals Act of Sierra Leone (2009),[19] the Constitution of the Republic of Liberia (1986),[20] and the Constitution of the Federal Republic of Nigeria.[21] With respect to Nigeria, matters concerning land use and natural resource exploitation are subjected to the combined provisions of the Petroleum Act,[22] Minerals and Mining Act,[23] the Constitution,[24] and the Land Use Act.[25] Pursuant to Section 1(1) of the Nigerian Petroleum Act, the absolute ownership and control of all petroleum in, under, or upon any lands is vested in the State.[26] The Act broadly applies to all lands, including lands covered by water.[27] This particular provision of the Petroleum Act was reinforced by the Nigerian Constitution, which states that

> the entire property in and control of all minerals, mineral oils and natural gas in, under or upon any land in Nigeria, under or upon the territorial waters and the exclusive economic zone of Nigeria shall vest in the government of the federation and shall be managed in such manner as may be prescribed by the national assembly.[28]

Similarly, the Nigerian Minerals and Mining Act[29] also broadly mandates that any lands upon which minerals have been discovered in Nigeria will be expropriated by the federal government in accordance with the Land Use Act.[30] Whereas, the Land Use Act for its part, divests the title of ownership in land from every entitled landowner in Nigeria (whether individual, collective, or customary), substituting it with rights of occupancy, and thereby vesting the original ownership title in the State government.[31] The Land Use Act effectively converts existing ownership interest in lands, whether customary or freehold, into a lesser right of occupancy; the effective ownership title now vests in the governor of the State where the land is situated, and who holds it on behalf of the State. Consequently, anyone who possesses ownership title to a parcel or parcels of land before the advent of the Land Use Act is now deemed a holder of a lesser *right of occupancy*.[32]

Interestingly, prior to the enactment of the Nigeria's Land Use Act, corporations carrying on extractive projects within lands occupied by the various indigenous communities treated such communities as the owners of their lands. To this extent, whenever those corporations planned to embark on any extractive project within lands occupied by indigenous communities, they would approach the leadership of the communities concerned, consult and negotiate terms concerning the project's implementation with them, as well as finalize an agreement on the terms for payment of land rents.[33] The Land Use Act, in many respects, overturned this type of arrangement. Hence, following its enactment, corporate entities deal with the national and state governments almost exclusively on every matter relating to land use and natural resources development. Corporations simply adjusted to the absence of a legal mandate compelling them to undertake the consultation and negotiation process with the communities.[34]

In a practical sense, weak or emasculating regulatory frameworks, such as those highlighted above, pose significant challenges, in terms of the implementation of right to consultation in Africa. Nevertheless, relatively vigorous constitutional and regulatory protections, which exist in few African countries, have not necessarily proven to be a panacea to overcome these challenges either.[35] Rather, the dismissive and lukewarm attitude of many African governments towards the notion of indigenous people's rights appears to be the most significant hurdle that has become too steep to surmount.[36]

Take for instance, the Ethiopian Constitution[37] that recognizes the right of existence of indigenous tribal nations and peoples in the country, and secures protection for their rights to environmental safeguards and consultation, especially with respect to any economic development activity that may be disruptive to their environmental or ecological balance.[38] Despite this clear constitutional protection, the government of Ethiopia failed to adhere to these constitutional provisions in the implementation of the *Gibe* III hydroelectric dam project. Construction of the dam project impacted many indigenous communities in the *Omo* River basin in southern Ethiopia.[39] In implementing the *Gibe* III hydroelectric dam project, the consultation right of the several indigenous communities affected by the project was either ignored by the government, or carried out in a manner that fell below the minimum standard of free, prior, and informed consent (FPIC).[40] The observation of James Anaya, the former UN Special Rapporteur on the Rights of Indigenous Peoples, who investigated the complaints of affected indigenous communities about the implementation of the Gibe III dam project, clearly expressed this predicament.

> [T]he Special Rapporteur expresses his concern that the consultations were carried out with the goal to "ensure [the project's] acceptance," which indicates that the consultations were carried out with a predetermined outcome. Under relevant international standards, consultations should involve a genuine

opportunity for indigenous peoples to present their views and to influence decision-making, and the option of not proceeding with the proposed project should not be foreclosed during these consultations . . . . In the present case, given the magnitude of the Gibe III dam project and its potential effects on indigenous peoples in surrounding areas, the Special Rapporteur notes that there is a need for concerted efforts to carry out adequate consultations with affected groups and to endeavor to reach consensus with them on all aspects of the project affecting them.[41]

In light of the discussion above, it is axiomatic that the disregard by many African countries for the rights of *indigenous peoples*, especially concerning their right to consultation, has persisted irrespective of whether or not those countries provide meaningful constitutional or regulatory protection for their indigenous populations. In a sense, the lack of enthusiasm to respect indigenous rights, as often displayed by many corporate entities operating within the African continent, merely mirrors the governments' lackadaisical attitude toward their *indigenous peoples*.

Latin America

Notwithstanding the political challenges in Latin America, the sub-region has been able to establish rich regulatory schemes and strong legal jurisprudence, with respect to indigenous people's rights. It should be pointed out that many Latin American countries have undergone a progressive constitutional and regulatory transformation in the past three decades,[42] resulting in a significant expansion of existing national legal frameworks in order to provide protection for the rights of *indigenous peoples*, including safeguarding their right to prior consultation.[43]

Unlike the situation in Africa, constitutional and legislative provisions specifically enacted to protect indigenous people's rights are burgeoning in many of the Latin American states. For instance, the Constitution of Ecuador directly dealt with matters concerning the rights of *indigenous peoples* in general, and the rights to participation and consultation in particular.[44] Likewise, the Constitution of Bolivia guarantees the rights of its indigenous populations to compulsory prior consultation before the government can implement any legislative or administrative measure that may affect indigenous peoples' communities, especially when such measures involve the exploitation of non-renewable natural resources within a territory occupied by them.[45]

On a similar note, in September of 2011, the legislature in Peru enacted a new law that was specifically intended to protect the consultation right of the indigenous peoples in that country.[46] The Peruvian law mandated the implementation of compulsory prior consultation in relation to any matter concerning indigenous communities in Peru.[47] The law requires the participation of *indigenous peoples* across the country in all activities that affect their collective human rights, whether relating to administrative or legal measures, or concerning developmental projects.[48]

Furthermore, the fact that a majority of Latin American countries ratified the ILO Convention No. 169 and voted in favor of the UNDRIP[49] constitutes a significant development in terms of securing the rights of *indigenous peoples* within the region. This is so because of the implication created by such ratification and adoption in relation to the concept of *legal monism*,[50] which is practiced by a majority of Latin American countries. Under the monist tradition, both international law and national law constitute a single legal system.[51] Essentially, *Monism* permits the direct incorporation of international instruments, such as treaties, into a domestic legal scheme, once the appropriate authority of the State validly ratifies them.[52] As a result, ratified international instruments may be construed either as having the same status as the national constitution (that is belonging to the same *constitutionality block*), or deemed inferior to the national constitution, but enjoy similar status accorded to any other domestic legislation.[53] According to one study, for example, Bolivia, Colombia, and Peru usually designate ratified international treaties as having constitutional status, while in Ecuador, they are treated as forming part of the country's statutory laws.[54]

The influence of *legal monism* was clearly amplified in the Constitution of Ecuador.[55] The constitution affirms that the collective rights of *indigenous peoples* in Ecuador shall be recognized and guaranteed "in conformity with the Constitution and human rights agreements, conventions, declarations, and other international instruments."[56] As a practical matter, *legal monism* provides an additional layer of protection for indigenous people within Latin America, because it creates the opportunity to directly apply firm international normative standards to local situations.[57] As an illustration, in the matter concerning the issue of right to consultation, and involving the *U'wa Indigenous Community* and the *Ministry of the Environment* in Columbia, the Constitutional Court of Colombia explained that the right of indigenous communities to participate in matters that affect them is a fundamental right protected by Article 40(2) of the Columbian Constitution and strengthened by ILO Convention No. 169, which was already ratified by the State.[58] The court concluded that ILO Convention No. 169 forms part of domestic legislation, and that in keeping with Articles 93 and 94 of the Columbian Constitution, ILO Convention No. 169 became part of the constitutionality block, which is intended to guarantee and make such participation effective.[59]

Notwithstanding the foregoing, *indigenous peoples* in Latin America continue to face challenges with regard to the protection of their right to consultation. These challenges are often related to the attitude of State governments who sometimes view the right to consultation as subservient to the interests of the State to pursue natural resource development.[60] In many cases, indigenous communities in Latin America have only succeeded in securing protection for their right to consultation after fierce legal contests or persistent public protests.[61]

APPRAISING THE OPERATIONAL FRAMEWORK FOR RIGHT TO CONSULTATION IN THE CONTEXT OF DEVELOPED COUNTRIES

North America

United States

In the United States, the right to consultation with respect to Native American tribes is unique in some sense, because, unlike in Latin America, it has a very limited constitutional guarantee. It is principally based on tribal treaties with the U.S. government;[62] general fiduciary trust obligation owed to the tribes by the United States;[63] federal statutes and regulations;[64] and presidential memorandum and executive orders.[65]

In keeping with the terms of the various treaties negotiated between Native American tribes and the U.S. federal government, the tribes possess significant jurisdictional powers over the lands they occupy and the resources therein.[66] In *Cherokee Nation v. Journeycake*, the U.S. Supreme Court concluded that lands and territories subject to treaties are the common property of all the tribal citizens subject to the treaties, and that concerned tribes possess full common rights and property interests in the designated territories.[67] As a result, tribes in the United States are able to establish consultation standards of their own and demand compliance with those standards before a non-tribal party may carry on any activities within tribal lands or implement projects relating to the resources therein.[68]

The trust obligation of the U.S. government is of particular importance in this context. This is because the underlying trust doctrine is one of the fundamental pillars of federal Indian law in the United States, and embodies the general fiduciary responsibility owed to the Native American tribes by the U.S. government, which in many ways reinforces the claim for meaningful prior consultation by the tribes.[69] It is worth noting that the foundational theme for the trust doctrine itself evolved from the *Marshall Trilogy*, a reference to the famous U.S. Supreme Court decisions handed down between 1823 and 1832, in the *Johnson v. McIntosh*,[70] *Cherokee Nation v. Georgia*,[71] and *Worcester v. Georgia*[72] cases.[73] It should be emphasized that the duty owed by the U.S. federal government to faithfully discharge its trust obligation is deeply rooted within the American legal landscape to the extent that tribes may validly bring an action in court against the U.S. government to enforce this obligation.[74]

In terms of regulatory protection, several U.S. federal statutes and regulations contain provisions mandating consultation with various tribal authorities before federal agencies can take any action that will affect tribal lands or interests. Federal legislations such as the Native Graves Protection and Repatriation Act (NAGPRA),[75] the National Historic Preservation Act (NHPA),[76] along with its implementing regulation,[77] and the National Environmental Policy Act (NEPA),[78] all contain mandates that instruct the appropriate federal agencies to consult with federally recognized tribes in all phases of implementing a measure or project that impacts tribes.[79]

Two important executive orders issued by former U.S. presidents reflect the broad regulatory and policy direction of the U.S. government as it concerns the consultation rights of Native American tribes. First, the federal Executive Order 13007 of May 24, 1996, which calls for consultation with regard to American Indian sacred sites.[80] And, second is Executive Order 13175 of November 6, 2000,[81] which covers consultation with Indian tribes generally. For example, the objective of Executive Order 13175 was stated as follows:

> To establish regular and meaningful consultation and collaboration with tribal officials in the development of Federal policies that have tribal implications, to strengthen the United States government-to-government relationships with Indian tribes, and to reduce the imposition of unfunded mandates upon Indian tribes.[82]

In an effort to discharge the foregoing commitment of the United States to engage in meaningful consultation and collaboration with tribal officials, the federal government, in 2009, issued a presidential memo calling on all heads of its executive departments and agencies to diligently honor the provisions of Executive Order 13175.[83] Subsequently, in 2010, the U.S. government also endorsed the UNDRIP, after abstaining from voting to support this landmark international instrument on indigenous rights protection since its adoption by the UN General Assembly in 2007.[84]

Additionally, in accordance with federal Indian law in the United States, Native American tribes also possess inherent sovereign self-governing power over tribal lands.[85] This power allows the tribes to play a significant role in the affairs of their territories, including the control and management of the natural resources found on tribal lands.[86] In contrast to the .situation of indigenous groups in Africa and Latin America, this inherent self-governing power put Native American tribes in a much better position to protect their right to consultation, and prevent unnecessary infraction of the right by both the government and corporate entities.[87]

Canada

In Canada, however, the foundational basis for the duty to consult with the Canadian First Nations is grounded both in law and equity.[88] That is, on one hand, it arises out of a trust-like relationship between the Crown (Canadian federal and provincial governments) and the First Nations. And on the other hand, it enjoys protection under the Canadian Constitution.[89] As the Supreme Court of Canada (SCC) explained in *Guerin v. The Queen*, the nature of the aboriginal title of First Nations, which is founded on historical occupation, imposes an enforceable fiduciary duty upon the Crown.[90]

The breadth of the consultation rights possessed by the First Nations in Canada was further highlighted by Lambert J. A. of Canada's Court of Appeal for British Columbia, when, in the case of *Haida Nation I,*[91] he stated that the fountainhead of the obligation to consult in Canada is the trust-like relationship which exists between the Crown and the Aboriginal people of Canada, and that such consultation duty is an enforceable legal and equitable one.[92]

The consultation right of the First Nations was accorded constitutional protection pursuant to Section 35 of the Constitution Act of Canada, which guaranteed their aboriginal and treaty rights.[93] The Canadian Constitution recognized, and affirmed, all existing aboriginal and treaty rights of the Aboriginal peoples of Canada.[94] Thus, in situations where the possibilities exist that the rights of any of the First Nations may be infringed, the government is duty-bound to consult with the affected groups.[95] Interestingly, the Canadian Constitution fully secures the right of any group claiming First Nation status. That is, the legal and fiduciary duty owed by the Crown arises whether or not the aboriginal group to be impacted has successfully proven the existence of their aboriginal or treaty right to the satisfaction of a judge of competent jurisdiction.[96] As pointed out by Lambert J. A in *Haida Nation I*:

> The manifestation of the fiduciary duty of the Crown to the aboriginal peoples is that it grounds a general guiding principle for s. 35(1) of the Constitution Act, 1982. It would be contrary to that guiding principle to interpret section 35(1) as if it required that before an aboriginal right could be recognized and affirmed, it first had to be made the subject matter of legal proceedings; then proved to the satisfaction of a judge of competent jurisdiction; and finally made the subject of a declaratory or other order of the court. That is not what section 35(1) says and it would be contrary to the guiding principles of section 35(1), as set out in R. v Sparrow (1990) 1 SCR 1075, to give it that interpretation.[97]

Clearly, in Canada, the duty to consult is principally imposed upon the Canadian government and its agencies. However, in appropriate circumstances, third parties, such as private corporate entities, may also incur the obligation to consult, especially in cases where the government has outsourced its own duty to consult to the private sector, or where a corporate

entity facilitates a breach of the duty to consult. In *Haida Nation I*,[98] the Court
of Appeal for British Columbia concluded that both the Crown and Weyer-
haeuser Company Limited had an obligation to consult the *Haida* people.[99]
The practical implication here is that even though the duty to consult is
incumbent upon the Crown, a private company could be liable for the breach
of the duty owed by the Crown to consult with First Nations, if the private
company had actual or constructive knowledge that the Crown is in breach
of its duty to consult, and the company assisted in perpetrating the breach.[100]
The Canadian Supreme Court, in the subsequent *Haida Nation II*[101] case,
therefore, emphasized that

> the fact that third parties are under no duty to consult or accommodate Aborigi-
> nal concerns does not mean that they can never be liable to Aboriginal peoples.
> If they act negligently in circumstances where they owe Aboriginal peoples a
> duty of care, or if they breach contracts with Aboriginal peoples or deal with
> them dishonestly, they may be held legally liable.[102]

Peculiarly, in the Canadian context, the right to consultation is not a preeminent tool, but one of the tools available to indigenous peoples in that
country for protecting their collective rights.[103] The reason for this is that,
unlike other jurisdictions, consultation, in the sense used under Canadian
jurisprudence, is not particularly designed to accomplish the FPIC standards,
but essentially to ensure that the interests of the First Nations are accommo-
dated.[104] In other words, it neither creates a duty incumbent upon the Crown
to simply accept demands made by the First Nations nor does it confer a right
on the First Nations to veto the actions of the Crown.[105] The duty here mainly
requires that the consultation be *adequate* and *sufficient* enough to support
any infringement by the Crown on aboriginal rights. Oftentimes, judicial contest becomes the common means of determining the adequacy or sufficiency
of any consultation conducted by the Crown and to enforce this duty.[106]

Australia

The legal basis for the protection of consultation rights of Aboriginal and
Torres Strait Islanders under the Australian system is somewhat interlaced.
This is because there are no direct constitutional protections for aboriginal
rights in general or right to consultation specifically.[107] Broadly speaking,
existing regulatory frameworks that protect indigenous people's rights in that
country are largely based on common law,[108] federal legislation, and laws
of the States and Territories.[109] The Common law foundation for aboriginal
rights in Australia has been unequivocally validated by the 1992 decision of
the High Court of Australia in *Mabo v. Queensland,* where the Court ruled

that the land title of the Aborigines and Torres Strait Islanders is valid and recognized at common law on the basis of concept of native title, and determined by traditional connection to, or occupation of, the land.[110]

Until 1976 when the Aboriginal Land Rights (Northern Territory) Act was enacted, no substantive legislation existed in that jurisdiction to protect the rights of Aboriginal and Torres Strait Islander peoples.[111] The Act was significant in many respects because it marked the first attempt by any tier of government in Australia to formally acknowledge the aboriginal system and the collective traditional association of the indigenous people in that country to their land by way of legislation.[112]

About two decades later, the Native Title Act,[113] another highly important piece of legislation in terms of aboriginal rights, was also enacted.[114] The Native Title Act calls for a notice to be served on aboriginal communities that may be impacted if any action relating to aboriginal lands or where mining of natural resources is being proposed by the national, State, or Territory authorities.[115] In order for such notice to be considered valid, it must contain sufficient details and should be addressed to any registered native title body corporate, registered native title claimants, or any representative Aboriginal or Torres Strait Islander traditional body that may be affected by the proposed action.[116]

A critical feature of the two legislations highlighted above is that they both conferred the right to be consulted on Aboriginal Australians. The consultation privileges created under these legislations guarantee the right of Aboriginal Australians to participate in the decision-making process concerning activities proposed to be undertaken on aboriginal lands and waters.[117] Unlike the situation in Canada, the scope of the right to consultation in Australia includes the right to say yes or no to the implementation of certain projects.[118] For instance, in accordance with Aboriginal Land Rights (Northern Territory) Act, the Australian government may not issue a permit or license to private persons or corporate entities for the purpose of extracting any natural resources on aboriginal lands unilaterally.[119]

More importantly, such permit or license can only be issued if the express consent of the *Land Council* for the area in which the land is situated was first sought and obtained, and the extractive project proponent has entered into an agreement (Indigenous Land Use Agreement) with the *Land Council* regarding the terms and conditions upon which the license will be granted.[120] Once the Indigenous Land Use Agreement containing the terms upon which the consent of *Land Council* was granted, has been registered, it immediately becomes binding on all the parties, including corporate entities.[121]

It is apparent from discussion throughout this chapter that while the international norms concerning the implementation of consultation with *indigenous peoples* before taking any action that affects them is well defined, its scope and operational scheme varies depending on the interplay of multiple factors existing at the regional and national levels. The various flaws and strengths highlighted throughout this chapter, in terms of how best to realize the objectives of consultation, demonstrate that challenges still abound, and a picture-perfect situation may not exist yet. However, the issues and cases discussed here may provide a good starting point for evaluating the flaws and limitations in national policies on consultation in other to improve such policies, and for establishing a mechanism to safeguard the areas of strength.

NOTES

1. See, for example, Constitution of the Republic of South Africa, Act No.108 of 1996, Chapter 2, particularly sections 32, 31, 25, 24, 19 and 16; Constitution of the Republic of Ghana 1992, sections 18, 20, 21, 38 (7)(8) & (9), and 37(2); Constitution of the Republic of Uganda 1995, sections 32, 36, 39, 41, 26, and 29. See, further, the African Charter of Human and Peoples Rights (1981), art. 13(1)—which states that "every citizen shall have the right to participate freely in the government of his country, either directly or through freely chosen representatives in accordance with the provisions of the law."

2. See the Constitution of Eritrea, 1997, Article 7(1).

3. See the Constitution of the Federal Republic of Nigeria, 1999, section 14(2) (c). But curiously, provisions contained under section 14 of the Nigerian Constitution form part of the *Fundamental Objectives and Directive Principles of State Policy*. In effect, all provisions included under that heading are largely not legally enforceable in Nigeria's courts.

4. See *Bogosi* Act of Republic of Botswana, 2008, section 3.

5. See *Id. Bogosi* Act (2008), sections 2,4,5, and 17–20.

6. See *Id. Bogosi* Act (2008), sections 2,4, and 5.

7. See *Id. Bogosi* Act (2008), sections 2,4,5 and 17–20. See also Constitution of Botswana (1966), particularly section 88(2), which allows for some form of consultation with tribal chiefs (House of Chiefs) before the enactment of any law that may affect tribal organization or tribal property. See further, *Report of the Special Rapporteur on the Situation of Human Rights and Fundamental Freedoms of Indigenous People*, James Anaya, Addendum on the Situation of Indigenous Peoples in Botswana, A/HRC/15/37/Add.2, June 2, 2010.

8. See generally, *Report of the Special Rapporteur on the Rights of Indigenous Peoples, James Anaya – Extractive Industries and Indigenous Peoples – A/HRC//24/41*, July 1, 2013.

9. See generally, *Report of the African Commission's Working Group of Expert on Indigenous Population/Communities*, adopted by the African Commission on Human and Peoples' Rights at its 28th ordinary session, 2005; Naomi Kipuri, The UN Declaration on the Rights of Indigenous Peoples in the African Context, cited in Claire Charters and Rodolfo Stavenhagen (eds.), *Making the Declaration Work: The United Nations Declaration on the Rights of Indigenous Peoples* (IWGIA, 2009).

10. See, for example, *Overview of State Ownership in the Global Minerals Industry: Long Term Trends and Future*, Extractive Industries for Development Series #20 (Raw Materials Group, World Bank, May 2011), p.15; Theodore Okonkwo, Ownership and Control of Natural Resources under the Nigerian Constitution 1999 and Its Implications for Environmental Law and Practice, *International Law Research*, Vol. 6, No. 1 (2017), Canadian Center of Science and Education. See also *Id.* Report of the African Commission's Working Group of Expert (28th ordinary session, 2005).

11. See S. James Anaya, International Human Rights and Indigenous Peoples: The Move Toward the Multicultural State, *Arizona Journal of International and Comparative Law*, Vol. 21 (2004), p. 13, at 35. See also George Mukundi Wachira, Indigenous Peoples' Rights to Land and Natural Resources, in Solomon Dersso (ed.), *Perspectives on the Rights of Minorities and Indigenous Peoples in Africa* (Pretoria University Law Press, 2010), p. 297.

12. See *Id. Report of the Special Rapporteur*, James Anaya (A/HRC//24/41 – 2013), para 49. It is, however, noted that the concept of State ownership of natural resources is common in Africa, although not completely typical of the continent. The Mining Law of Ecuador, Constitution of Peru (article 66), Constitution of Venezuela, as well as the Chinese Constitution have all vested the right to minerals and other natural resources upon the States. These provisions may, however, be contrasted with those of the United States and Canada, which appear to allow either private ownership or a form of qualified ownership by the state, or perhaps a kind of arrangement that leaves the control and benefits of the natural resources to be determined at the level of the constituent provinces. See, for example, The Indian Mineral Leasing Act of 1938 (25 USC 396a–g); Energy Policy Act of 1992 (42 U.S.C. § 13201); and Nicholas Haysom and Sean Kane, *Negotiating Natural Resources for Peace: Ownership, Control and Wealth-sharing* (Centre for Humanitarian Dialogue, October 2009), pp.8 and 10. But See Constitution of the Republic of Namibia (1990), which article 100 also seems to accommodate very limited private ownership of natural resources as property.

13. See John Ghazvinian, *Untapped: The Scramble for Africa's Oil* (Harcourt Books, 2007).

14. See Statement by Alfred Ilenre, human rights activist and leader of the Ethnic and Minority Rights Organization of Africa (EMIROAF), in *Id.*, John Ghazvinian, *Untapped* (2007), p. 70.

15. See the Minerals and Mining Act (2006), Act 703 of Republic of Ghana, article 1.

16. See *Id.* the Minerals and Mining Act (Ghana, 2006), article 2.

17. See *Id.* the Minerals and Mining Act (Ghana, 2006), articles 2,4,9, and 10.

18. See Constitution of the Democratic Republic of Congo (2005), article 9.

19. See Mines and Minerals Act of Sierra Leone (2009), section 2.

20. See Constitution of the Republic of Liberia (1986), Article 22.

21. See Constitution of the Federal Republic of Nigeria, 1999, section 44(3).

22. See the Petroleum Act of 1969, Cap 350, Laws of the Federation of Nigeria (LFN) 1990.

23. See Nigerian Minerals and Mining Act 2007 (Act No. 20 of 2007). This Act No. 20 repeals the former Minerals and Mining Act (No. 34 of 1999) and re-enacts the

Nigerian Minerals and Mining Act, 2007 for the purposes of regulating all "Aspects of the Exploration and Exploitation of Solid Minerals in Nigeria."

24. See Constitution of the Federal Republic of Nigeria (1999).

25. See the Land Use Acts of 1978, Cap 202 Laws of the Federal Republic of Nigeria (LFN) 1990.

26. See *Id.*, the Petroleum Act (Cap 350 LFN, 1990), section 1(2). Note also that Nigeria's Land Use Act (1978), and other land holding legislations in the country exclude rights claimed by any persons or entity, to minerals or natural resources attached to a land or real estate, as a derivative of ownership.

27. See *Id.*, the Petroleum Act (Cap 350 LFN, 1990), section 1.

28. See *Id.*, Constitution of the Federal Republic of Nigeria (1999), section 44(3).

29. See *Id.,* Nigerian Minerals and Mining Act (2007).

30. See *Id.,* Nigerian Minerals and Mining Act (2007), section 1 (2).

31. See *Id.*, Land Use Acts of 1978 (Cap 202 LFN 1990), section 1.

32. See I.O. Smith, *Practical Approach to Law of Real Property in Nigeria* (Ecowatch Publications, 1999), p. 69. Nigeria's Land Use Act is not an isolated legislation—it appears to be parallel (in effects) to other national laws around the continent. For instance, the Tribal Territories Act (1933) and the Tribal Land Act (1968) in Botswana also merely allowed lands within tribal areas to be administered and held by tribes as *de facto* custodians, but does not vest any legal ownership rights in those tribes. See *Id., Report of the Special Rapporteur*, James Anaya (Botswana—A/HRC/15/37/Add.2—2010). See also Kwame Frimpong, The Administration of Tribal Lands in Botswana, *Journal of African Law*, Vol. 30, No. 1 (Spring, 1986), pp. 51–54.

33. See, generally, *Land, Oil and Human Rights in Nigeria's Delta Region* (CRP Publications, 1999).

34. See *Id. Land, Oil and Human Rights in Nigeria's Delta Region*, p.15.

35. There are a few examples of constitutions and laws in Africa that directly address the issues concerning protections for indigenous peoples. See, generally: Constitution of the Republic of Kenya 2010; Republic of Congo Law on the Promotion and Protection of Indigenous Populations, Act No. 5-2011 of February 25, 2011; Constitution of the Federal Democratic Republic of Ethiopia 1995; and Central African Republic (CAR) Ratification of ILO Convention No. 169. (30/08/2010)—Republique Centrafricaine, Instrument De Ratification, Autorisant La Ratification De La Convention De L'organization Internationale Du Travail Du Juin 27, 1989 Relative Aux Peuples Indigenes Et Tribaux.

36. See, for example, *Id., Report of the African Commission's Working Group of Expert* (28th ordinary session, 2005).

37. See Constitution of the Federal Democratic Republic of Ethiopia (1995).

38. See *Id.* Constitution of Ethiopia (1995), articles 39, 44, 92, and 93.

39. See, generally, Terri Hathaway, *Facing Gibe 3 Dam: Indigenous Communities of Ethiopia's Lower Omo Valley, Public Consultation Practices for the Gibe 3 Dam Project* (International Rivers, January 2009). See also Xan Rice, Ethiopia's Rush to Build Mega Dams Sparks Protests, *Guardian News UK*, Thursday, March 25, 2010; Peter Bosshard, How a Big Dam Fuels Land Grabs, Hunger and Conflict in Ethiopia, *Huffington Post*, September 12, 2011.

40. See *Report by the Special Rapporteur on the Rights of Indigenous Peoples*, James Anaya, A/HRC/18/35/Add.1, August 22, 2011, Annex IV [ETH 1/2011], paras 10–13.

41. See *Id., Report by the Special Rapporteur*, James Anaya A/HRC/18/35/ Add.1, Annex IV [ETH 1/2011], paras 12 and 13.

42. See, for example, Roberto Gargarella, Recent Constitutional Reforms in Latin America: A Preliminary Study, *Desarrollo Economico*, Vol. 36, No. 144 (January–March, 1997), 971–990. See also Roberto Gargarella, *Latin American Constitutionalism, 1810–2010: The Engine Room of the Constitution* (Oxford University Press, 2013).

43. See Christian Courtis, Notes on the Implementation by Latin American Countries of the ILO Convention 169 on Indigenous Peoples, *Sur – Revista Internacional de Direitos Humanos*, Vol. 6, No. 10 (Sao Paulo, June 2009).

44. See Constitution of the Republic of Ecuador 2008, chapters 4 and 5.

45. See Constitution of the Plurinational State of Bolivia 2009, article 30(15).

46. See Law on the Right of Consultation of Indigenous Peoples (Peru), L. 29785, EL PERUANO (E.P.) (September 7, 2011). Formally, Ley 29785 del Derecho a la Consulta Previa a los Pueblos Indígenas u Originiarios Reconocido en el Convenio 169 de la Organización Internacional delTrabajo (OIT), 2011.

47. See *Id.*, Law on the Right of Consultation of Indigenous Peoples (Peru-2011), articles 2, 4, 5, and 6.

48. See *Id.*, Law on the Right of Consultation of Indigenous Peoples (Peru-2011), articles 2, 4, 5, and 6.

49. As of July 12, 2019, twenty-three countries have ratified the ILO Convention No. 169. More than half of those countries are from Latin America, including Bolivia, Ecuador, Peru, and Nicaragua. Interestingly, the Central African Republic (CAR) is the sole African country on the ratification roll. See https://www.ilo.org/dyn/normle x/en/f?p=NORMLEXPUB:11300:0::NO::P11300_INSTRUMENT_ID:%20312314 (last accessed on July 12, 2019).

50. See, for example, Paul Gragl, *Legal Monism: Law, Philosophy, and Politics* (Oxford, 2018); and *Id.* Christian Courtis, *Notes on the implementation by Latin American countries of the ILO No. 169* (2009).

51. See *Id.*, Paul Gragl, *Legal Monism* (2018); and, *Id.* Christian Courtis, *Notes on the Implementation by Latin American Countries of the ILO No. 169* (2009), paras 3.1–3.2. See also, J.G. Starke, *Studies in International Law* (London: Butterworth, 1965), pp. 1–19.

52. See, for example, *Id.* Christian Courtis, *Notes on the Implementation by Latin American Countries of the ILO No. 169* (2009), paras 3.1–3.2.

53. See María Clara Galvis (ed.), *The Right of Indigenous Peoples to Prior Consultation: The Situation in Bolivia, Colombia, Ecuador, and Peru* (DPLF/Oxfam, 2011), p.3; and, *Id.* Christian Courtis, *Notes on the implementation by Latin American countries of the ILO No. 169* (2009), paras 3.1–3.2.

54. See *Id.* María Clara Galvis (ed.), *The Right of Indigenous Peoples to Prior Consultation* (2011), p.3.

55. See *Id.*, Constitution of the Republic of Ecuador 2008, articles 56–58.

56. See *Id.,* Constitution of the Republic of Ecuador 2008, article 57. See also, *Indigenous and Tribal Peoples' Rights Over Their Ancestral Lands and Natural Resources: Norms and Jurisprudence of the Inter-American Human Rights System,* IACHR, OEA/Ser.L/V/II.Doc. 56/09 30 (December 2009).

57. See the *Application of Convention No. 169 by Domestic and International Courts in Latin America: A Casebook* (ILO Programme, 2009), p.69.

58. See *U'wa Indigenous Community Case,* Constitutional Court of Colombia, Judgment SU-039/97, February 3, 1997.

59. See *Id. U'wa Indigenous Community Case* (1997). See further Constitutional Court of Bolivia—Constitutional Judgment 0045/2006, File 2005-12440-25-RDL, Judgment of June 2, 2006; and, *Id., Application of Convention No. 169 by Domestic and International Courts in Latin America* (2009), 69.

60. See Gonzalo Bustamante, The Right to Consultation and Free, Prior and Informed Consent in Latin America: The Governmentality of The Extraction of Natural Resources, *Québec Journal of International Law,* Special Issue (March 2015), p. 179. See also *Right to Free, Prior, and Informed Consultation and Consent in Latin America: Progress and Challenges in Bolivia, Brazil, Chile, Colombia, Guatemala, and Peru* (Due Process of Law Foundation, 2015).

61. See *Id. Right to Free, Prior, and Informed Consultation and Consent in Latin America.*

See *Id.,* Bustamante, *The Right to Consultation and Free, Prior and Informed Consent in Latin America*; and, *Id., Right to Free, Prior, and Informed Consultation and Consent in Latin America.*

62. See, for example, Article 7 of the 1854 Treaty made between the Peoria Tribe of Indians of Oklahoma and the U.S. federal government on May 30, 1854. See also *Peoria Tribe of Oklahoma v United States,* 390 U.S. 468, 88 S.Ct. 1137, 20 L.Ed.2d 39 (1968). See, further, Phillip M. Kannan, Reinstating Treaty-Making with Native American Tribes, William & Mary Bill of Rights *Journal* Vol. 16 (2008), p. 809; Arthur Spirling, US Treaty-making with American Indians: Institutional Change and Relative Power, 1784–1911, *American Journal of Political Science,* Vol. 56, No. 1 (January 2012), pp. 84–97; and Felix Cohen, *Cohen's Handbook of Federal Indian Law* (Lexis-Nexis, 2005).

63. See, for example, Janice Aitken, The Trust Doctrine in Federal Indian Law: A Look at Its Development and at How Its Analysis Under Social Contract Theory Might Expand Its Scope, *Northern Illinois University Law Review,* Vol. 18 (1997), p. 115.

64. See, for example, National Environmental Policy Act (NEPA), 42 U.S.C. §§ 4321 et seq. (2006); and, Federal Historic Preservation Regulations, 36 C.F.R. Part 800 (2008).

65. One of the most famous of these types of Orders was that issued following the landmark meeting between President Bill Clinton and representatives of Tribal governments at the White House on April 29, 1995. See Executive Order 13175 of November 6, 2000: "Consultation and Coordination with Indian Tribal Governments," *US Federal Register,* Vol. 65, No. 218, Thursday, November 9, 2000.

66. See *Id.,* Phillip M. Kannan, *Reinstating Treaty-Making with Native American Tribes.* See also, *Morton v. Mancari,* 417 U.S. 535 (1974).

67. See *Cherokee Nation v. Journeycake*, 155 U.S. 196 (1894).

68. See, for example, Galanda, *The Federal Indian Consultation Right: A Front-line Defense Against Tribal Sovereignty Incursion*, Government Affairs Practice Committee Newsletter (ABA, Winter 2010–2011, Vol. 1).

69. See *Id.*, Galanda, *The Federal Indian Consultation Right*, Vol. 1. See also Colette Routel and Jeffrey Holth, Toward Genuine Tribal Consultation in the 21st Century, University of Michigan Journal of Law Reform, Vol. 46 (2013), p. 417. See also *Id.*, Janice Aitken, The Trust Doctrine in Federal Indian Law.

70. See *Johnson v McIntosh*, 21 U.S. (8 Wheat.) 543 (1823).

71. See *Cherokee Nation v. Georgia*, 30 U.S. (5 Pet.) 1 (1831).

72. See *Worcester v Georgia*, 31 U.S. (6 Pet.) 515 (1832).

73. See, further, David Getches, Charles Wilkinson, Robert Williams, Matthew Fletcher, and Kristen Carpenter, *Cases and Materials on Federal Indian Law*, 7th Ed. American Casebook Series (West Academic, 2016).

74. See for example *Jicarilla Apache Tribe v Supron Energy Corp.*, 782 F.2d 855 (10th Cir. 1986). The court concluded that the U.S. government owed fiduciary duty to tribes in administering tribal oil and gas reserves, and in determining what royalties the tribe is owed. See also *United States v Mitchell* (Mitchell II) 463 U.S. 206, 218 (1983).

75. See 25 U.S.C. §§ 3001–3013. (2006).

76. See NHPA of 1966 as amended (2000), 16 U.S.C. §§ 470a et seq.

77. See Federal Historic Preservation Regulations, 36 C.F.R. Part 800 (2008).

78. See 42 U.S.C. §§ 4321 et seq. (2006).

79. See, generally, Walter E. Stern, *Developing Energy Projects on Federal Lands: Tribal Rights, Roles, Consultation, and Other Interests – A Developer's Perspective*, Rocky Mountain Mineral Law Foundation's Special Institute on Energy Development, Paper No. 15A (2009).

80. See Executive Order 13007 of May 24, 1996, U.S. Federal Register, Vol. 61, No. 104, Wednesday, May 29, 1996.

81. See Executive Order 13175 of November 6, 2000, *U.S. Federal Register*, Vol. 65, No. 218, Thursday, November 9, 2000.

82. See *Id.*, Executive Order 13175 (November 2000), preamble. Section 5 of this Executive Order further provides that each agency shall put in place an accountability process to ensure meaningful and timely input by tribal officials in the development of regulatory policies that have tribal implications. *Id.*

83. See Memorandum for the Heads of Executive Departments and Agencies, of November 5, 2009, Federal Register, Vol. 74, No. 215, Monday, November 9, 2009. In carrying out the instructions of Executive Order 13175, the U.S. Department of Interior issued a new Comprehensive Tribal Consultation Policy framework, which provides a greater role for tribes in federal decisions affecting Indian Country. See U.S. Department of Interior Order No. 3317: Department of Interior Policy on Consultation with Indian Tribes, December 1, 2011.

84. See U.S. Department of State, Announcement of U.S. Support for the United Nations Declaration on the Rights of Indigenous Peoples, January 12, 2011. Available at https://2009-2017.state.gov/documents/organization/154782.pdf (last accessed on 05/05/2019).

85. See, generally, *Id.*, Stern, *Developing Energy Projects on Federal Lands*; and, *Id.*, *Jicarilla Apache Tribe v Supron Energy Corp.* (1986).

86. See, for example,, The Indian Mineral Leasing Act of 1938 (25 USC 396a–g); and Energy Policy Act of 1992 (42 U.S.C. § 13201). Section 2604 directs that "the Secretary of the Interior is authorized to make annual grants to Indian tribes for the purpose of assisting Indian tribes in the development, administration, implementation, and enforcement of tribal laws and regulations governing the development of energy resources on Indian reservations."

87. See, for example, *Id. Jicarilla Apache Tribe v Supron Energy Corp.* (1986).

See further Mark Allen, Native American Control of Tribal Natural Resource Development in the Context of the Federal Trust and Tribal Self-Determination, *Boston College Environmental Affairs Law Review, Vol16* (1989), *p.* 857; S. James Anaya and Robert A. Williams, Jr., The Protection of Indigenous Peoples' Rights over Lands and Natural Resources Under the Inter-American Human Rights System, *Harvard Law School Human Rights Journal* Vol. 14 (2001), p. 33.

88. See, for example, Supreme Court of Canada (SCC) in *Guerin v The Queen*, [1984] 2 S.C.R. 335.

89. See the Constitution Act of Canada, 1982, section 35.

90. See *Id.*, *Guerin v The Queen* (1984). The SCC added that it is an inherent right that existed prior to the Royal Proclamation of 1763, and properly founded upon historical occupation. *Id.*

91. See *Haida Nation v. British Columbia–Ministry of Forests* (Haida Nation I), [2002] 6 W.W.R. 243.

92. See *Id.*, Haida Nation I (2002), paras 33, at 256 and 262. See further, *Taku River Tlingit First Nation v British Columbia* (Project Assessment Director), 2004 SCC 74, [2004] 3 SCR 550; and, *Mikisew Cree First Nation v Canada* (Minister of Canadian Heritage), 2005 SCC 69, [2005] 3 SCR 388.

93. The written Constitution is composed of the British North America Act of 1867, the Statute of Westminster of 1931 (to the extent that it applies to Canada), the Canada Act of 1982, and the Constitution Act of 1982. But See the Constitution Act, 1982, being Schedule B to the Canada Act 1982 (UK), 1982, c 11.

94. See *Id.* the Constitution Act of Canada, 1982, sections 35(1)–(4).

95. Consultation in the sense used under Canadian jurisprudence is not particularly designed to achieve free prior and informed consent (FPIC). That is, it is neither a duty to agree, nor does it confer on First Nations a right of veto. But mainly requires that the consultation be adequate and sufficient enough to support any infringement by the Crown on aboriginal rights. Oftentimes, judicial contest or litigation is the common means of determining the adequacy or sufficiency of the consultation provided by the Crown. See, generally, Thomas Isaac and Anthony Knox, The Crown's Duty to Consult Aboriginal People, *Alberta Law Review*, Vol. 41 (2003–2004), p. 49.

96. See *Id.*, *Haida Nation I* (2002), paras 36 and 37. See also *Taku River Tlingit First Nation v Tulsequah Chief Mine Project* (2002) 4 W.W.R. 19.

97. See *Id.*, *Haida Nation I* (2002), paras 36 and 37, per Lambert J. A.

98. See *Id.*, *Haida Nation I* (2002), para 48.

99. See *Id.*, *Haida Nation I* (2002), para 48.

100. See *Id., Haida Nation I* (2002), paras 48, and 54–55.

101. See *Haida Nation v British Columbia—Minister of Forests* (Haida Nation II) (2004) 3 S.C.R. 511, 2004 SCC 73. The Court in *Haida Nation II* established a test to determine the situation where the duty to consult would arise. They are, inter alia (1) the Crown's real or constructive knowledge of a potential aboriginal claim or right; (2) contemplated Crown conduct; and (3) the potential that the contemplated conduct may adversely affect an aboriginal claim or right. *Id.*

102. See *Id., Haida Nation II* (2004), para 56.

103. See *Rio Tinto Alcan v Carrier Sekani Tribal Council*, 2010 SCC 43, [2010] 2 SCR 650, para 46; and, *Upper Nicola Indian Band v British Columbia (Environment)*, 2011 BCSC 388, [2011] 2 CNLR 348, paras 121–125.

104. See generally *Id., Haida Nation I* (2002); and, *Id., Haida Nation II* (2004).

105. See *Id., Haida Nation II* (2004), para 48.

106. See generally, Isaac and Knox, The Crown's Duty to Consult Aboriginal People,; and, Chris Sanderson, Keith Bergner, and Michelle Jones, The Crown's Duty to Consult Aboriginal Peoples: Towards an Understanding of The Source, Purpose, and Limits of the Duty, *Alberta Law Review*, Vol. 49, No. 4 (2012), p. 821.

107. See, for example, The Australian Constitution, 1900 (An Act to constitute the Commonwealth of Australia [July 9, 1900]). See also, generally, *Report by the Special Rapporteur on the Situation of Human Rights and Fundamental Freedoms of Indigenous People: Situation of Indigenous Peoples in Australia*, James Anaya, A/HRC/15/37/Add.4, June 1, 2010.

108. See *Mabo v Queensland* (No. 2) (1992), 175 CLR 1.

109. See, for example, Aboriginal Land Rights Act 1983 (New South Wales); Anangu Pitjantjatjara Yankunytjatjara Land Rights Act, 1981; Aboriginal Land Act, 1991; the Torres Strait Islander Land Act, 1991; and The Mineral Resources Act, 1989 (Queensland). See also, *Id., Report by the Special Rapporteur*, James Anaya—Australia (A/HRC/15/37/Add.4, 1 - 2010).

110. See *Id., Mabo v Queensland* (1992), paras 120, 121, and 129.

111. See Aboriginal Land Rights (Northern Territory) Act of 1976 (No. 191, 1976).

112. As the long title of the Act suggests, "An Act providing for the granting of Traditional Aboriginal Land in the Northern Territory for the benefit of Aboriginals, and for other purposes." See further, *Id.* Aboriginal Land Rights (Northern Territory) Act, 1976, part II.

113. See Native Title Act 1993, Act No. 110 of 1993 as amended.

114. This particular Act was passed in response to the decision in *Id. Mabo v Queensland*. It was an attempt to establish a framework for the protection and recognition of native title. The legislation entered into force on January 1, 1994.

115. See *Id.* Native Title Act 1993, part 1(3) and (4), Part 2, Division 2, sub-div. B 22EA, sub-div. C 22H.

116. See *Id.* Native Title Act 1993, part 1(3) and (4), Part 2, Division 2, sub-div. B 22EA, sub-div. C 22H; Division 3, sub-div. A, 24AA and 24AB.

117. See, generally, *Id.* Aboriginal Land Rights (Northern Territory) Act, 1976, part IV.

118. See, *Id.* Aboriginal Land Rights (Northern Territory) Act, 1976, part IV, sections 41, 41A and 42.

119. See *Id.* Aboriginal Land Rights (Northern Territory) Act, 1976, part IV, section 40 (a).

120. See, *Id.* Aboriginal Land Rights (Northern Territory) Act, 1976, part IV, sections 40, 41, and 41A.

121. See *Id* Native Title Act 1993, part 2, Division 3, Sub-div. B.

Chapter 7

Corporate Responsibility to Consult and Dimensions of Implementation

PERCEPTIONS, PRACTICES, AND CORPORATE APPROACHES TO CONSULTATION

As noted in chapter 6, under the international indigenous rights framework, the legal duty to consult with *indigenous peoples* was allocated to States only.[1] Nevertheless, corporations bear a responsibility to respect human rights in general, in accordance with the human rights due diligence duty placed upon them under international law, especially pursuant to the "UN Protect, Respect, and Remedy" Framework.[2] However, this due diligence duty also requires that corporations avoid any violation of the consultation right of *indigenous peoples*, by ensuring that they conduct good faith consultation with indigenous groups who may be impacted by their operational activities.[3] That is, corporations have a particular responsibility to respect the human rights of *indigenous peoples*, including their consultation right. As James Anaya put it:

Independent of States' basic responsibility to consult with indigenous peoples prior to the implementation of measures affecting them, and the assumption that States alone should perform that task, companies also bear a responsibility to respect indigenous peoples' right to participate in decisions with regard to such measures, including through the holding of consultations to keep them informed. Such consultations are particularly important in connection with impact studies, compensation measures and benefit sharing.[4]

Great challenges still lie ahead, in terms of ensuring that corporate operational conduct fully respects the consultation right of *indigenous peoples*. It is, however, worth noting that corporations are gradually embracing the importance of incorporating the practice of good faith consultation as a key component of their human rights' due diligence compliance protocol.[5] Some companies have even taken steps to develop formal internal policies on how best to fulfill their consultation responsibility. [6]

According to scholars, beyond the requirement of the human rights due diligence duty, a central goal of any corporate operational policy should be to engage with the host communities as stakeholders, and to do so at the earliest opportunity.[7] The rationale used to justify this viewpoint is that it is economically expedient for corporations over the long term, in relation to their bottom line, if the core component of any corporate social responsibility approach that they implement is defined by good faith engagement with those stakeholders that may be impacted by the corporations' business operations.[8]

Except for the legal obligation allotted to States under international law, the human rights due diligence duty owed by corporations does not impose a legally binding obligation. Corporate human rights due diligence duty, as considered here, largely evolved as an ethical, or, at best, a moral construct.[9] Certainly, the successful articulation of the human rights' due diligence duty clearly marked an important step, at the global level, towards ensuring that corporations conform with international human rights norms. Nonetheless, it is difficult to reconcile the current non-binding nature of the human rights due diligence duty to consult placed on corporations, in view of the broad consensus among indigenous scholars and advocates about the essentiality of the consultation right to the fulfillment of all other types of indigenous peoples rights.[10] This is especially challenging in this modern era, where corporate activities, evidently, affect the socio-cultural and economic well-being of the society as much as State actions. Whereas, under the prevailing situation, the legal burden to respect this critical indigenous right to consultation was not pragmatically imposed on all of the potential violators, whether States or corporate entities.

Another challenging obstacle impeding efforts to protect the consultation right of indigenous peoples, especially in developing countries, is the misperception of consultation as a concept, in a way to suggest that its centerpiece is mere *information*. To this extent, the way in which the substance and the scope of consultation are perceived in these parts of the world does not adequately reflect the global normative standards[11] as articulated by UNDRIP[12] and ILO Convention No. 169.[13] Against this background, the fact that many African countries brushed off the idea that certain groups claiming to be *indigenous* within their jurisdictions deserve special protection under the rubric of indigenous rights contributed both to the disregard for indigenous people's rights generally, and particularly, the treatment of the right to consultation as if less consequential than as conceived under UNDRIP and ILO Convention No. 169.[14]

Besides, in many developing countries where the concept of State owner-ship of lands or natural resources are prevalent, those lands and the natural resources therein are treated as national property, irrespective of claims by indigenous groups who use and occupy these lands.[15] As a result, the con-cerned indigenous groups are often viewed as undeserving of a prior consul-tation right, and even if consultation occurs, the nature of such consultation process is substandard and typically not meant to align with the principle of free, prior, and informed consent (FPIC) as required by the ILO Convention No. 162 and UNDRIP. Rather, such consultations are commonly carried out to serve the purpose of notification to the indigenous people concerned about an impending project. Oftentimes, this is done in accordance with a predetermined goal to ensure the project's advancement.[16] In practice, any consultation conducted in this sense is usually not meant to seek consensual agreement as to whether or not the project can safely be implemented in a way respectful of the peoples' rights.[17] Contrastingly, the fundamental fea-tures of the right to consultation as envisaged under Articles 18 and 19 of UNDRIP, and Articles 6 and 7 of ILO Convention No. 169, was to signal to all relevant parties, including corporate investors, governmental agencies, and the impacted territories, that the *indigenous peoples* concerned have rights and interests that should be protected in the process of implementing projects or developmental measures.[18]

An understanding of the various challenges highlighted above, along with a clear-sighted view of how States' actions impel corporate responsibility, is pertinent, in terms of evaluating corporate approaches to consultation, and their effectiveness. This is because, in many of the cases where breaches of indigenous peoples' human rights or right to consultation occur, and there is corporate complicity, such corporations frequently walk in the shadow of governments and their agencies, either through active collaboration, acquies-cence, or inaction.[19]

In Nigeria, for example, the Department of Petroleum Services (DPR), which is the regulatory body vested with the power to supervise all petroleum extraction operations in the country,[20] mainly requires a public notification of the environmental impact assessment (EIA) regarding any proposed oil extraction project impacting local communities.[21] The public notice about the EIA report is often perceived as adequate fulfillment of community engage-ment needs. Thus, notification, not good faith consultation, appears to be the main requirement prescribed by the DPR prior to the issuance of a pros-pecting or mining license to corporations intending to engage in operational activities that may impact indigenous communities.[22] This particular require-ment is conceived, in many respects, as an informational process rather than a deliberative and consultative one. The DPR guidelines fail to incorporate the principle of FPIC,[23] in keeping with international standards on consultation, as the basis upon which engagement with the impacted community should be conducted.[24]

In addition to that, once an exploration license has been validly granted by the Nigerian regulatory authority, the benefiting corporate entity, as the licensee, generally becomes vested with the power to gain extensive access to the host communities' lands, without having any compelling legal obligation to consult with those communities for the purpose of entering upon their lands.[25] Typically, pursuant to the grant of an oil exploration license, a supplementary license to engage in the establishment and maintenance of pipelines and other activities incidental to the exploration will also accompany the grant.[26] The applicable law in Nigeria explicitly confers upon the licensee the right to enter on any land along the route specified in the permit or reasonably close to such route in order to

> survey and take levels of the land; to dig and bore into the soil and subsoil; to cut and remove such trees and other vegetation as may impede the purposes specified in this subsection; and to do all other acts necessary to ascertain the suitability of establishment of an oil pipeline or ancillary installations.[27]

It is evident from the above provision that a corporation acting pursuant to a license grant, may, without obligation to conduct meaningful consultation with the affected host community, direct its officers, agents, servants, or equipment to enter lands specified in the license, including adjacent lands, to the extent necessary or convenient for the purpose of obtaining access to the areas specified in the license.[28]

A better depiction of the problem associated with the misperception about the essence of consultation can be deduced from the observation of James Anaya, former UN Special Rapporteur on the Rights of Indigenous Peoples.[29] During Anaya's visit to Botswana in March of 2009, representatives of the government of Botswana maintained that consultation with the various local communities in relation to decisions affecting those communities was adopted as a key planning principle of the government.[30]

However, independent reports gathered by Anaya during a field trip to impacted communities contradicted the assertion made by the government. It quickly became apparent that the government had a different understanding of the nature of the consultation right that is due to the communities. In one of the accounts relating to a Wildlife Management project implemented by the government at the time, the *indigenous people* in *Mababe* village, which is located in the North-West District of Botswana, disclosed that they were simply informed of the decision by the government to subject their traditional lands to the restrictive regime of the Wildlife Management Areas scheme without being allowed to take part in the decision-making process.[31]

This particular Wildlife Management project significantly constrained the rights of the villagers, by limiting how they use their natural resources, including requiring them to seek special permits from the government in order to hunt for games in the forest. In his evaluation of the situation between the members of the *Mababe* village and governmental authorities in Botswana, Anaya observed that

> the sentiment repeatedly expressed was that decisions are made by the government at the national or district levels and that *Kgotla* [public community meetings] or other local community processes are usually at best opportunities to comment on development planning with little real influence in outcomes of that planning.[32]

The foregoing observation clearly demonstrates that the government of Botswana's understanding of the nature and scope of consultation is at variance with existing internationally recognized standards. As Anaya articulated in a different report:

> Under relevant international standards, consultations should involve a genuine opportunity for indigenous peoples to present their views and to influence decision-making, and the option of not proceeding with the proposed project should not be foreclosed during these consultations.[33]

The problem associated with the misconstruction of consultation right was similarly highlighted by Victoria Tauli-Corpuz, the Special Rapporteur on the Rights of Indigenous Peoples, in her recent address during the 39th Session of Human Rights Council:

> A common pattern is that large-scale projects are frequently undertaken without consulting the indigenous peoples concerned, nor is their free, prior and informed consent sought. When measures have been undertaken to consult with indigenous peoples, these have often been culturally inappropriate, lacked good faith and been driven primarily by an incentive to have already elaborated projects rubber-stamped, with no intention of allowing for genuine review or participation in their design and execution.[34]

The consequence of the misperceptions and common practices highlighted above, especially on the part of governmental authorities, is that it influences corporate attitudes inversely. Over the years, corporations have tended to view consultation as a kind of excessive demand by *indigenous peoples*, as opposed to a substantive right that is of fundamental importance to all indigenous groups. Corporations appear to treat demand for implementation of meaningful consultation, along with its core principle of FPIC, as an unnecessary burden that should be carried out, largely, as a matter of courtesy, rather than as a crucial process meant to safeguard the collective rights of those indigenous communities who may be impacted by corporate projects.[35]

RIGHT TO CONSULTATION AND THE
PROBLEM OF AMALGAMATED INTERESTS

No doubt, in today's modern interconnected society, corporate operational activities have a significant impact on our communities as much as governmental actions. It is interesting to note that those corporate projects which oftentimes affect the rights and interests of *indigenous peoples*, and which form the basis for the violation of their prior consultation privilege, are usually carried on either to further the economic development agenda of governments, or are simply a joint commercial pursuit between private corporations and States.[36] Put differently, under this kind of situation, a convergence of interests defines the relationship between the States and corporations, especially in developing countries, evolving from the melding of States' desires for economic development with the large reserves of financial capital and influence possessed by corporations.

The ramifications of this convergence of interests were well illustrated in the cases of *Sarei v. Rio Tinto PLC*,[37] *Bowoto v ChevronTexaco*,[38] and the *Wiwa v Royal Dutch Petroleum* trilogy.[39] In the *Sarei* Case, members of the Bougainville communities, an island province in Papua New Guinea (PNG) filed a lawsuit against Rio Tinto, a multinational mining corporation with a global office in the United Kingdom. This case concerned a copper mine operated by the company in the Bougainville's village of Panguna under a joint enterprise with the PNG government.[40] The plaintiffs alleged that Rio Tinto, in collaboration with the PNG government, harmed their health and environment, engaged in racial discrimination, and committed serious human rights violations against the communities.[41] A protest organized by members of the communities to oppose Rio Tinto's practices eventually turned violent. According to the allegations, Rio Tinto induced the PNG government to suppress the protest in order to keep business operations at the mine running.[42] The PNG government, at the behest of Rio Tinto, ultimately launched an attack on the communities, resulting in the destruction of properties, displacements, injuries, and several deaths.[43]

In the *Bowoto* case,[44] the complaints before the U.S. District Court of Northern California were that ChevronTexaco, operating through Chevron Nigeria Limited (CNL), acted in concert with the Nigerian military and police to plan, order, and carry out attacks on members of the local communities who had been protesting the company's environmental pollutions and human rights abuses within their territory.[45] The communities alleged that, during one of the protests at the *Parabe* oil platform, CNL prompted the Nigerian military and police to fire weapons at the crowd staging a protest around the oil platforms, and two protesters were killed as a result.[46] According to the allegations, CNL's helicopter, operated by the company's pilots, transported members of the Nigerian military and police forces across the communities of *Opia* and *Ikenyan* where they opened fire on the villagers.[47] It was further alleged that, in a subsequent but coordinated attack, CNL sea trucks also ferried company personnel and members of the Nigerian military and police during an assault on these communities, which caused the destruction of many village settlements, and deaths of several villagers and livestock.[48]

Similarly, in the *Wiwa* cases,[49] Royal Dutch Petroleum, its Nigerian subsidiary Shell Petroleum Development Company Nigeria Limited (SPDC), and Brian Anderson, the then head of Shell operations in Nigeria, were accused by members of the Ogoni communities of being complicit in furthering human rights violations and crimes against humanity in Ogoniland, in a crisis which led to the execution of nine prominent leaders of the Ogoni people.[50] The complaints alleged that Shell had cultivated a close relationship with the Nigerian military regimes at the time, and had collaborated with those regimes by providing monetary and logistical support, in their efforts to use deadly force on the Ogoni people in order to suppress mounting outcry against the company's adverse extractive project.[51] After a series of protracted litigations in various U.S. courts, the company eventually settled with the plaintiffs, agreeing to pay compensation of about US$15.5 million.[52]

In other instances, the interests of State governments and corporations may not simply be in alignment; they can also be contractually fused. As an illustration, in *Sarei*, the Panguna copper mine in dispute was operated as a joint venture between Rio Tinto and the PNG government.[53] Rio Tinto had tendered 19.1 percent of the mine to the PNG government as a means to secure government assistance for the project.[54] Furthermore, in the *U'wa* case,[55] an action was filed by the U'wa indigenous community in northeastern Colombia against Columbia's Ministry of the Environment and Sociedad Occidental Del Colombia Inc., for the violation of the community's collective right to prior consultation regarding the Ministry's license permitting Sociedad Occidental to undertake hydrocarbon exploration activities with respect to *Bloque Samoré* project located within U'wa lands.[56]

The court in *U'wa* ultimately concluded that the government failed in its duty to engage in the process of prior consultation with the U'wa people, thereby violating the community's right to participation, including their right to sociocultural survival and economic integrity. An order which suspended the hydrocarbon exploration license was therefore entered by the court.[57]

What is notable in this case is that the *Bloque Samoré* project was a joint venture between Colombia's state-owned company, ECOPETROL, Occidental Petroleum, and Shell.[58] According to reports, Occidental, rather than implement good faith consultation, took advantage of the absence of a concrete governmental consultation process, by promoting discord and division within the U'wa community as a strategy to secure support for continuing the *Bloque Samoré* project.[59]

This kind of government-corporation contractual arrangement is not unusual. For instance, one of the biggest gemstone mining operations in the Republic of Botswana is owned by Debswana Diamond Company, a 50/50 joint venture between the government of Botswana and De Beers Group, a multinational corporation based in London.[60] Similarly, virtually all the major oil and gas exploration and production projects executed in Nigeria by private corporations have been carried on under a form of joint venture agreement or production sharing contracts between private corporations and the national government-owned Nigerian National Petroleum Corporation (NNPC).[61]

The situation highlighted above creates a perplexing challenge in terms of how to appropriately place consultation obligation. Currently, States are allotted the legal obligation to consult, but corporate entities that act as an extension of those State governments, at least in a commercial sense, are not under a legal obligation to consult. Corporations, especially big multinational companies, have tended to evaluate what level of consultation to engage in with indigenous communities based on the strength of the corporation's commercial alliance with State governments and agencies.

A call for a reevaluation of the degree of the duty owed by corporations to indigenous communities, who host corporate projects, is therefore not unreasonable. Particularly, considering the reality of this intricate government-corporation interconnection,[62] and the practice of abdication of the duty to consult by State governments prevalent in developing countries. The African Commission on Human and Peoples Rights confronted this dilemma in *SERAC v. Nigeria*,[63] when it concluded that the Nigerian government failed in its duty to consult by withholding information from the Ogoni communities about the dangers created by the oil exploration activities being conducted by Shell Petroleum Development Corporation (SPDC), an entity of which the Nigerian government, through the National Petroleum Corporation, holds more than 50 percent share as a joint venture partner.[64] The African Commission determined that the Nigerian government actively placed the legal and military powers of the State at the disposal of the SPDC, and in doing so condoned and actively facilitated the violations of the rights of the Ogoni people.[65]

Likewise, in the *Endorois* Case,[66] the government of Kenya granted concession to a private company, under an arrangement that is financially beneficial to the government, for ruby mining on Endorois people's traditional land, without adequate consultation with the communities.[67] The government of Kenya continued with the implementation of this mining project despite the clear request made by the African Commission to the president of Kenya to suspend the mining activities pending the outcome of the case brought by the communities.[68]

Similar conclusions, concerning abdication by governments of their duty to consult, were reached in the *Awas Tingni* Case,[69] and the case *of Maya Indigenous Community of the Toledo District v. Belize*.[70] Particularly, in *Awas Tingni*, one of the most important contemporary jurisprudential sources for international indigenous rights advocacy, the government of Nicaragua in 1995 granted a thirty-year logging concession to a Korean-owned company Sol de Caribe SA (SOLCARSA), without prior consultation. The government permitted the commercial exploitation of nearly 62,000 hectares (about 160,000 acres) of tropical forest belonging to the Awas Tingni community in Nicaragua's municipality of Waspan.[71] In February 1997, the Constitutional Court of the Supreme Court of Justice of Nicaragua declared the concession granted to SOLCARSA as unconstitutional, on the grounds that the government did not consult with the Awas Tingni people prior to the issuance of the timber concession, including failure to procure the required signatures from certain regional officials signifying that approval of the indigenous communities had been obtained.[72] Despite the Supreme Court's ruling, the state neglected to take measures to halt SOLCARSA's operations and continued to act as if the concession were valid.[73]

After a series of protracted legal contests that ultimately reached the Inter-American Court of Human Rights, the regional court in its 2001 decision concluded that Nicaragua, in tolerating the activities of SOLCARSA, violated the right of the Awas Tingni community to property which was protected by Article 21 of the American Convention on Human Rights of 1969.[74] The government of Nicaragua was ordered to abstain from any acts that might lead it, or SOLCARSA, as third parties acting with the government's acquiescence or tolerance, to affect the existence, value, use, or enjoyment of the property of the Awas Tingni community.[75]

It is evident from the issues discussed throughout chapters 5, 6, and 7 of this book that consultation if conducted in accordance with FPIC principle is a crucial tool for safeguarding the collective rights of *indigenous peoples* and ensuring their socio-cultural and economic survival. It has become an internationally recognized standard that where the interests and territories of *indigenous peoples* will be impacted by a project, action, or measure, the indigenous peoples concerned should be consulted in order to secure their FPIC.[76] However, in spite of this global recognition, the distinction between the legal duty of states and social responsibility of corporations still presents a challenge in terms of the effectiveness of consultation right as a valuable safeguard that indigenous communities can count on. As many of the cases and examples evaluated throughout this part show, corporations have demonstrated a strong tendency to exploit this complexity to the detriment of indigenous communities who host extractive projects. Ian Gary offered a fitting characterization of this problem when he stated the following:

> Imagine if a company paid the government to mine for gold or drill for oil in your backyard—but didn't ask for your permission, pay you, or give you important information about the project. Right now, oil, gas, and mining companies are doing this all around the world, often in the poorest countries.[77]

There is no doubt that a review of this *legal duty–social responsibility* distinction has now become necessary. The reality of our modern society demands the blurring of this dividing line. The adoption of a binding international regulation that defines corporate human rights obligation is essential. If the goal is to achieve meaningful accountability for violations of human rights of *indigenous peoples*, both State and corporate actors must be held to legally binding standards.

NOTES

1. See, for example, *Report of the Special Rapporteur on the Situation of Human Rights and Fundamental Freedoms of Indigenous Peoples*, James Anaya, A/HRC/12/34, July 15, 2009, paras 36–38. See also, *Report of the Special Rapporteur on the Situation of Human Rights and Fundamental Freedoms of Indigenous Peoples*, James Anaya, A/HRC/15/37 July 2010, paras 35 & 60.

2. See generally the *UN Guiding Principles on Business and Human Rights: Implementing the United Nations "Protect, Respect and Remedy" Framework* (United Nations, 2011).

3. See *Id., UN Guiding Principles on Business and Human Rights*, paras 18–19 and 22–23.

4. See *Id., Report of the Special Rapporteur*, James Anaya (A/HRC/15/37–2010), para 67.

5. See, for example, Cathal Doyle and Jill Cariño, *Making Free Prior & Informed Consent a Reality: Indigenous Peoples and the Extractive Sector* (PIPLinks/Middlesex University/ECCR, 2013), p. 40.

6. See *Id.*, Cathal Doyle and Jill Cariño, *Making Free Prior & Informed Consent a Reality*, p. 40.

7. See, for example, David Grayson and Adrian Hodges, *Everybody's Business: Managing Risks and Opportunities in Today's Global Society* (Dorling Kindersley, 2001), p. 260, step 6.

8. See David Grayson and Adrian Hodges, *Everybody's Business* (2001), p. 260. The focus is to ensure an effective stakeholder engagement, which should involve

open, two-way communication, the commitment of fellow managers and employees, active involvement in public policy, maintenance of stakeholder partnerships, an appreciation of the needs of the community, and an understanding of how business may address those needs. *Id.*, pp. 20–261.

9. See *UN Guiding Principles on Business and Human Rights*, General Principles, p. 1.

10. See, for example, *IACHR Highlights the Importance of Respecting Indigenous Peoples' Right to Prior Consultation*, Inter-American Commission on Human Rights Press Release No. 88/11, August 9, 2011. See also *Id. Report of the Special Rapporteur*, James Anaya (A/HRC/12/34 – 2009).

11. For an illustration of similar challenges with respect to indigenous communities in the Americas, see, for example, *U'wa Community v Ministry of the Environment and Sociedad Occidental Del Colombia Inc*, Case SU-039/97, Corte Constitucional, exp. No. T- 84771 [Constitutional Court of Colombia] February 3, 1997; and, *Maya Indigenous Community of the Toledo District v Belize*, Case 12.053, Report No.40/04, Inter-Am. C.H.R., OEA/Ser.L/V/II.122 Doc. 5 rev. 1 at 727 (2004).

12. See UNDRIP, adopted by the UN General Assembly in September 2007, articles 18–24. See also *Id.*, articles 10–11, 15–17, 28–32, and 36–38.

13. See the ILO Convention (No. 169) Concerning Indigenous and Tribal Peoples in Independent Countries, adopted by the General Conference of the International Labour Organization in June 1989, articles 6–7.

14. See, for example, Naomi Kipuri, The UN Declaration on the Rights of Indigenous Peoples in the African Context, in Claire Charters and Rodolfo Stavenhagen (eds.), *Making the Declaration Work: The United Nations Declaration on the Rights of Indigenous Peoples* (IWGIA, 2009).

15. See, for example, Theodore Okonkwo, Ownership and Control of Natural Resources under the Nigerian Constitution 1999 and Its Implications for Environmental Law and Practice, *International Law Research*, Vol. 6, No. 1 (2017), Canadian Center of Science and Education; Report of the African Commission's Working Group of Expert on Indigenous Population/Communities, adopted by the African Commission on Human and Peoples' Rights at its 28th ordinary session, 2005; and, *Overview of State Ownership in the Global Minerals Industry: Long Term Trends and Future*, Extractive Industries for Development Series #20 (Raw Materials Group, World Bank, May 2011), p. 15.

16. See *Report by the Special Rapporteur on the Rights of Indigenous Peoples*, James Anaya, A/HRC/18/35/Add.1, August 22, 2011, paras 10–13, at para 12.

17. See *Id., Report by the Special Rapporteur*, James Anaya (A/HRC/18/35/Add.1—2011), para 12.

18. See Joji Carino, Indigenous Peoples' Right to Free, Prior, Informed Consent: Reflections on Concepts and Practice, *Arizona Journal of International and Comparative Law*, Vol. 22 (2005), pp. 19, 25.

19. See generally, Florian Wettstein, The Duty to Protect: Corporate Complicity, Political Responsibility, and Human Rights Advocacy, *Journal of Business Ethics*, Vol. 96, No. 1 (September 2010), pp. 33–47; and *Corporate Complicity & Legal Accountability*, Report of the International Commission of Jurists Expert Legal Panel

on Corporate Complicity in International Crimes (Vol. 1, Corporate Complicity & Legal Accountability, ICJ, Geneva, 2008).

20. See Department of Petroleum Resources, Historical Background and Functions, available at https://www.dpr.gov.ng/functions-of-dpr/ (last accessed April 06, 2019).

21. See, for example, Guidelines for the Establishment of Hydrocarbon Process Plants (Petroleum Refinery and Petrochemicals Plants) In Nigeria, DPR July 2008, para 3.6.2.

22. See, *Id.*, Guidelines for the Establishment of Hydrocarbon Process Plants in Nigeria (DPR, 2008), para 3.6.2. See also, Environmental Impact Assessment Decree No. 86 of 1992, Laws of the Federation of Nigeria (LFN) 1992, part I section 7.

23. See *Id.*, UNDRIP, articles 18–19; and, ILO Convention No. 169, articles 6–7.

24. See DPR Guidelines, Requirements and Forms, for the Application for Oil and Gas Industry Services Permit of January 2012. See also *Id.*, Guidelines for the Establishment of Hydrocarbon Process Plants in Nigeria (DPR, 2008), para 3.6.2. It should be emphasized that, as a practical matter, a statutory rule requiring a public hearing on the environmental impact assessment report of any proposed natural resource extraction project merely directs the supervising government agency to give an opportunity to members of the public or relevant experts and interested groups to comment on the environmental impact of the activity proposed. The intent of the statutory requirement is not to foster a serious dialogue with, or solicit the consent of, affected communities. See *Id.*, Environmental Impact Assessment Decree, (LFN) 1992, part I section 7.

25. See, for example, Oil Pipelines Act, Chapter 338, Laws of the Federation of Nigeria (LFN) 1990, section 5.

26. See generally, *Id.*, Oil Pipelines Act (LFN, 1990).

27. See, *Id.,* Oil Pipelines Act (LFN, 1990), section 5(1) (a)–(d).

28. See *Id.,* Oil Pipelines Act (LFN, 1990), section 5. The Oil Pipelines Act only requires that the licensee give the land occupier at least 14 days' notice of intention to enter the land. However, this provision in practice does not operate as good faith consultation, but as a mere notice of intention to enter. *Id.*, section 6.

29. See Report of the Special Rapporteur on the situation of human Rights and fundamental freedoms of Indigenous People, James Anaya, Addendum on the situation of indigenous peoples in Botswana, A/HRC/15/37/Add.2, June 2, 2010.

30. See *Id., Report of the Special Rapporteur*, James Anaya – Botswana (A/HRC/15/37/Add.2 – 2010), para 48 and 52.

31. See *Id., Report of the Special Rapporteur*, James Anaya – Botswana (A/HRC/15/37/Add.2 – 2010), para 54.

32. See *Id., Report of the Special Rapporteur*, James Anaya – Botswana (A/HRC/15/37/Add.2 – 2010), para 53.

33. See *Id., Report by the Special Rapporteur*, James Anaya (A/HRC/18/35/Add.1 – 2011), para 12.

34. See Statement of Ms. Victoria Tauli-Corpuz, Special Rapporteur on the rights of indigenous peoples to the Human Rights Council 39th Session, Geneva, September 19, 2018. Available at http://unsr.vtaulicorpuz.org/site/index.php/en/statements/25 2-hrc-2018 (last accessed June 19, 2019).

35. See *Id.*, UNDRIP, articles 18–19; *Id.*, Joji Carino, *Indigenous Peoples' Right to Free, Prior, Informed Consent* (2005), p. 25; and, Constitutional Court of Bolivia, Constitutional Judgment 0045/2006, File 2005-12440-25-RDL, Judgment of June 2, 2006.

36. There are several instances where governments have direct ownership stake in extractive ventures, either as the sole owner of the commercial entity or form partnership with other private entities to create an operating corporation. See *State Participation in Oil, Gas and Mining, Natural Resource Governance Institute*, Parliamentary Briefing January 2015, https://resourcegovernance.org/sites/default/files/nrgi_Stat eParticipation_20150311.pdf (last accessed April 11, 2019). See also, *Joint Ventures / Government Shareholding in Project Company, Public-Private-Partnership Legal Resource Center*, the World Bank Group (2016-07-13). Available at https://ppp.wor ldbank.org/public-private-partnership/agreements/joint-ventures-empresas-mixtas (last accessed April 11, 2019).

37. See *Sarei v. Rio Tinto, PLC*, 487 F. 3d 1193 – Court of Appeals, 9th Circuit (2007).

38. See *Larry Bowoto et al. v. Chevron Texaco Corp.*, et al., 312 F.Supp.2d 1229 (2004), US District Court, N.D. California, March 2004. See also *Larry Bowoto et al. v Chevron Texaco Corp. et al*, Superior Court for the State of California, Case No. CGC-03-417580, (January 2008).

39. These three cases are Wiwa v Royal Dutch Petroleum, No. 96 CIV. 8386 (S.D.N.Y. Nov. 1996); Wiwa v Brian Anderson, Case 1:01-CV-01909-KMW-HBP (S.D.N.Y. March 2001); and Wiwa v Shell Petroleum Development, No. 04 CIV. 2665 (S.D.N.Y. April, 2004).

40. See *Id.*, *Sarei v. Rio Tinto* (2007), at 1198.

41. See *Id.*, *Sarei v. Rio Tinto* (2007), at 1198.

42. See *Id.*, *Sarei v. Rio Tinto* (2007), at 1198.

43. See *Id.*, *Sarei v. Rio Tinto* (2007), at 1198. Although the case was ultimately dismissed in 2011 by the United States Court of Appeals (9th Circuit) on technicality for lack of jurisdiction, the company was unable to resume operation at the mine, and eventually walked away from the project. See *Sarei v. Rio Tinto, PLC*, 671 F. 3d 736 – Court of Appeals, 9th Circuit 2011. See also Daniel Flitton, *Rio Tinto's billion-dollar mess: unprincipled, shameful and evil*, the Sidney Morning Herald, August 19, 2016.

44. See *Id. Larry Bowoto v. Chevron Texaco Corp.* (2004); *Id.*, *Larry Bowoto v Chevron Texaco Corp.* (2008).

45. See *Id. Larry Bowoto v. Chevron Texaco Corp.* (2004); *Id.*, *Larry Bowoto v. Chevron Texaco Corp.* (2008).

46. See *Id. Larry Bowoto v. Chevron Texaco Corp.* (2004); *Id.*, *Larry Bowoto v Chevron Texaco Corp.* (2008).

47. See *Id. Larry Bowoto v. Chevron Texaco Corp.* (2004); *Id.*, *Larry Bowoto v. Chevron Texaco Corp.* (2008). See also Richard C. Paddock, Jury Urged to find Chevron Liable in Oil Platform Assault, *Los Angeles Times,* November 26, 2008.

48. See *Id. Larry Bowoto v. Chevron Texaco Corp.* (2004); *Id.*, *Larry Bowoto v. Chevron Texaco Corp.* (2008). See also *Bowoto v. Chevron: Peaceful Protest, Military*

Response: Chevron's Complicity in Murder and Torture in Nigeria, EarthRights International, available at https://earthrights.org/case/bowoto-v-chevron-2/#docume ntsff69-1a905f26-f4b6 (last accessed May 13, 2019).

49. See *Id.*, *Wiwa v. Royal Dutch Petroleum* (1996); *Id.*, *Wiwa v. Brian Anderson* (2001); and, *Id.*, *Wiwa v. Shell Petroleum Development* (2004).

50. See *Id.*, *Wiwa v. Royal Dutch Petroleum* (1996); *Id.*, *Wiwa v. Brian Anderson* (2001); and, *Id.*, *Wiwa v. Shell Petroleum Development* (2004). See also Hannah Summers, Amnesty Seeks Criminal Inquiry into Shell over alleged Complicity in Murder and Torture in Nigeria, *The Guardian*, November 28, 2017.

51. See *Id.*, *Wiwa v. Royal Dutch Petroleum* (1996); *Id.*, *Wiwa v. Brian Anderson (2001)*; *Id.*, *Wiwa v. Shell Petroleum Development* (2004); and, *Id.* Hannah Summers, *Amnesty Seeks Criminal Inquiry into Shell* (November 2017).

52. See *Wiwa v. Shell Petroleum Development* – Settlement Agreement and Mutual Release (S.D.N.Y. 2009). See also Ingrid Wuerth, Wiwa v. Shell: The $15.5 Million Settlement, Insights, *The American Society of International Law*, Vol. 13, No. 14 (September 9, 2009).

53. See *Id.*, *Sarei v. Rio Tinto* (2007), at 1198.

54. See *Id.*, *Sarei v. Rio Tinto* (2007), at 1198.

55. See *U'wa Community v. Ministry of the Environment and Sociedad Occidental Del Colombia Inc*, Case SU-039/97, Corte Constitucional, exp. No.T- 84771 [Constitutional Court of Colombia] February 3, 1997.

56. See *Id.*, *U'wa Community*, Case SU-039/97 (1997). See also Daniel Bonilla, The Principle of Political Unity and Cultural Minorities' Self-Government, *Florida Journal of International Law,* [vii] No. 3 (2005), p. 525.

57. See *Id.*, *U'wa Community,* Case SU-039/97 (1997).

58. See *Id.*, *U'wa Community,* Case SU-039/97 (1997). See also Luis Carlos Arenas, The U'wa Community's Battle Against the Oil Companies: A Local Struggle Turned Global, in Boaventura de Sousa Santos (ed.), *Another Knowledge is Possible: Beyond Northern Epistemologies* (Verso, 2007), p. 120 at 125.

59. See *Id.*, *U'wa Community,* Case SU-039/97 (1997); and, *Id.*, Luis Carlos Arenas, *The U'wa Community's Battle Against the Oil Companies* (2007), p. 126.

60. See De Beers Group at http://botswana.debeersgroup.com/en/who-we-are/ de-beers-in-botswana.html (last accessed April 13, 2019). See also Botswana and De Beers Announce Milestone Agreement Marking New Era for Botswana Diamonds, *The Anglo American*, September 16, 2011.

61. See Nigerian National Petroleum Corporation (NNPC), https://www.nnpcgrou p.com/NNPCBusiness/UpstreamVentures/OilProduction.aspx (last accessed April 13, 2019). See also Okechukwu Nnodim, Nigeria Investing $7bn in Joint Ventures Annually — NNPC, *The Punch Newspapers*, May 13, 2018; and, Joint Ventures in The Nigeria Oil and Gas Industry, Oil & Gas Law Department – Resolution Law Firm, available at https://resolutionlawng.com/joint-venture-in-the-nigeria-oil-and-gas-industry/ (last accessed April 13, 2019).

62. See, for example, William B. Werther Jr and David Chandler, *Strategic Corporate Social Responsibility: Stakeholders in a Global Environment* (Sage, 2006), p. 5.

63. See *Social and Economic Rights Action Centre (SERAC) & Another v. Nigeria* (2001) AHRLR 60 (ACHPR 2001). Communication 155/96, Decided at the 30th ordinary session, October 2001.

64. See *Id.*, *SERAC v. Nigeria* (2001), para 57. See also *SHELL, SPDC and its Joint Venture Partners*, available at https://www.shell.com.ng/about-us/what-we-do/spdc.html (last accessed April 23, 2019).

65. See *Id.*, *SERAC v. Nigeria* (2001) para 3.

66. See Centre for Minority Rights Development (Kenya) and Minority Rights Group International on behalf of Endorois Welfare Council v Kenya (Communication 276/2003), decision adopted by the African Commission in May 2009 and endorsed by the African Union on February 4, 2010. *(Endorois Case).*

67. See generally *Id.*, *Endorois Case* (2010).

68. See *Id.*, *Endorois Case* (2010), paras 1–21, at 14.

69. See *Case of the Mayagna (Sumo) Awas Tingni Community v. Nicaragua*, I/A Court H.R., Merits, Reparations and Costs, Judgment of August 31, 2001. Series C No. 79. See also Claudio Grossman, Awas Tingni v. Nicaragua: A Landmark Case for the Inter-American System, *American University Washington College of Law Human Rights Brief: 8 No. 3 Human Rights Brief* 2 (2001), p. 2.

70. See *Maya Indigenous Community of the Toledo District v Belize*, Case 12.053, Report No.40/04, Inter-Am. C.H.R., OEA/Ser.L/V/II.122 Doc. 5 rev. 1 at 727 (2004).

71. See *Id, Mayagna (Sumo) Awas Tingni Community v Nicaragua* (2001). See also S. James Anaya and Claudio Grossman, The Case of Awas Tingni v. Nicaragua: A New Step in the International Law of Indigenous Peoples, *Arizona Journal of International and Comparative Law*, Vol. 19, No. 1 (2002).

72. See *Id, Mayagna (Sumo) Awas Tingni Community v Nicaragua* (2001), para 17.

73. See *Id, Mayagna (Sumo) Awas Tingni Community v Nicaragua* (2001), para 17. See also *Id.* S. James Anaya and Claudio Grossman, *The Case of Awas Tingni v. Nicaragua* (2002).

74. See *Id, Mayagna (Sumo) Awas Tingni Community v Nicaragua* (2001), paras 155 and 173.

75. See *Id, Mayagna (Sumo) Awas Tingni Community v Nicaragua* (2001), paras 153, 155, 164, and 173.

76. See Inter-American Court of Human Rights in *Kichwa Indigenous People of Sarayaku v Ecuador*, Judgment of June 27, 2012 (Merits and Reparations), paragraphs 164–166. See also Lisi Brunner and Karla Quintana, The Duty to Consult in the Inter-American System: Legal Standards after Sarayaku, *ASIL-Insights*, Vol. 16, No. 35 (November 28, 2012); and, *Id. Report of the Special Rapporteur*, James Anaya (A/HRC/12/34 – 2009), paras 61–69.

77. See Ian Gary, Gas Money, Where Is it Really Going? *Huffington Post*, January 26, 2010.

Chapter 8

Indigenous Rights and Corporate Responsibility in Perspective

THE OUTLOOK

Discussions throughout this book show that *indigenous peoples* generally have a special connection to the environment where they live and the traditional lands they use and occupy. *Indigenous peoples* remain among the world's most vulnerable, disadvantaged, and marginalized groups in our society.[1] The sociocultural and economic growth of indigenous communities has, for a long time, been significantly undermined, and their continued existence threatened by the commercial pursuits of both governmental authorities and corporations. Various measures were, as a result, adopted at the international and national levels to address issues concerning *indigenous peoples*, and to safeguard their rights as a unit.

Admittedly, only States have the legal obligation to protect and respect human rights under international law. More so, there is no universal legally binding instrument currently in existence to address corporate human rights obligation. In light of this, the need to impose some form of universal binding human rights obligation on corporations is now more glaring than ever before. Without a doubt, corporations play a vital role in driving global development, and they add immense value to the socioeconomic growth happening across various national boundaries. Nevertheless, the establishment of binding standards to regulate corporate conduct, especially with respect to human rights violations, has become inescapable. This is particularly so, considering the staggering instances of monumental adverse impacts caused by corporate activities around the world, some of which were discussed in this book.

Despite the daunting challenges, a global effort to establish a workable binding human rights code of conduct for corporations persists.[2] The fact that a framework for indigenous rights, embodying the collective human rights of *indigenous peoples*, was successfully established at the international level constitutes a remarkable achievement.[3] This indigenous rights framework provides the normative standards for the protection and promotion of the rights of indigenous peoples all over the world.[4]

In addition, at the national level, in keeping with these new international indigenous rights norms, countries have been enacting new laws or modifying existing regulatory schemes, to make indigenous rights normative standards directly applicable to corporate entities within their domestic jurisdictions.[5] Furthermore, many international human rights treaties' monitoring bodies have equally found ways to expand their implementation processes and thematic focus by using preexisting traditional international human rights instruments to promote and protect the rights of *indigenous peoples*.[6]

If the rapid momentum already gained by the expansion of indigenous peoples' rights, and the strengthening of enforcement mechanisms by State governments and international governance institutions are any indication, it is important for corporations to align their operational activities and corporate responsibility approaches with these normative standards on human rights of *indigenous peoples*.[7]

Undoubtedly, States have an abiding obligation to respect and protect human rights, and must avoid the abdication of this obligation. Nevertheless, it is important for corporate entities to realize that a State's non-recognition of indigenous peoples' rights, lack of well-defined legal protections for such rights, or abdication by the State of its own duty to respect and protect human rights does not excuse a corporation from applying the minimum international normative standards concerning human rights of individuals and groups.[8] To this extent, corporations should refrain from violating human rights in general, and the rights of indigenous peoples in particular. If violations occur, any adverse impacts caused thereby should be addressed.[9]

Integration of Indigenous Peoples Rights' Compliance Measures as a Day-to-Day Corporate Practice

Corporations should develop, in alignment with internationally recognized norms, substantive internal standards by way of formal corporate policy to address human rights and indigenous rights issues. Acquiring greater knowledge and understanding about indigenous human rights norms, indigenous peoples, and important issues concerning them, at both top management and field operation levels, would be very helpful in facilitating constructive and beneficial engagement with any compliance challenges that may arise. Development of pragmatic corporate human rights compliance policy, backed by genuine internal commitment at the top management level, can serve as an effective tool for ensuring that the rights and interests of host communities are not jeopardized by corporate operational activities. This viewpoint is consistent with the observation expressed by the UN High Commission for Human Rights in its report on business and human rights, that

> experience to date suggests that the development of a human rights policy requires a commitment to implement that policy. This depends on finding appropriate ways to institutionalize concern for human rights into the decision-making and operational structure of a business.[10]

In this regard, corporations, as part of their human rights' due diligence duty, should, prior to commencing any activities that may impact indigenous communities, identify the particular indigenous groups involved, and apply the formal corporate policy already developed, to address the concerns of those indigenous groups.[11] The corporate policy or any other compliance approach adopted should align with recognized normative standards on human rights of indigenous peoples. Adequate attention should be paid to issues relating to the recognition of the indigenous groups concerned, and claims pertaining to their traditional occupation and use of the lands and natural resources affected, as well as whether or not the groups' right to prior consultation was safeguarded.[12]

It is therefore important that corporations become conversant with issues and trends in the areas of human rights in general, and indigenous rights in particular. Corporations should develop necessary formal protocols or policies required for compliance with the rights of any indigenous groups that may be impacted by the corporations' activity. In relation to consultation, any formal policy must be based on the principle of *free, prior, and informed consent* (FPIC).[13] Such consultation engagement should, necessarily, occur prior to the commencement of the corporate activity, be conducted in good faith, and with the ultimate goal of obtaining the consent or agreement of the indigenous group impacted.[14]

It should be the goal and deliberate policy of corporations to engage with their host communities at the earliest stage and consult with them on how best to ensure that the company's operational activities are respectful of the communities' rights. In many cases when corporations abide by the law and show respect for the human rights of *indigenous peoples* in the course of conducting their business activities or implementing projects, it results in broad support for the company's operations, and boosts the corporate image and brand equity within the host community, as well as in the market place.[15] As some business experts describe it, in today's corporate environment, the continuing success and sustainability of companies is heavily contingent on how well those companies secure and maintain their social license to operate wherever they do business.[16] It is now the case, as some have predicted, that an inclusive community relationship fostered by corporations is now one of the most important factors in determining commercial viability and business success.[17] However, to be beneficial, this type of engagement should be proactive, rather than reactive.[18]

Respect for human rights by corporations is not just a moral or legal thing to do; it is the economically wise thing to do. Corporations are, in many ways, acting in their own self-interest when they respect human rights in places where they operate.[19] This is so because failure to observe human rights rules can expose corporations to unnecessary risks and pecuniary losses, including penalty for infraction of both local and international norms, disruptive and costly project delays when communities protest and demand respect for their rights, reputational damage and depreciation of brand equity, and, of course, expensive protracted litigation.

In today's globalized socio-economic environment, human rights compliance has become, and will continue to be, a key barometer for measuring economic performance and social relevance of corporations around the world.[20] Therefore, to underscore the consequential nature of this reality, corporations are encouraged to, at the minimum, incorporate certain task list as integral components of their routine operational policies.[21] These action items, consistent with the suggestion highlighted in the report by the UN High Commission for Human Rights, may include the following:

- Identify any potential human rights issues that the corporation might encounter in implementing a proposed activity or project.
- Develop corporate human rights policy options, particularly in accordance with recognized human rights normative standards and good practice.
- Operationalize the human rights policy options developed, and make sure that they become part of the corporations' everyday practice.
- Undertake, at the earliest, thoughtful dialogue, outreach, or collaboration with stakeholders and any group that may be affected by a proposed corporate activity or project.
- Educate and train key personnel of the corporation to ensure that every person with the capacity to act or make a decision that can implicate the corporation's human rights responsibility is knowledgeable about the policy options and the applicable human rights standards.
- Develop appropriate internal capacity and expertise. This can be done, for instance, through institution of human rights specialists that can help the corporation deal properly with complex issue, effectively monitor fast-changing business environment, engage meaningfully with stakeholders and impacted groups, manage situations where the corporation's human rights policy is violated, and ensure that appropriate company personnel are held accountable for faulty implementation.
- Communicate with business partners, including vendors and subcontractors, to ensure that they fully understand and act upon the corporation's human rights policy and applicable human rights standards.

- Maintain internal accountability, by establishing performance benchmarks and making sure that personnel designated to apply the corporate policy on human rights are held responsible for any implementation lapse.
- Adopt independent verification and public reporting practices. This can be a valuable positive reinforcement mechanism for the corporations' social responsibility practice, and could help boost its image in the public arena.[22]

It is important to point out here that, in developing any formal human rights compliance policy, corporations must ensure that such policy accommodates specific measures that directly address the human rights of indigenous peoples. The reason is that, although the traditional human rights framework generally applies to the situation of indigenous peoples, the nature of indigenous peoples' rights and the protections it embodies is characteristically unique.[23]

Certainly, significant progress has been accomplished in terms of the advancement of indigenous rights as a concept. But there is still a long way to go, particularly with respect to curbing the rampant violations of indigenous people's rights around the world. Indigenous communities, notably in developing countries, are increasingly concerned about the continuing disregard for their human rights, the land they occupy, and the natural resources they rely upon. Oftentimes, these violations involve situations relating to the implementation of extractive or development projects.

In light of the foregoing, encounters and experiences of many indigenous groups have informed different approaches to safeguard their rights and interests, and to ensure that they fully participate in the decision-making process concerning the execution of projects or initiatives that may affect them. One view frequently shared by indigenous rights advocates is that, along with consultation, adequate safeguards that include comprehensive environmental, socio-cultural, and economic impact assessments, impact prevention and mitigation programs, and fair compensation and benefit sharing measures should form the core component of any implementation plan involving projects occurring within or near the territories of *indigenous peoples*.[24]

Adoption of Evolving Patterns in Project Development and Implementation as a Safeguard for Indigenous Peoples Rights

Proactive Participation of Indigenous Peoples in Natural Resource Development

As noted above, violations of human rights of *indigenous peoples* frequently occur in situations involving implementation of natural resource extraction or development projects on or near indigenous territories, by States and corporate entities. These extraction projects are, oftentimes, coupled with severe

162

adverse effects on the environment and well-being of the *indigenous peoples* concerned. In many of the cases, these extractive projects involve an outside private corporate entity acting in concert with the government, and the indigenous communities impacted are usually not a part of the decision-making process relating to such projects. As a result, these indigenous communities lack meaningful opportunity to express their concerns or the power to reject the project, if going forward is indeed averse to their rights and interests. As James Anaya noted, there will surely be cases in which extractive projects are "simply incompatible with indigenous peoples' own aspirations and priorities for development."[25]

Anaya, however, emphasized that it should not be automatically presumed that, in all cases, the interests pursued by extractive projects "are entirely or always at odds" with those of *indigenous peoples.*[26] According to Anaya, there are instances where *indigenous peoples* have expressed the desire to be involved in commercial extraction of resources found within their own territory, in a manner that safeguards their collective rights and protects their interests.[27] And in such instance, those *indigenous peoples* desire to play active rather than a passive role. This desire to be an active participant is compatible with various protections available to *indigenous peoples* under international law, which guarantees that all peoples have the right of self-determination, and may, for their own ends, freely dispose of their natural wealth and resources.[28] On this point, Victoria Tauli-Corpuz, the Special Rapporteur on the Rights of Indigenous Peoples, in her recent report to the UN Human Rights Council, reiterated that

> indigenous peoples' right to self-governance is closely linked to their right to exercise self-determination, as it allows them to be in control of their own destiny and self-determined development. . . . Self-determination for indigenous peoples is also a matter of cultural self-determination, which has been described as the right to recapture their identity, reinvigorate their ways of life, reconnect with the Earth, regain their traditional lands, protect their heritage, revitalize their languages and manifest their culture, all of which are considered "as important to indigenous people as the right to make final decisions in their internal political, judicial, and economic settings."[29]

Usually, natural resource projects are undertaken within lands used and occupied by *indigenous people* solely by a government or a private corporation, or perhaps jointly. Thus, accommodating only minimal involvement, if any, of the affected indigenous community and with little or no economic benefit to the community.[30] Hence, as Anaya explained, going forward, the preferred model for natural resource development within indigenous territories should be one in which the *indigenous peoples* are concerned, through their own enterprise or partnership arrangements actively participate in the development, implementation, and management of the natural resource projects taking place on their lands.[31]

Of course, this preferred model for natural resource development within indigenous territories comes with challenges in terms of the immense technical capacity and capital required on the part of *indigenous peoples*. While these challenges are formidable, they are not insurmountable, as there have been successful co-partnership and other collaborative arrangements between *indigenous peoples* and private companies that could be further developed to advance this preferred model.[32]

When *indigenous people* actively participate in how natural resource extraction is developed and implemented within their territories, they are provided an opportunity to ensure that adequate safeguards are in place to protect their rights and interests, and make certain that the project is implemented in accordance with international standards and best practices. According to Anaya:

> In contrast to the prevailing model in which natural resource extraction within indigenous territories is under the control of and primarily for the benefit of others, indigenous peoples in some cases are establishing and implementing their own enterprises to extract and develop natural resources. This alternative of indigenous-controlled resource extraction, by its very nature, is more conducive to the exercise of indigenous peoples' rights to self-determination, lands and resources, culturally appropriate development and related rights, in accordance with the United Nations Declaration on the Rights of Indigenous Peoples and other international sources of authority.[33]

Essentially, with this preferred model, the rights of *indigenous peoples* to their traditional lands, natural resources, culture, self-determination, and all other rights are safeguarded and potentially strengthened.

Independent Third-party Monitoring of Project

Another important development in the area of natural resource extraction projects involving territories used and occupied by *indigenous peoples* is the implementation of a third-party monitoring and auditing. The goal of this process is to ensure that, by allowing the involvement of an independent auditing body or a third party, implementation of projects is guided properly so that they align with international standards on human rights, and fully respect the rights, culture, way of life, and environment of the indigenous communities concerned.

One example of such third-party auditing body is Equitable Origin, an independent and non-profit organization that supports communities and project developers in ensuring responsible natural resource project implementation and management. Equitable Origin established the first independent credible verification and certification system that incentivizes compliant project implementation in the area of energy development, particularly as it affects indigenous communities.[34] The EQ 100 Standards, a framework for responsible energy project implementation developed by Equitable Origin, ensures that energy projects abide by international standards concerning *indigenous peoples*.[35] There are also other initiatives in existence,[36] including the Aluminium Stewardship Initiative (ASI),[37] which established various performance standards to ensure responsible project implementation in several areas including bauxite mining and alumina refining.[38]

NOTES

1. The United Nations Declaration on the Rights of Indigenous Peoples: A Manual for National Human Rights Institutions, APF/OHCHR, August 2013.

2. See, for example, Karolin Seitz, One Step Further towards Global Regulation of Business, *Global Policy Forum*, Briefing January 2018, p. 3, https://www.globalpolicy.org/images/pdfs/GPF-Briefing_One_step_further_Report_of_the_3rd_session_on_the_Treaty.pdf (last accessed April 15, 2019).

3. See *UN Declaration on the Rights of Indigenous Peoples* (UNDRIP) 2007, and The ILO Convention (No. 169) Concerning Indigenous and Tribal Peoples in Independent Countries (1989). See also generally S. James Anaya, *International Human Rights and Indigenous Peoples* (Aspen, 2009).

4. See *Id*., UNDRIP 2007; and, *Id*., ILO Convention (No. 169) 1989.

5. See, for example, Constitution of the Republic of Ecuador 2008, chapters 4 & 5; Constitution of the Plurinational State of Bolivia 2009; Indigenous Peoples Rights Act of Philippine 1997; Constitution of the Republic of Kenya 2010; and, Law on the Promotion and Protection of Indigenous Populations, Act No. 5-2011 of Republic of Congo, 2011.

6. For example, Article 27 of the International Covenant on Civil and Political Rights have been widely applied to indigenous issues. See, for example, General Comment 23, UN Human Rights Committee, U.N. Doc. CCPR/C/21/Rev.1/Add.5. Similarly, the UN Committee on the Elimination of Racial Discrimination (CERD) has made effort to protect indigenous rights using the general normative framework of the non-discrimination under the Convention on the Elimination of All Forms of Racial Discrimination. See CERD, General Recommendation 23: Indigenous Peoples, U.N. Doc. A/52/18, Annex V.

7. See *Report of the Special Rapporteur on the Situation of Human Rights and Fundamental Freedoms of Indigenous People*, James Anaya, A/HRC/15/37, July 19, 2010, paras 39–46.

8. *Id*., *Reports of Special Rapporteur*, James Anaya (A/HRC/15/37 – 2010), paras 49–52.

9. See *UN Guiding Principles on Business and Human Rights: Implementing the United Nations "Protect, Respect and Remedy" Framework* (United Nations, 2011), para 11, p.13. See also David Weissbrodt, Human Rights Standards Concerning Transnational Corporations and Other Business Entities, *Minnesota Journal of International Law*, Vol. 23 (2014), p. 135.

10. See *Business and Human Rights: A Progress Report*, Office of the United Nations High Commissioner for Human Rights (OHCHR, Geneva, 2000), p.16. Available at https://www.ohchr.org/Documents/Publications/BusinessHRen.pdf (last accessed June 18, 2019).

11. See *Id.*, *Report of the Special Rapporteur*, James Anaya (A/HRC/15/37 – 2010), para 46. See also *Id.*, *UN Guiding Principles on Business and Human Rights* (2011).

12. See generally *Id.*, *Report of the Special Rapporteur*, James Anaya (A/HRC/15/37 – 2010).

13. See *Id.* UNDRIP 2007, article 19; and, *Id.* ILO Convention (No. 169) of 1989, article 6(2). See also *Report of the Special Rapporteur on the Situation of Human Rights and Fundamental Freedoms of Indigenous People*, James Anaya, A/HRC/12/34, July 15, 2009.

14. See *Id.* UNDRIP 2007, article 19; *Id.* ILO Convention (No. 169) of 1989, article 6(2); and, *Id.*, *Report of the Special Rapporteur*, James Anaya (A/HRC/12/34 – 2009), paras 54–57.

15. See generally, Steven Herz, Antonio La Vina, and Jonathan Sohn, *Development Without Consent: The Business Case for Community Consent* (World Resources Institute, 2007); and, Kathleen Wilburn and Ralph Wilburn, Achieving Social License to Operate Using Stakeholder Theory, Journal *of International* Business Ethics, Vol. 4 (2011), pp. 3–16.

16. See, for example, Charles Goodyear, Chief Executive Officer, BHP Billiton (BHP Mining), *The BHP Billiton Sustainability Report* (Full Report 2007); and, David Grayson and Adrian Hodges, *Everybody's Business: Managing Risks and Opportunities in Today's Global Society* (DK Publishing 2002).

17. See, for example, David Wheeler and Maria Sillanpaa, *The Stakeholder Corporation: The Body Shop Blueprint for Maximizing Stakeholder Value* (Pitman, 1997), p. ix. See also *Id.*, David Grayson and Adrian Hodges, *Everybody's Business* (2002), p. 260.

18. See, *Id.*, David Wheeler and Maria Sillanpaa, *The Stakeholder Corporation* (1997), p. ix; and *Id.*, David Grayson and Adrian Hodges, *Everybody's Business* (2002), p. 261.

19. See John Kamm, The Role of Businesses in Promoting Respect for Human Rights in China, *Business Ethics in China*, Vol. 1, No. 1 (1997); and *International Business Ethics Review*, Nov. 1 (1997). See particularly Ralph G. Steinhartdt, Soft Law, Hard Markets: Competitive Self-Interest and the Emergence of Human Rights Responsibilities for Multinational Corporations, *Brooklyn Journal of International Law* Vol. 33, No. 3 (2008), p. 933, at 943.

20. See Geordan Graetz and Daniel M. Franks, Incorporating Human Rights into the Corporate Domain: Due Diligence, Impact Assessment and Integrated Risk

Management, *Impact Assessment and Project Appraisal*, Vol. 31, No. 2 (2013), pp. 97–106. See also, generally, *Id., Business and Human Rights: A Progress Report* (OHCHR, 2000).

21. See *Id., Business and Human Rights: A Progress Report* (OHCHR, 2000), p. 20.

22. See *Id., Business and Human Rights: A Progress Report* (OHCHR, 2000), pp. 20–22.

23. See *Report of the Special Rapporteur on the Rights of Indigenous Peoples*, James Anaya, A/66/288, August 10, 2011, at para 92.

24. See, for example, Lisa Laplante and Suzanne Spears, Out of the Conflict Zone: The Case for Community Consent Processes in the Extractive Sector, *Yale Human Rights and Development Law Journal*, Vol. 11 (2008), p. 69.

25. See *Report of the Special Rapporteur on the Rights of Indigenous Peoples on Extractive Industries and Indigenous Peoples*, James Anaya, A/HRC/24/41, July 1, 2013, paras 1–4.

26. See *Id. Report of the Special Rapporteur*, James Anaya (A/HRC/24/41 – 2013), paras 1–4.

27. See *Id. Report of the Special Rapporteur*, James Anaya (A/HRC/24/41 – 2013), para 2.

28. See, for example, International Covenant on Civil and Political Rights (ICCPR) 1966, articles 1(1)-(2); International Covenant on Economic, Social and Cultural Rights (ICESCR) 1966, articles 1(1)-(2); and *Id.*, UNDRIP 2007, article 3.

29. See *Report of the Special Rapporteur of the Human Rights Council on the Rights of Indigenous Peoples*, Victoria Tauli-Corpuz, A/73/176, July 17, 2018, para 35.

30. See *Id. Report of the Special Rapporteur*, James Anaya (A/HRC/24/41 – 2013), paras 8 and 9.

31. See *Id. Report of the Special Rapporteur*, James Anaya (A/HRC/24/41 – 2013), paras 8 & 9. See further Claudia Notzke, A New Perspective in Aboriginal Natural Resource Management: Co-management, *Geoforum*, Vol. 26, No. 2 (May 1995), pp. 187–209.

32. See, for example, Clayton Blood, Owning Our Future: A Perspective on Oil and Natural Gas Development, *Context Magazine*, November 26, 2018; Jean Yuen, *First Nations-Private Sector Partnerships – Tips for Success*, Boughton Law Corporation, June 2015, https://www.boughtonlaw.com/2015/06/first-nations-private-sector-partnerships-tips-for-success/ (last accessed May 18, 2019); EDF Renewables Canada in Partnership with the Blood Tribe Secures Wind Project in Alberta, *Business Wire*, December 18, 2018; Kristin Butler, How Colorado's Southern Utes Took Control of Their Economic Destiny, *Indian Country Today*, February 16, 2017; *Indigena Capital's Partnership with Various Indigenous Nations*, https://indigenacapital.com/ (last accessed May 18, 2019); and, *Id.*, Lisa Laplante and Suzanne Spears, *Out of the Conflict Zone* (2008).

33. See *Id. Report of the Special Rapporteur*, James Anaya (A/HRC/24/41 – 2013), para 8.

34. See Equitable Origin, available at https://www.equitableorigin.org/# (last accessed May 16, 2019).

35. See EO100™ Standard for Responsible Energy, https://www.equitableorig in.org/eo100-for-responsible-energy/overview/ (last accessed May 16, 2019).

36. It should be pointed out that other monitoring or certification systems exist in the area of forest resource management and indigenous peoples. See, for example, The Programme for the Endorsement of Forest Certification (PEFC) (https://www. pefc.org/). See also A. V. Tikina, J. L. Innes, R. L. Trosper, and B. C. Larson, Aborig-inal Peoples and Forest Certification: A Review of the Canadian Situation, *Ecology and Society*, Vol. 15, No. 3 (2010), p. 33.

37. See Aluminum Stewardship Initiative, https://aluminium-stewardship.org/ (last accessed May 16, 2019).

38. See, for example, *ASI Performance Standard* (Version 2, December 2017).

Index

Note: Page numbers followed by "n" refer to notes.

About the Author

Jide James-Eluyode teaches at the Arizona State University School of Social and Behavioral Sciences in the MA Program in Social Justice and Human Rights. His research and teaching interests lie at the intersection of human rights and social justice, law and development, indigenous peoples' rights, globalization, international business and economic development, environmental law, and international and comparative law. A recipient of the Advanced Graduate Study Certificate in Global Policy from Northwestern University, Jide James-Eluyode also holds an SJD degree, with a focus in international human rights, from the University of Arizona Rogers College of Law, and an LLM degree, with specialization in international business and trade, from the UIC John Marshall Law School.

CPSIA information can be obtained
at www.ICGtesting.com
Printed in the USA
LVHW111456080120
642934LV00009B/140/P